BIG 4 ENCYCLOPEDIA

A GUIDE TO THE METAL MUSIC OF

METALLICA, SLAYER, MEGADETH & ANTHRAX

A SCRAPBOOK OF LISTS, ARTICLES & REVIEWS

NEIL DANIELS

BIG 4 ENCYCLOPEDIA

A GUIDE TO THE METAL MUSIC OF

METALLICA, SLAYER, MEGADETH & ANTHRAX

BY

NEIL DANIELS

NEIL DANIELS

Big 4 Encyclopedia – A Guide To The Metal Music Of Metallica, Slayer, Megadeth & Anthrax

First edition published, 2016

ISBN-13: 978-1515073833

ISBN-10: 1515073831

Copyright Neil Daniels © 2016

Visit Createspace at www.createspace.com

Visit Neil Daniels at www.neildanielsbooks.com

All rights reserved. No part of this publication may be reproduced, stored in a retrieval system, or transmitted in any form or by any means, electronic, mechanical, photocopy, recording or otherwise, without prior written permission of the copyright owner. Nor can it be circulated in any form of binding or cover other than that in which it is published and without similar condition including this condition being imposed on a subsequent purchaser.

NEIL DANIELS

"Lars does love Diamond Head and he is mentioned in the book [Am I Evil?] a lot. I have followed Metallica's ascent to the top for over twenty-five years".

- **Brian Tatler (Diamond Head) 2009**

"As it [Violent Storm] progressed I thought, well, yeah, the materials good but there's things lacking, you know, to sort of bring it up to a certain standard these days when you're competing with the likes of Metallica and Maiden and everybody, you know".

- **K.K. Downing (Judas Priest) 2006**

"Metallica have just put a big piece on a new documentary that's coming out about Saxon and they've just done a fantastic thing for us... British heavy metal was a big influence on them. I know Dave Mustaine as well; obviously he was in Metallica at that time ['81-'83] as well".

- **Biff Byford (Saxon) 2008**

"They're great and we're still on the road with them. We get along really well and it makes the tour a lot more enjoyable. I toured with them in the States when I was in Priest with John [Bush] singing. I'm a fan of Anthrax and I'm friends with them. They've been great with us and the *fans have been great with us. For an opening tour without a record, it's been great. I remind my band of this every day. This isn't a tour a band would usually go on without an album out. I'll tell you what; I think that the UK was the best so far. I think the [London] Astoria was probably the best show".*

- **Tim "Ripper" Owens (Beyond Fear) 2006**

"I love the first four Metallica albums but I love Megadeth, too. If we're looking at both band's entire outputs, then Mustaine edges it, just, for me, as he's more consistent but, equally, I don't think he has anything in his repertoire that matches the first four Metallica albums".

- **Harry Paterson (Author/Music Journalist) 2013**

"As far as actual songs, I prefer Megadeth over Metallica. I just think Dave Mustaine is such a unique songwriter and guitarist, especially in the early years".

- **Bob Nalbandian (Music Journalist/Broadcaster) 2011**

"To witness a stop on the now legendary co-headlining tour with Metallica was something special. There was noticeable tension in the air after Metallica's set and the hour's long wait until Guns went on. The

show was solid enough, but crashed and burned during 'Knockin' On Heaven's Door' when someone threw a cup of ice or a lighter or something which hit Axl on the leg. He stalked off mid-song leaving Duff McKagan to finish with horribly out of tune vocals".

- **Michael Christopher (Music Journalist) 2013**

"To promote the release of Re-Load, Metallica wanted to perform an outdoor free show in the American city that got the most votes via a toll-free number. Philadelphia won, but due to lawsuits and threats from local politicians concerned with noise levels and rowdy attendees, the show literally came down to the last minute. 30,000 fans showed up, the band ripped through a 14 song set that included rarities like 'Helpless', 'The Wait' and 'The Thing That Should Not Be'".

- **Michael Christopher (Music Journalist) 2013**

"Metallica – a secret gig at the 100 Club in London's Oxford Street, a few days before Donington in 1987. It was hellishly hot and the sweat was dripping off the walls. The stage was tiny, and people kept flying over the moshpit and landing at the band's feet. I had gone along with The Mission, who had brought John Paul Jones from Led Zeppelin, who was producing them at the time. After the gig he was stunned, I think he'd not been out much since Zeppelin split, and he was shaking his head, saying, 'I didn't know bands could do stuff like this'. Some footage of this gig recently surfaced on YouTube, not great quality but you get an idea of the general sense of excitement and chaos (and how hot it was)".

- **Neil Perry (Music Journalist) 2010**

"Blame it on Xavier Russell, back in the early Kerrang! days. I was living rough at the time, sleeping on couches and floors, toting around a portable typewriter and a plastic carrier bag full of my possessions. This one night I ended up back at X's. He gave me Wild Turkey and a squash racket, then put on 'Creeping Death' and the two of us stood there riffing out on our squash rackets to it. I thought I was tripping, the music was so immense. He also introduced me to Molly Hatchet properly that night. I was very ill the next day".

- **Mick Wall (Author/Music Journalist) 2010**

"I first saw Metallica on the ... And Justice For All tour at the Meadowlands in New Jersey. They just seemed superhuman. The instruments were like extensions of their bodies. I was watching and listening and thinking – 'This is impossible! Nobody can play like that!' But there they were".

- **Mike McPadden (Author/Music Journalist) 2013**

BIG 4 ENCYCLOPEDIA

RIP

Ian Fraser "Lemmy" Kilmister

(24 December 1945 – 28 December 2015)

MOTÖRHEAD FOREVER

CONTENTS

FOREWORD BY BRIAN TATLER OF DIAMOND HEAD

INTRODUCTION

A-Z

DISCOGRAPHY

ASSORTED REVIEWS

AFTERWORD BY BOB NALBANDIAN

APPENDECIES

BIBLIOGRAPHY & SOURCES

ACKNOWLEDGEMENTS

DISCLAIMER

ABOUT THE AUTHOR

PUBLISHED BOOKS BY NEIL DANIELS

PRAISE FOR THE AUTHOR'S PREVIOUS WORKS

ALSO AVAILABLE FROM NEIL DANIELS BOOKS

BIG 4 ENCYCLOPEDIA

FOREWORD BY

BRIAN TATLER

OF

DIAMOND HEAD

January 24 2011. The hand of Lars is upon us! Promoter's Kilimanjaro called me to offer Diamond Head the fantastic opportunity of opening on the main stage for the Big 4 – that is Metallica, Slayer, Megadeth and Anthrax in case you did not know! – at 2011's Sonisphere Festival at Knebworth on Friday 8 July. I thought *yeah, I might be tempted*; I of course said 'Yes please!' and quickly let everyone know by phone or email. This would be Diamond Head's biggest ever show and myself and the other band members were very excited and were looking forward to what was an historic event. Knebworth is one of those venues you only dream of playing; I saw Led Zeppelin there in 1979. I was in the audience along with 200,000 rockers, and never imagined that one day I would be on that stage, it proves the saying 'anything is possible!' It also meant I got to see my friends in Metallica and Megadeth once again which is always fun, I owe both Lars Ulrich and Dave Mustaine a beer.

Lars called me on the July 6 (two days before the show) and asked if I would like to join the Big 4 onstage for a jam of either 'Am I Evil?' or 'Helpless'. I was mega flattered to be asked and voted for 'Am I Evil?'. I caught up with Lars and James Hetfield in the Metallica dressing room area and was impressed to see both of them sitting together looking and sounding very relaxed whereas I had been panicking about stuff for hours. I wondered what it must feel like playing on the same stage with the Big 4 to all those people, especially as I had seen the clips on YouTube from Sofia, Bulgaria in 2010.

After Diamond Head's afternoon spot, the rest of the band left to catch the 9pm ferry and I visited Metallica's production office where I was given an itinerary explaining in detail how I was getting to France in time for the following day's gig at 3.25pm.

I was invited by Lars to attend the pre gig jam session in the warm up room which was a very nice set up inside the back of a trailer, with all the gear, monitors and what looked like a ProTools rig running in case one of them came up with a riff. It sounded fantastic as they ran through 'Shortest Straw'. Around 8.30pm Metallica went onstage and completely owned the whole event.

I made my way to a section under a part of the stage where the road crew live tuning guitars and basses. James' guitar tech Chad, loaned me a 1980 white Gibson Flying V to warm up on, he adjusted the strap up a bit for me and when Metallica came off for the last song of the set, some extra backline was added and James introduced Slayer, Megadeth, Anthrax and Brian Tatler from Diamond Head! A huge roar greeted our arrival and I plugged in and stood between Kerry King from Slayer and James Hetfield for a powerful rendition of 'Am I Evil?'. An awesome, truly memorable experience that I will never forget.

Here are some extracts from my autobiography *Am I Evil?*, written with noted NWOBHM historian/author John Tucker.

On 14th October 1990, Sean was invited to sing 'It's Electric' with Megadeth at Wembley Arena, and this began our friendship with Dave Mustaine. We knew he liked Diamond Head and when I first met him at the Cambridge Corn Exchange a year later, he said he would help us any way he could, as a producer, guitarist, writer, advisor, anything we needed. He struck me as a very intelligent, switched-on guy.

Dave Mustaine, who'd earlier offered to help out, agreed to mix a couple of tracks. It was fantastic that he wanted to be part of it, so around October 1992 we sent two 24 track masters to him and Max Norman in Burbank, California. Dave called up Sean and said, "Would you mind if I put some guitar on it?" Sean said, "No, course not; please do", telling me it needed that 'killer tone'. I had not yet put down the solo so we sent them a DAT tape of a solo I had recorded for the demo and they flew it in. Dave did a brilliant job playing guitar, editing and mixing the song 'Truckin''. I understand they ran out of time to mix the second track which was 'Paradise'. Dave had said in *Kerrang!* at the time, "I saw Sean and Brian in England. I've always really loved Diamond Head and what they have done and everything, and so I said, 'Man, I'm a young, hungry producer and I would like nothing more than to produce a Diamond Head record, because I know how to produce good. I mean, I'm not great, but I'm really good'. I thought that, given the brilliance of their songwriting and my determination to make an instrument sound the absolute best an instrument can, and with their capabilities and my knowledge of technology, we could make a kick-ass record". Sean said something like, "Pretty sure of yourself, aren't you mate?" And I went, 'What was that? Are you pissed off or something?' The next thing you know, they'd sent over a tape with two songs on it, and said, 'Do what you want. Play on it, produce it, mix it...'

Bronze Records announced in the press that there would be an EP called, *Intestate*, released on 17th May with 'Truckin'', 'The Prince' and 'It's Electric' from *Lightning To The Nations* and 'Borrowed

Time' from the John Brown 8-track demos. This was a complete non-starter because of ownership issues so we all just aimed at getting the most out of the big Metallica gig. Originally, the bill was going to be Metallica, Megadeth and Alice In Chains, but once Alice In Chains pulled out Diamond Head and The Almighty were added. A limited number of promo EPs on the Bronze/Castle Communications label were pressed up and featured 'Truckin", 'Calling Your Name', 'Run' and 'Starcrossed'. A hundred autographed copies were given away in a *Kerrang!* competition.

I got in touch with Dave Mustaine and made the offer that if he ever wanted to write with me to let me know. Dave responded, explaining that he had done one side project already called MD45 and thought it would be great to do one with me. I bought a VS880 and began writing music for it, following his guidelines that "It should be really heavy and a cross between the first Diamond Head album and EP, and Megadeth's *Killing Is My Business* and *Peace Sells, But Who's Buying"*. I raided my riff tapes and recorded a first batch of eight songs that I posted over to Dave in Arizona on cassette. Dave said "The drummer should be a session guy (at least as good as Jimmy De Grasso) for learning and recording so as not to spend a fortune chopping drums", and added, "Do you know Chris Cornell? He would make an interesting vocalist". I thought, 'Wow, Chris Cornell! Only about the best rock vocalist in the world at that time'.

Dave suggested we meet up when he next came over to the UK and so on 5th Dec 2000 we got together in an office at Sanctuary Records. Dave suggested I get a Pro Tools rig and we could send ideas back and forth across the net. This was a bit of a learning curve for me as I had no idea how to use Pro Tools. I carried on working on the VS and sent more song ideas over on cassette. I hadn't written much since 1994 so it forced me to pull my finger out and come up with as much as possible; I didn't want Dave to think the muse had deserted me. Dave loved some of my ideas and sent notes back about which ones he did and didn't like. By the way, did anyone notice how similar the Megadeth song 'When' is to 'Am I Evil?'

Dave had been recording a new Megadeth album called *The World Needs A Hero* and was in the process of negotiating a new record deal with Sanctuary. He said "I got a side amendment (promissory contract) from Sanctuary for our project", – by which I took it to mean that he'd had the project added to his deal with Sanctuary – "and we are on our way. I talked to my old art director yesterday too, the guy that did *Youthanasia* and *Countdown To Extinction*. He would be a good candidate for the cover". He also told me his manager; Steve

Woods, was on board and "Will make sure this project gets done". I began to think that this could be really great, although thought I'd better let Lars know; he'd done so much for me and Diamond Head over the years and I didn't want to piss him off now that I was writing with an ex-Metallica member, but Lars was cool about it. He knows like everyone else that a man's got to eat!

I continued writing material for the Dave Mustaine project and, by June, Dave had received thirty-four song ideas from me. Rachel and I went to see Megadeth supporting AC/DC and The Offspring at Milton Keynes Bowl on 8th June 2001. I caught up with Dave backstage and later Malcolm Dome collared me to do a quick on-air interview for *Total Rock* radio. As the Megadeth tour ran from March through to November I had to be patient and wait for Dave to finish before he could commit to our project.

I was getting frustrated waiting for The Dave Mustaine Project to happen. Dave had had all my songs for about eight months. I had an e-mail in December 2001 where Dave talked about writing lyrics and said he was coming to England soon and would visit me. Another email came in January 2002 to say he was spending some time with his family. On 26th March a third email made my heart sink. "I am sorry to inform you that I have hurt my arm real bad and am currently in physiotherapy three days a week for the unforeseeable future. The Docs say a year and even then I may never play again. This means our project is not going to happen. I am very, very sad about this". On 3rd April a press statement was released: 'Dave Mustaine, founder, vocalist and lead guitarist of metal pioneers Megadeth suffers serious injury. Announces departure from Megadeth. Group disbanding after nearly 20 years'. The condition is called 'Saturday Night Palsy' and it's similar to when you wake up after lying on your arm all night and you feel like you've a trapped nerve or something. So it was serious shit and I had to take it on the chin. I was disappointed that it had all been building up and building up and then came to nothing. But I was used to disappointment by then.

    Back home again, a couple of months later, in June, I had an e-mail from Steve Guard saying that Sean had written a full album's worth of material. I started going to Sean's house again and we worked on some new songs together. Sean had bought a new Akai 16 track digital recorder for his home studio. I had given him some of my demos from the now defunct Dave Mustaine project and Sean had come up with a great vocal to one of them called 'Shine On Me'. We also demoed 'Music Box', 'Forever 16' and 'Voodoo Sky', left-overs from *Death And Progress*, and at the end of July, Sean handed me a six-track demo with "I hope we can do the business together" scrawled on it. Plans for a new Diamond Head album started taking shape.

We were now being managed by Steve Guard who also doubled as booking agent (taking 20% of all live fees), and he put together a fourteen-date UK tour. Karl flew back over at the end of August for four days' rehearsal at Arcadia. We added 'Shine On Me' to the set after rehearsing it for about an hour as it sounded fantastic. The tour began at the Bloodstock 2002 indoor festival on 31st August at the Assembly Rooms, Derby, for which we received a fee of £1,500. It was a big success, with a turnout of at least 600, headlined by Blind Guardian with their unbelievable ten-foot high drum riser (from top to bottom, the bill was Blind Guardian, Gamma Ray, Diamond Head, Threshold, Balance Of Power, Freedom Call and Biomechanical). The next gig was awful by comparison; the Transport Club in Rochdale (fee £250) was a working men's club that was almost exclusively booked tribute bands. We examined the poster of 'forthcoming events' to find we were the only band that wrote our own tunes. About 60 people turned out to stare at this novelty; it was grim...

I was now living with Rachel and renting out my house. I built a little studio in her old cloakroom, using my VS880. Nick, who worked for Telewest, fitting phone lines, would drop in with an idea whenever he was in the area, and if it sounded good he would return the next day with a fleshed-out verse or chorus. This went on all summer, and we utilised some material from the Dave Mustaine Project as well. Nick's energy and enthusiasm helped push things along and in August I called Sean and told him I was going to continue Diamond Head with another singer and would not be working with Host. I'd had enough. I figured that life's too short, and that there are enough obstacles to overcome without someone actually creating more. I couldn't release the album without Sean's permission, he couldn't release it without mine; the whole thing had reached a stalemate so the best thing was to end it now and get on with our lives. I don't think he expected this. I posted a message on the Diamond Head website about "The departure of Sean Harris" and he posted a reply on *melodicrock.com* that he was "Shocked by the news". But at least I was now back in control of my own destiny. And in all honesty, that felt good.

Before Karl went back to the US, he and Steve said that the reformed Megadeth were touring the UK in February and that maybe I should email Dave Mustaine to offer our services as support band. Dave rang me straight back: "Oh my God! What a great idea!" At first I presumed we would just do the eight dates in the UK and Ireland, but Dave said we should do the whole European tour – 22 dates on the road with MegaDave! For us, this was a great opportunity. The last European tour we had undertaken was over 20 years ago with Black Sabbath, and we were a very different band back then. I was in the process of sending out CDs of the new album to record labels but because we were about to play to 35,000 people on the Megadeth tour in less than two months' time we decided to press a limited edition batch of 1,000 copies ourselves, sell them on the tour to help cover costs and seek a deal when we were home once more. Mick Payton and I quickly began work on a sleeve and Steve Guard priced it up. All the while I was thanking my lucky stars that we had done that JB's date, otherwise Nick's first show would have been in front of 2,000 people.

Dave and his manager said they would make up a joint Megadeth/Diamond Head T-shirt and that we could have half the profits. This was very generous as, as far as I am aware, no-one has ever done that. They also suggested that we put our gear into their truck which would save us money on transportation. Dave was so keen to make it happen he even said that he would cover any losses.

Steve and I began costing a tour bus for the European leg and a mini bus for the UK, and just before Christmas we were confirmed as support for the whole tour. Rachel booked the ferries and hotels on-line and we were pretty much ready to roll.

I spent 13th January mastering the album with engineer Tony Dixon at Masterpiece studio. Steve called to tell me that Livewire/Cargo liked the album and would offer a deal. All of a sudden, things seemed to be moving quite quickly. We completed the artwork with an image of a solar eclipse, which we also used for the front of a run of 500 T-shirts. Eleven days later, Karl arrived for three days of rehearsals, and on the 28th the gear was packed up and dropped off to travel with Megadeth's to Dublin and the start of the tour, which kicked off on 1st February.

I kept a tour diary for the first time ever and posted it on the website for posterity (Setlist: 'It's Electric'/'Mine All Mine'/'The Prince'/'Give It To Me'/'Truckin''/'In The Heat Of The Night'/'Broken Pieces'/'Helpless'/'Am I Evil?').

Diamond Head's first ever gig in Ireland was at the Dublin Ambassador. The crossing was very rough and we all felt sick but we'd heard that the Irish crowds were good and they were in fact far crazier than we were expecting. This got us off to a flying start and gave this line-up the confidence it needed. Dave came into our dressing room after the gig and welcomed us all to the tour, adding, "If there's anything you need, we will arrange for it; if anything breaks, we'll fix it for you". The next day we drove to Belfast and our hotel in County

Antrim where we enjoyed a good meal and a shower (a step-up from the night before when we slept in a cheap youth hostel, eight of us in one room with four bunk beds). The gig was at the famous Ulster Hall, a big 2,000 capacity venue. We had a long soundcheck and played to another brilliant crowd. We even got a mosh pit going, and thought that this reaction would be hard to beat elsewhere. And we were all amazed to see lifelong Diamond Head superfan Mike Lace turn up in his wheelchair.

The ferry crossing from Belfast to Stranraer was fortunately smoother than the Holyhead to Dublin trip. We changed the set slightly and went down a storm at the Glasgow Academy. On Dave's suggestion, all of us went on stage with Megadeth to sing backing vocals on 'Back In The Day' which we did for the rest of the tour. We were nervous at first but got into it, especially Eddie who would often do something crazy and, at one gig, Dave could not sing for laughing.

It took drum tech/driver Andy Bailey under five hours to whisk us from a Glasgow Travelodge to the Birmingham Academy on 4th February. It was very weird arriving at the venue and seeing a long queue waiting to get in as we'd got used to the gig being empty until we were virtually due to go on. As this was our hometown show, we had friends and family on the guestlist which of course made us much more anxious. My fiancée Rachel brought her two children to the soundcheck where they met Dave who happened to be sitting out front at the lighting desk. A lot of the gigs on this tour started early and at this one we were on at 6.45 and off at 7.30 (Megadeth did 8pm till 10pm) so a few people unfortunately missed our show or arrived halfway through...

INTRODUCTION

On June 22, 2010, Metallica, Megadeth, Slayer and Anthrax – known in metal circles as the Big Four – performed on the same bill at the Vasil Levski National Stadium in Sofia, Bulgaria. The concert was part of an event where the Big Four would, for the first time, tour together as part of the popular Sonisphere Festival. The Bulgaria show was the third in a succession of seven such events but what made it especially popular was that it was transmitted live via satellite to 800 cinemas worldwide; and later released on DVD. It also provided a mouth-watering moment for metal fans as every member of the Big Four (bar Tom Araya, Kerry King and Jeff Hanneman of Slayer) grouped together onstage for an historic version of Diamond Head's classic NWOBHM track 'Am I Evil?'.

 Lars Ulrich explained to *Revolver* magazine in 2011: "The reason we picked 'Am I Evil?' is because obviously playing a Metallica song would've seemed a little selfish. All of the musicians would certainly share that thread in Diamond Head in terms of influence. It's probably difficult to find a band that's more responsible for, or at least indirectly responsible, for thrash metal. And 'Am I Evil?' is just a great, anthem-like song that also has the quality of not being super complicated. So it just seemed like the right kind of vibe to share with everybody for five minutes that wasn't necessarily going to send people back to the rehearsal room for days on end. [Dave] Mustaine and a bunch of these guys obviously knew the riff, too, and it just seemed like a logical choice".

The Big Four popularised thrash metal in the 1980s although there would be discontent and some ill-feelings between various members for quite some time. Nevertheless, what the event did show is that thrash metal is as popular now as ever before.

Metallica's peers included many bands in the North California area which became known as the Bay Area thrash scene with bands such as Exodus, Testament, Sadus and Possessed while there were also thrash metal outfits in South California such as Slayer and the Dave Mustaine's new outfit, Megadeth. This led to the rise of American thrash and death metal and was heavily inspired by UK bands; primarily the originators of heavy metal, the Midlands bands Black Sabbath and Judas Priest, and also the New Wave Of British Heavy Metal bands whilst not forgetting the mighty punk-metal crossover monster, Motörhead. Meanwhile, the New York thrash outfit Anthrax that formed in 1981 and released their killer debut *Fistful Of Metal* in 1984 were leaders of the East Coast thrash metal scene along with the

New Jersey band Overkill.

"I trace most of what's going on today back to 1976 in England, when the punk movement started. Most of today's metal scene is inspired by that – when all the bands in England said, 'Fuck the excess, fuck the grandeur'. It was brought back to a minimalist approach of people wanting to do their own records, not caring about sellable images", Lars Ulrich said to *Married To Metal* in 1985.

Collectively, Metallica, Slayer, Megadeth and Anthrax became known as "The Big Four", though it has been argued since that three of the four bands are certainly nowhere near as popular while Metallica – their enormous global success cannot be denied – have soldiered on simply as a great live band because their studio output has been mediocre at best since 1991's *Metallica* opus.

Thrash wasn't specifically located to America although it may have seemed that way: the German thrash trio Sodom had formed in 1981 while Destruction and Kreator both formed in 1982. They were the pioneers of European technical thrash and death metal and became known as 'the three kings' of Teutonic thrash metal. Suffice it to say there were regional thrash metal scenes all over the world but it was spearheaded primarily by American and German bands. Later, Brazil were found a growing metal scene led by the band, Stress and

Canada spawned Anvil, Exciter, Voivod and later in the decade, Annihilator. Many of these bands stayed on a cult level without the mass appeal that would be given to Metallica. Jeff Waters of Annihilator told the author in 2006: "...when I was younger I had dreams of being [in] Metallica; just as a kid you dream about getting to this level and over the years you get slapped down to reality and you realise you should be happy where you are".

This isn't a book to debate the difference between speed metal and thrash metal but suffice it to say thrash evolved from speed metal. A band liked Anvil and Exciter (both from Canada) have been dubbed speed while the Big Four bands are thrash.

Exciter's John Ricci told the author in 2011: "Speed metal is closer in style to power metal which is like big power chords played fast with melodic vocals; thrash is more like a guitar riff with a whole bunch of notes crammed in a very short space in the music therefore you can't really distinguish the riff and once this fast riffing is combined with lots of distortion you have thrash".

It is important to know the difference between thrash and speed and what makes Metallica a thrash band. Speed metal evolved from such songs as 'Communication Breakdown' by Led Zeppelin, 'Highway Star' and 'Fireball' by Deep Purple, 'Sheer Heart Attack' and

'Stone Cold Crazy' by Queen and much of Motörhead's back catalogue, including 'Bomber', 'Overkill'.

David Konow – author of *Bang Your Head: The Rise And Fall Of Heavy Metal* – spoke to the author in 2011 about the difference between speed metal and thrash and what specifically pigeon-holed Metallica in the latter subgenre of metal. He stated: "I always found the subgenre labels of metal, like many found them, to be a bit confusing and head scratching, especially these days with screamo, this, that, whatever... It was never properly defined to me in all my years as a metalhead, speed metal was supposed to be mostly fast, thrash had slower 'mosh' parts and things like that is how I vaguely remember it being once defined. Metallica always strove very hard to leave all that stuff behind and not be pigeonholed into that category. It's a big reason I always liked their music, it had more to it than Venom and Slayer, who I loved as well, but their style was more one dimensional. Metallica had more variety to what they were doing, they were really good musicians too, and it's also what I loved about Megadeth's first two albums, the musicianship was up to a much higher standard and they were more experimental with what they were doing. Although they always knew they'd get cries of sell out, Metallica were smart to expand their sound early and not get stuck in one thing, where a lot of bands painted themselves in a corner with their style and couldn't expand on what they were doing. But getting back to your original question, I think with say death metal it's obvious what the difference is, and what defines that sound, and even back in the 1980s there were all these category names like speed core, grindcore was probably defined around 1987, etc. I still dig a lot of it, and I guess the all purpose term these days is extreme metal, which a lot of this stuff fits under just fine".

The American thrash metal scene that was located on both ends of California, the East Coast and also South Florida was the complete opposite to the LA hair metal scene. The LA area in the early 1980s was dominated by glam rock and hair metal bands led by the likes of Mötley Crüe, Poison, Quiet Riot, Dokken, Ratt, W.A.S.P. and Stryper. There were lots of others bands too but the aforementioned ones were some of the more popular and commercially successful outfits. "They [Metallica] were certainly different from anything going on in LA at the time or really in the USA as they were so influenced by the New Wave Of British Heavy metal and European style metal", said Brian Slagel in 2011.

The glam and hair metal scene wasn't specifically centered around the Sunset Strip as Black 'N Blue came from Oregon, Bon Jovi came from New Jersey and Twister Sister hailed from Long Island. Metallica and their ilk had distanced themselves from the LA hair metal scene. For them, metal was more technical and intricate, heavy and fast, and certainly not focused on fashion and hairstyles.

There were many other thrash bands, but none of them as wildly successful or popular as Metallica. Metal photographer Bill Hale who shot the rise of Metallica and Megadeth in the early days says it rather well, as he told the author in 2011: "Way before Metallica and Megadeth came along, the Bay Area had some great bands already: Vicious Rumors, Exodus, Trauma, Griffin, Anvil Chorus, Death Angel, Testament, Lääz Rockit, Heathen, Forbidden, Blind Illusion, Ruffians, Vio-lence, Possessed, just to name a few... But somehow Metallica rose to the top of the 'Thrash Metal Heap'. The Bay Area has always been a hot bed for music. The 1980s was just the heavy metal chapter!"

Long gone were the days of bands like Sabbath and Purple. The rise of American metal had begun!

This book – told in A to Z format – is a guide to the Big Four bands; it does not purport to be a definitive work but rather a scrapbook of the musicians, the music, the tours, the influences and those who have been influenced by the Big Four bands however directly or indirectly. It is a compilation of lists, articles and reviews that I have written over the years as well as some new pieces. It does not include every album or song but some of the hits (and misses) as well as the people that made the music; those on and off stage and in front of and behind the microphone. Perfect for time spent reading on the loo!

Neil Daniels

www.neildanielsbooks.com

A

A YEAR AND A HALF IN THE LIFE OF METALLICA

A two part documentary about the making of *The Black Album* released on video in 1992.

AEROSMITH

By far one of the most universally successful American rock bands of all time, Aerosmith have sold over 150 million albums, almost half of which have been sold in the US alone. They regularly feature in polls of greatest bands and have been inducted into both the Rock And Roll Hall Of Fame and the Songwriters Hall Of Fame. The band is made up of singer Steven Tyler, guitarist Joe Perry and Brad Whitford, drummer Joey Kramer and bassist Tom Hamilton. Some of their famous albums include *Permanent Vacation* (1987), *Pump* (1989), *Get A Grip* (1993) with such well-known and enduring singles as 'Sweet Emotion', 'Back In The Saddle', 'Dude (Looks Like A Lady')', 'Ragdoll', 'Cryin'' and 'Pink'. The band are still touring and recording. Tyler even had a stint as an *American Idol* judge. Aerosmith are an influence on each of the Big Four bands. Kirk Hammett and James Hetfield are big 'smith fans.

AIN'T MY BITCH

A promo single from Metallica issued in Mexico and culled from *Load*, their sixth album.

ALL NIGHTMARE LONG

The fifth single from Metallica's ninth album *Death Magnetic*. It was released in December 2008.

AMERICAN HEAD CHARGE

American Head Charge's breakthrough album was 2001's *The Art Of War*, produced by Rick Rubin and released through his label American Recordings. Their debut album *Trepanation* was independently released in 1999. Although they're often touted as an industrial metal outfit some argue they fell into the nu-metal mould after touring with the likes of Cold Chamber and Mudvayne. They've toured/shared the bill with a number of other high-profile metal bands, including Hatebreed, System Of A Down, Ministry, Static-X and Biohazard *et al*. They also played on the 2001 Ozzfest with bands such as Linkin Park. Formed in Minneapolis in 1997, the band have had their fair share of inner turmoil, mostly due to drug abuse. They were released from their record deal with Rubin's label and their third album *The Feeding* was issued in 2005 through DRT Entertainment/Nitrus. Guitarist Bryan Ottoson died in 2005, aged just 27; it was alleged that his death was caused by an accidental drug overdose (the drugs were medically prescribed). Things have been quiet with the band since the release of 2007's live CD/DVD set *Can't Stop The Machine*. They finally released their latest studio album (their Napalm Records debut) *Tango Umbrella* in 2015. There have been a number of line-up changes in AHC, as they are affectionately known by fans, but the 2009 line-up is: singer Cameron Heacock, bassist Chad Hanks, keyboardist Justin Fowler, guitarists Karma Singh Cheema and Ted Hallows and drummer Chris Emery.

AMONG THE LVIING

This is a seminal thrash metal release by Anthrax. It was issued in 1990 and was undoubtedly the band's breakthrough release.

...AND JUSTICE FOR ALL (ALBUM)

Metallica ended 1987 with some rehearsals as they were planning ideas for their fourth album. In many respects this would be a pivotal album in the early years of Metallica's career because not only was it the first not to feature Cliff Burton but they had a lot to live up to after the critical success of *Kill 'Em All*, *Ride The Lightning* and *Master Of Puppets*.

On January 28, 1988, Metallica entered One On One Recording Studios in Los Angeles to begin work on what was to be the first album to feature James Newsted; the band's fourth album in total. They have always been very particular about their choice of recording studio; making sure each studio had exactly what they needed such as the size of the control room and recording suites. The band did prefer to work at Sweet Silence Studios in Copenhagen where they recorded *Ride The Lightning* and *Master Of Puppets*. In Europe – as opposed to the United States – the studios have in-house engineers, which is how they met Flemming Rasmussen who produced the latter two albums and the band had been impressed with Rasmussen's work with the English rock band Rainbow (founded by former Deep Purple guitarist Ritchie Blackmore) on their 1983 opus *Difficult To Cure*. For the fourth release, Metallica's record company had set up a tour of LA's recording studios and had Hetfield choose one suitable for the band's needs.

Producer Flemming Rasmussen who had co-produced with the band *Ride The Lightning* and *Master Of Puppets* was unavailable so the band opted to work with Mike Clink who had made a name for himself with Guns N' Roses debut album *Appetite For Destruction*. However, the relationship between Clink and Metallica was to be short-lived and after two months Rasmussen entered the picture to replace Clink once he was free of his other production duties. Clink was credited with engineering the drums on 'The Shortest Straw' and 'Harvester Of Sorrow' and for the recording two cover versions: 'Breadfan' and 'The Prince' which were initially used as B-sides on the single 'Harvester Of Sorrow' and were later used on the double CD *Garage Inc*. Ulrich explained (Borivoj Krgin interview, *Metal Forces*, 1988): "Mike did a fine job and did us all a big favour by coming into the studio and helping us out, but Flemming is the only one who can record Metallica and Mike understood that perfectly before he came to work with us".

Kirk Hammett (*Rolling Stone*, 'Pretty Hate Machine', 1996): "We're the master procrastinators. We tend to work eighty percent of the time on the first ten percent of the album and spend the other twenty percent of the time on the last ninety percent of the record. We tend to sweat and toil on the beginning of a record, and a lot of that has to do with establishing a stride that works for us. And sometimes establishing that momentum is very difficult".

They came out of the studio on May 1, 1988. Though *...And Justice For All* is not a concept album per se there are consistent themes running rippling throughout the nine lengthy tracks. Perhaps inspired by futuristic novels like George Orwell's *1984*, the themes present in the album include political, legal and social injustice in a world of censorship, war and nuclear weapons.

And Justice For All was released in August 1988 and was the band's first Top 10 hit in the USA, reaching Number 6. Whatever criticisms that were aimed at the album clearly had no effect on its sales. It did great for the band in the UK peaking at Number 4. 'Harvester Of Sorrow' was a hit single in the UK reaching Number 20 and 'Eye Of The Beholder' reached Number 27. The band also released '...And Justice For All' as a single. With a hit album had Metallica now become a mainstream band?

Fans had waited two and a half years since *Master Of Puppets* and some felt it was too long but the band had a lot to deal with: they committed themselves to an eleven month world tour, they released an EP and VHS tape and they had to deal with the death of Cliff Burton and also James Hetfield's skateboarding accident. They were not sitting around idly. Metallica were fortunate enough to have control over their music; they were effectively self-employed and ran their own business.

Metal Forces co-founder and editor Bernard Doe said to the author in 2011: "*Master Of Puppets* was always going to be a hard album to top, but for me ...*And Justice For All* was still a disappointment at the time, apart from 'One' of course which is arguably up there as one of Metallica's finest moments. I also found the production rather limp-wristed. Far less accessible than previous releases, much of the material from the album was quickly dropped from the band's live set or stripped down and relegated to the '...And Justice For All Medley', which spoke volumes at the time".

Critical opinion was mostly very positive with rave reviews in *Kerrang!* and *Metal Hammer*. Upon the album's original release, Michael Azerrad wrote in *Rolling Stone:* "Thrash is too demeaning a term for this metametal, a marvel of precisely channeled aggression. There are few verse-chorus structures, just collages done at Mach 8. The album is crammed with diatribes about nuclear winter, the right to die and judicial corruption, delivered in an aggressive bark by rhythm guitarist James Hetfield".

Azerrad reviewed ...*And Justice For All* with Bon Jovi's *New Jersey* (also released in 1988) and concluded his review by saying, "Bon Jovi's trick is to use heavy-metal chords and still sound absolutely safe. Rock 'n' roll used to be rebellion disguised as commercialism; now so much of it is commercialism disguised as rebellion. Bon Jovi is safe as milk; Metallica harks back to the time when rock's bite was worse than its bark".

The famed American rock critic gave the album a rating of C+ in his historic *Consumer Guide Reviews* and merely said: "Problem isn't that it's more self-conscious than *Master Of Puppets*, which is inevitable when your stock in trade is compositions not songs. Problem is that it goes on longer – which is also inevitable when your stock in trade is compositions not songs. Just ask Yes".

Bill Hale who photographed the band during the first few years said to the author: "I would say the first three albums, never heard the fourth. The fans over here [California] wanted/needed to have a band all their own. Yeah, we all dug Motörhead, Diamond Head, Maiden, Angel Witch but they were not one of us. Metallica was! They unlikely friends in a band and being his band Lars of course had big plans. Ron [McGovney] was the first to go followed by Mustaine. Musically, the band was straight from the gut: no filler, no fluff, just pure young angry metal riffs. Of yeah, they 'borrowed' from the British bands but the sound that they made was all their own!"

In time, the album would continue to receive adulation. Here's what the rock and metal scribes said in the noughties:

Steve Huey's astute review at *MSN Music* said: "The most immediately noticeable aspect of *...And Justice For All* isn't Metallica's still-growing compositional sophistication or the apocalyptic lyrical portrait of a society in decay. It's the weird, bone-dry production. The guitars buzz thinly, the drums click more than pound, and Jason Newsted's bass is nearly inaudible".

He continued: "It's a shame that the cold, flat sound obscures some of the sonic details, because ...*And Justice For All* is Metallica's most complex, ambitious work; every song is an expanded suite, with only two of the nine tracks clocking in at under six minutes".

Punk News stated: "*Justice* contains Metallica's most sophisticated, heaviest riffs yet. A lot of changing tempos, a lot of weird rhythms, a lot of palm-muted guitars and a lot of excellent solos courtesy of one Kirk Hammett, specifically 'One', 'Blackened' and 'Dyers Eve'. What's interesting about this record is how most of its solos are actually divided in two, with a small break in between".

Sputnikmusic enthused: "Overall this album has a very angst feel. No, this is not for anyone who watches *Alley Mcbeal* [*sic*.] The lyrics are violent, the riffs are fast, it truly makes you want to kick some ass. To be more specific a lot of lyrics were pretty much insulting our countries leaders. You can here [*sic*] the really feel the aggression in James' vocals as they flow through the speakers".

BBC Music offered a mixed review but said: "This album sounds different to every other Metallica record, vocally gruffer but with thinner orchestration. Drums tick and pop, rather than bang, the guitars sound dryer and thinner, and there's little in the way of bass... The songs are longer too. And as the sound has become thinner and tauter the songs have grown grander and more epic. These are musicians becoming more ambitious craftsmen and experimenting as a result".

Martin Popoff – the Canadian metal historian and author – gave the author his opinion of *...And Justice For All*: "My views on this album aren't all that innovative or different from anybody else's. One thing I do remember though, I definitely didn't draw as much value out of this album I did the previous two. I love the fact it was proggy and anti-commercial; I didn't even have complaints with the production job. It was just kind of cool hearing a very extreme, obscure production job, when there was so much wetness on hair metal albums, although don't get me wrong, I totally dug most of those hair metal bands as well, hating only Bon Jovi, Poison and Cinderella, really. But yeah, everybody complained about the production, they complained about the long songs, and yes, truth be told, it was a little extreme. Metallica on this record evoked that same reservation I had with the first record, where everybody crouched around and paid homage to riff. Only this time, there was less logic to it. Whereas on *Kill 'Em All*, you felt that there were two or three perfectly fine riffs stuck together, forced to live together, and presto, here's our song, with *Justice*, there were more like fourteen riffs per song, and still, they didn't all necessarily have to be there, or all necessarily work with each other, intro upon intro. So yeah, I suppose this album is the band's *Sin After Sin*, or their *Far Beyond Driven*, which is perfectly admirable, although like I say, it's a cool, intellectual album, and not so much one for the heart, like the previous two".

The legacy of *...And Justice For All* like it's three predecessors is assured and though many claim the band's fourth album to be a flaw masterpiece it is a significant album in Metallica's might arsenal of studios opuses. It was awarded Platinum status in the United States twelve times and remains a popular metal album; since 1991 alone it has sold over five million copies. 'One' was ranked at Number 7 in the '100 Greatest Guitar Solos Of All Time' by *Guitar World* while *IGN Music* placed the album at Number 9 in the list of 'The Top 25 Metal Albums' and it is also featured in the hefty reference tome *1001 Albums You Must Hear Before You Die*.

In time members of Metallica would later re-evaluate their opinion about *...And Justice For All*. "I must admit that listening to

...*Justice* now, I do wonder why we put three minute intros onto some of the stuff". Ulrich commented in 1990. "Obviously that's what we were into at the time, but right now, I'm more into the songwriting style we had on *Ride The Lightning*. I also know a lot of people found ...*Justice* difficult to get into but I'm not gonna sit here and apologise for that. I mean, out of all the Metallica albums to date, it's no secret that ...*Justice* is by far the less accessible of them all, I just find it funny that it's sold better than the others by over three to one..."

James Hetfield confessed almost a decade later (Douglas J Noble, *Guitar Magazine*, 'Load Era 1', 1996): "[... *And Justice For All*] was really, really anal. Every little bit was worked out. The arrangement was so orchestrated that it got really stiff, and when we were on tour it got really boring. So we knew we had to move on..."

...AND JUSTICE FOR ALL (SINGLE)

'...And Justice For All' was the second single from Metallica's album of the same name.

ANNIHILATOR

Canada's Annihilator are surely one of the most underrated bands in metal. Sure, thrash fans are familiar with Jeff Waters and his numerous cohorts from over the years, but do people really acknowledge their technical brilliance and mind-melting songs? The band was formed in 1984 by Jeff Waters and former singer John Bates. Their first two albums *Alice In Hell* and *Never, Neverland* remain their true masterpieces. They continue to this day though Waters is the only consistent member. They released *Suicide Society* in 2015. Waters spoke to the author about his love of Slayer for the author's book on Texan metal band Pantera:

"I would meet them [Pantera] at their shows in Vancouver for years to come. The most memorable was on the *Reinventing The Steel* tour. I'd followed them in the '90s on through music video channels and, of course, everybody was wearing Pantera shirts. I knew they were a big band but I didn't really get it until I saw that last *Reinventing The Steel* tour. Kerry King or Tom Araya (Slayer) had me on their guestlist and, to be safe, I got Phil Anselmo to put me on his, too! I love Slayer; one of my top three favourite bands. Fucking awesome! I know these guys! Early in the afternoon, I hung with the band and crew, talked about old times and spent the rest of the day with Phil. I just assumed it was a double bill or that Pantera were a special guest. I'm standing on Kerry's side of the stage watching Slayer. The kids are going crazy. It was an awesome reaction, as always, for Slayer. I thought, How the fuck does Pantera follow that? How do you follow what I just saw from Slayer? Jesus Christ! And what happens next? Pantera came out with a slick light show, a bigger stage show, bigger explosions, pyro, flames, massive, powerful riffs, grooves and sounds and then I realized: Oh my god, they're the fucking headliners! Slayer are the guests! That blew my mind and I realized that Pantera were even bigger than I thought they were! I was like, Jeff, you idiot, you're still getting it wrong after all these years. It was amazing to see full hockey arenas, with two bands of this calibre, playing in these venues. This was an era where traditional heavy music was literally banished to the underground by labels, press, the industry...unless you were playing a new kind of metal".

ANSELMO, PHIL

Phil Anselmo was born Philip Hansen Anselmo on June 30, 1968 in New Orleans, Louisiana. He went to Grace King High School in Metairie whilst his dad owned a restaurant in the suburban Metairie called Anselmo's, which closed after Hurricane Katrina of August 2005. Right from an early age, Anselmo discovered a passion and deep interest in horror films and culture; he would eventually accumulate an extensive personal library of horror films and an expert knowledge of the genre. "I didn't like school. I didn't like it at all!", he told *Kerrang!* writer Mörat in 1994. "I was smart enough; I made good grades when I applied myself. My folks used to get on at me, so I'd apply a little bit and I did good, but my head wasn't there".

A buddy of his named Thomas Gromaskas turned him on to Black Sabbath and they'd trade metal albums with each other. They listened to Sabbath's *Paranoid* or Venom's *Black Metal* and got stoned and talked for hours about metal. It was just Anselmo and Gromaskas; they didn't belong to a gang. They were the dudes that would hang around the school halls wearing Maiden or Sabbath T-shirts and jeans. They'd also jam with each other but as they got older their circle of friends grew. They really dug the satanic imagery of Venom; the power and evil nature of their music.

"...it [singer/musician] was something that I just really knew at a very young age", he said to Rafi at *VampireFreaks*. "At about 6 or 7 I knew that I wanted to be in music or I was going to be a professional wrestler... I fell in love with it; I was raised in a house of music".

Anselmo would play air guitar to Queen's *A Night At The Opera* and KISS *Alive!*. Similarly to Darrell, Anselmo would dress up as a member of KISS and practice his moves in the isolation of his bedroom.

One day when Anselmo was putting on the full KISS gear and applying the make-up in front of the bathroom mirror listening to his KISS albums his dad walked and just shook his head disapprovingly.

His parents were liberals and dug music by The Beatles and King Crimson but Anselmo was into harder rock bands. "I used to skip school and pretend I was sick", he told *Kerrang!*'s Robyn Doreian in 1991. "I remember one particular time when I built this fake guitar out of all this wood, and painted it blue".

Anselmo was between thirteen and fourteen years of age when he knew he wanted to be in a band. Anselmo's first major band was Samhain (not to be confused with Glen Danzig's band which he fronted between Misfits and Danzig). It was a big turning point for Anselmo as he'd never played music with a bunch of guys before that had their own instruments and a garage to practice in. The drummer in the band had his own kit and it was the first time Anselmo had heard experienced the powerful sound of the drums first-hand. Anselmo was taking guitar lessons at the time although his friends told him he should be a singer but he wasn't ready for that; not yet. Even though they played covers, Anselmo was eager to play original material and he began to develop his own. He would even show his guitar teacher some new riffs he was developing.

A reportedly quiet and sky kid who spent time working on fishing boats, Anselmo was a huge Judas Priest fan and in his next band Razor White, they covered the Priest classics. Anselmo's other favourite bands included Slayer, the British metal band Venom and the Swiss metal monsters Hellhammer. "When I first heard Hellhammer it truly disturbed me", he enthused to *VampireFreaks*' Rafi. "That is the key to a band, that their music stays with you and that you cannot deny its effect on you".

Anselmo was also interested in football and played the Defensive End and as he grew older he became a Defensive Tackle, Linebacker and then a Quarterback in Junior High. But music was his calling card; not sport and certainly not academia. He left school aged sixteen for a life in music, not sport or anything else.

The young singer and metal enthusiast made an instant connection with Hellhammer just as he did with the British band Venom. He came to love those bands and began a quest to seek out more bands that had the same kind of brutality, which he found a connection with. He even found emotion in this kind of music. It became a lifelong love. Metal was his life. Period.

The New Orleans bands were aware of the Bay Area scene over in North California and just in the state of Louisiana alone there were over twenty rock clubs. There was a thriving rock and metal movement in the South especially in Texas and Florida. Bands could play every day in a week in Louisiana and not play the same club twice. It was the perfect time for Anselmo to make a name for himself and build up some contacts. Lillian Axe and Razor White would run in and out of Texas and bump into bands like Pantera, Sweet Savage and a band called Stiff with Ron Taylor, Jon Ster and Rob Stratton who actually moved over to Lillian Axe before they got their first record deal.

Razor White was the next up-starting New Orleans melodic metal band and they opened up for Lillian Axe a number of times. Anselmo would always be found hanging out in the dressing room where he'd be asking Blaze or his cohorts how to play certain songs on the guitar. They mentored him in a way. One time Lillian Axe was opening for Ratt on a few dates and they ended up in Texas where they met Darrell, Vinnie and Brown. They told Blaze that they were looking for a new singer and he recommended Anselmo because he was an up and coming guy with a good voice, stage presence and enthusiasm.

When Anselmo joined in 1987 he was amazed at how Darrell could create a guitar sound that is best described as "shredding".

"...once again I gotta turn to Metallica to say they were the first ones to really bring that bite to the fucking guitars", said Phil Anselmo to *Examiner*'s Elliot Levin twenty years later, "so they really upped the game. But I also have to say this. Dimebag Darrell had known James Hetfield, and Lars, and all those guys a long time, even before I'd met them".

Darrell used to tell Anselmo stories about how he taught James Hetfield a few things on the guitar like scales and Hetfield used to tell Darrell how to get a certain sound through the amps. Anselmo really dug those stories because he was a huge Metallica fan. Pantera was definitely influenced by Metallica; there's no question about it. Certainly Diamond Darrell was inspired by James Hetfield too and probably Kirk Hammett, the band's lead guitarist. Pantera was a well-established regional band. They were well known, regionally but also nationally and Anselmo had a plan to turn Pantera's fortunes around and make them a nationwide band.

1988 saw the release of Pantera's fourth album, *Power Metal*; the first opus featuring Phil Anselmo's vocals. It was a far more aggressive and heavier album than fans had come to expect from Pantera.

It was around this time that the band met Slayer; one of the fiercest metal bands in the country. Still stuck on the seemingly never ending Texan club circuit, Pantera were booked for a show in Dallas on a Friday when Slayer were due to play on the Saturday evening as part of their recently commenced *South Of Heaven* tour and Anselmo, being an avid fan, had already bought his ticket for the show. As it happened, all members of Slayer par drummer Dave Lombardo went to see Pantera perform on the Friday night much to Anselmo's delight.

Speaking to Rafi at *VampireFreaks* about his first meeting with the legendary Kerry King, Anselmo enthused: "...Kerry King ended up getting on stage with us and played 'Reign In Blood'. After that me and him got to talking and hit it off really well".

The Pantera singer and Kerry King chatted about Judas Priest as they were both committed fans. They found a common bond and exchanged phone numbers. Anselmo continued to tell the story that just a few weeks later his phone rang but he could not understand who was on the other end of the line. It turned out that it was Kerry King. Anselmo was totally stoked. It really was Kerry King of Slayer! Anselmo struck up a close friendship with Kerry King and learnt a lot from him in due course, and although Slayer's 1988 album *South Of Heaven* received mixed reviews they had a masterpiece to their name with *Reign In Blood*; released in 1986. A mutual interest of course was the mighty Judas Priest – Slayer had covered Priest and Maiden songs at club dates in the early days.

Anselmo continued to tell *VampireFreaks'* Rafi: "The first time he just came to hang out, the second time he called me and said 'look this time I don't want to just come down for no reason'".

King told Anselmo that he wanted to jam. When King went down to jam with Pantera it was an amazing feeling for Anselmo who was such a fan of Slayer and their thrash metal peers. Indeed when Slayer next visited Texas, Kerry joined Pantera onstage and they blitzed through some classic material, including songs from Pantera's own opus *Power Metal* as well as Slayer's 'South Of Heaven' and 'Reign In Blood', and even some old Priest songs too. When King hooked up with Darrell he taught him a few new tricks; things that were going on in the burgeoning underground American metal scene at the time which was a world away from what Darrell's was influenced by, namely, Randy Rhoads, Eddie Van Halen and Ace Frehley. Kerry King played out of key and at an incredibly fast speed which was totally different from the way Darrell and his heroes played the guitar, so Darrell was taught a new perspective on how to make a metal riff. It was at this point in the late 1980s when Pantera began to develop their sound, which was evidently inspired by Anselmo's new heroes, Slayer.

Kerry King became an instrumental figure once Anselmo had joined Pantera. He would call Anselmo and joke that he wanted to join Pantera and he'd watch Pantera at local gigs. King even joined Pantera onstage at one point and the band had quickly developed a twin-guitar sound that recalled their heroes, Judas Priest. Diamond Darrell learned the Slayer songs and noticed how dense and intricate Slayer's riffs actually are. Many bands imitated Slayer, but not Pantera. Pantera began to develop their own sound.

The single 'Goddamn Electric' from Pantera's *Reinventing The Steel* features a guitar spot by Kerry King of Slayer and references Slayer and Black Sabbath. King's guest solo was recorded backstage at an Ozzfest show in Dallas (July 13) on a portable tape machine.

ANTHRAX

Formed in New York City in 1981, Anthrax was founded by guitarists Scott Ian and Danny Lilker. They would become part of the Big Four of thrash metal making them one of the genre's fundamental bands. The band has had a number of line-up changes and several internal complications, notably going through three singers: Neil Turbin, Joey Belladonna, Dan Nelson and John Bush. The classic line-up is most certainly from the *Among The Living* era with singer Joey Belladonna, guitarists Dan Spitz and Scott Ian, bassist Frank Bello and drummer Charlie Benante. They continue to tour regularly though their studio output has slowed down in recent years; mostly due to complications with their singers. They released their latest studio album *Worship Music* in 2011.

Some of their best albums are *Spreading The Disease* (1985), *Among The Living* (1987), *State Of Euphoria* (1988) and *Persistence Of Time* (1990).

CURRENT MEMBERS:

Scott Ian (Rhythm guitar/backing-lead vocals, 1981–)

Charlie Benante (Drums/percussion/lead guitar, 1983–)

Frank Bello (Bass guitar/backing vocals, 1984–2004, 2005–)

Joey Belladonna (Lead vocals, 1984–1992, 2005–2007, 2010–)

Jonathan Donais (Lead guitar, 2013–)

FORMER MEMBERS:

Bob Berry (Lead guitar, 1983)

John Bush (Lead vocals, 1992-2005, 2009-2010)

Rob Caggiano (Lead guitar, 2001-2005, 2007-2013)

John Connelly (Lead vocals, 1981)

Paul Crook (Lead guitar, 1995-2001)

Greg D'Angelo (Drums, 1981-1983)

Matt Fallon (Leads vocals, 1984)

Paul Kahn (Bass, 1981)

Dirk Kennedy (Lead vocals, 1981)

Kenny Kushner (Bass, 1981)

Dan Lilker (Bass, 1981-1984)

Dan Nelson (Lead vocals, 2007-2009)

Jason Rosenfeld (Lead vocals, 1981-1982)

Dan Spitz (Lead guitar, 1983-1995, 2005-2007)

Neil Turbin (Lead guitar, 1982-1984)

Joey Vera (Bass, 2004-2005)

Greg Walls (Lead guitar, 1981-1983)

David Weiss AKA "v.d". (Drums 1981)

Tommy Wise (Lead vocals, 1982)

SESSION MUSICIANS:

Alison Chesley (Cello, 2008-2011 – *We've Come For You All*)

GUEST MUSICIANS:

Phil Anselmo – 'Killing Box' from *Volume 8: The Threat Is Real* (1998)

Roger Daltrey – 'Taking The Music Back' from *We've Come For You All* (2003)

Dimebag Darrell – 'King Size' and 'Riding Shotgun' from *Stomp 442* (1995), 'Inside Out' and 'Born Again Idiot' from *Volume 8: The Threat Is Real* (1998) and 'Strap It On' and 'Cadillac Rock Box' from *We've Come For You All* (2003)

Public Enemy – 'Bring The Noise' from *Attack Of The Killer B's* (1991)

TOURING MUSICIANS:

Jason Bittner (Drums, 2006, 2011, 2012)

Jon Dette (Drums, 2012-2013)

Gene Hoglan (Drums, 2012)

Andreas Kisser (Guitar, 2011)

Dave Sabo (Guitar, 2000)

Joey Vera (Bass, 2004–2005, 2008, 2012)

ARAYA, TOM

Bassist and lead singer in Slayer, Araya is one of the most recognizable frontmen in metal. He was voted fifty-eight in *Hit Parader*'s list of '100 Greatest Metal Vocalists Of All Time'. His earnings as a respiratory therapist helped finance Slayer's debut album.

ATTITUDE ADJUSTMENT

Formed in 1985 in the Bay Area of San Francisco, Attitude Adjustment were one of the most notable thrash bands of the Northern California metal scene. They released their thrash-hardcore crossover album *American Paranoia* in 1985. Their second and final album *Out Of Hand* was released in 1991. The band's founder Chris Kontos went on to form the very successful metal band Machine Head with Robb Flynn of the thrash band Vio-Lence.

Their best known work is *American Paranoia* (1985) and *Out Of Hand* (1991).

B

BANG YOUR HEAD THAT DOESN'T BANG TOUR

On November 16 1984, the band kicked off the Bang Your Head That Doesn't Bang Tour with support from the cult British metal band Tank. Bang That Head That Doesn't Bang was printed on the top of the back of the original pressing of Metallica's debut album but was dropped on the 1988 reissue and later versions. This was Metallica's first major headlining tour of Europe where they played to around 1,300 fans each night.

Frontman James Hetfield had mastered the role of singer and rhythm guitarist with aplomb. "I had piano training when I was younger, and a piano is a 'two sides of the brain' thing, as is singing while playing rhythm", he said to *Guitar Magazine* in 1991. "Obviously some of our songs are easier than others, so I work harder on the more difficult ones... It's all a case of concentrating more on one role than the other in the appropriate places. But it's more or less second nature now".

Much of Metallica's set was dominated by the interplay between Hetfield and Ulrich with Hammett playing the lead breaks. Ulrich has never been the most versitile or technical drummer; not on par with such professionals as, say, Neil Peart of Rush or perhaps Nicko McBrain from Iron Maiden. "It was always a kind of contest – who could down-pick the fastest – and mostly it was a battle between me and Lars, actually", said Hetfield in 1991 to *Guitar Magazine*. "It's a hard thing to do well, because your timing has got to be dead on... If you're playing eighth or sixteenth notes then you've got to get cooking. A lot of practice is called for to build up your strength. A lot of wanking too!"

Metallica ended the Bang That Head That Doesn't Bang Tour on December 20 after 25 dates. Metallica would soon be a force to be reckoned with on a global scale.

BELLADONNA, JOEY

Belladonna was the frontman in Anthrax from 1984 to 1992 and returned to the fold in 2005 in a reunion of the classic-line-up with Dan Spitz, Scott Ian, Frank Bello and Charlie Benante. Belladonna continues to front the band.

BETTER THAN YOU

Winner of the 1999 Grammy Award for 'Best Metal Performance'. The song is taken from Metallica's *ReLoad*.

BEYOND MAGNETIC

A Metallica EP that was released digitally alongside the band's 30th Anniversary performances in 2011. The songs featured were recorded during the *Death Magnetic* sessions but never made the final cut. It was issued on CD in January 2012.

THE BIG FOUR: LIVE FROM SOFIA, BULGARIA

The DVD of the Big Four concert recorded at Sonisphere Festival at Vasil Leyski National Stadium on June 22, 2010. The concert was shown at 450 cinemas in the USA and 350 across Europe.

BLACK SABBATH

The true originators of heavy metal Black Sabbath are undoubtedly the biggest influence on all of the Big Four bands. The original line-up of singer Ozzy Osborune, guitarist Tony Iommi, bassist Geezer Butler and drummer Bill Ward have had their ups and downs over the years but the music speaks for itself. There have been various line-up changes and reunions as well as the spin-off of the Dio era led band, Heaven & Hell (named after the awesome Sabbath album), but the original line-up is the most iconic with albums such as their self-titled debut, *Paranoid*, *Vol.4*, *Sabbath Bloody Sabbath* and *Sabotage*. The band continues this day minus drummer Bill Ward. They released *13*, their latest album, in 2013. A farewell tour and album is planned.

Anthrax guitarist and co-founder Scott Ian said to the author: "Sabbath were the ones that started it all but Priest took it to another level. Sabbath and Priest, to me anyway, are the two metal bands that there's really not much of a touchstone before them to hear where they came from, exactly…They didn't really sound like any bands that came before them. Those bands, to me, really came out of nowhere were as with most other bands, you can see the influences more directly. You can see it direct or listen to it direct… I love Iron Maiden but you can hear them in Wishbone Ash and Thin Lizzy. Without Thin Lizzy there's no Iron Maiden. Whereas for me with Priest, I don't hear the bands that came before them…or any other bands in their sound. It's just Priest, man".

BLEEDING ME

A promo single issued to the radio in 1997 culled from Metallica's '96 album *Load*.

BLIND ILLUSION

Blind Illusion were heavily influenced by prog rock bands Rush and

Jethro Tull hence their progressive tinged thrash sound. The band was formed in 1979 while guitarist and songwriter Marc Biedermann was still at high school. The band went through many line-up changes throughout its history with Biedermann as its only member. Their debut album *The Sane Asylum* was released in 1988 but they wouldn't release their second album until 2010's *Demon Master*. The band had actually broken up in 1989 and then reformed in 2009 hence the length between releases.

Check out *The Sane Asylum* (1988) and *Demon Master* (2010).

BLITZKRIEG

Blitzkrieg's Brian Ross reflected his second encounter with Metallica to the author in 2011: "My next contact with Metallica was when Lars called Neat Records to get my home telephone number so that he could call me. He did call me, and after an oratory of how much a fan he was of mine and Blitzkrieg, he asked if I would give Metallica permission to do a cover of the song 'Blitzkrieg'. I gave my permission and the rest as they say is history. Since that time I have always made sure that my record company has sent them a copy of each album that I have recorded. I met them briefly at Donington Festival. That was the year [1991] that AC DC headlined and Queensrÿche and Mötley Crüe were also on the bill. As yet, I have never got up on stage with them to play 'Blitzkrieg' but I would love to do it. Who knows? One day I may get the chance!"

BREADFAN

A song from 1973 by the Welch band Budgie. This was covered by Metallica and included as a B-side on their 1988 single 'Harvester Of Sorrow'. It was then included on the covers album *Garage Inc*. The band have played it live regularly ever since.

BROKEN, BEAT & SCARRED

The sixth single released from Metallica's opus, *Death Magnetic*. It was issued in April 2009.

BURTON, CLIFF

Ulrich and Hetfield went to a gig by Californian band Trauma at the iconic West Hollywood drinking hole Whisky A-Go-Go. A bassist by the name of Cliff Burton stunned Ulrich and Hetfield so much so that McGovney was forced out of the band in December and thus Burton was invited to join Metallica. They caught up with Burton the following night at The Troubadour. Hetfield called an anecdote about the show to *Metal Hammer* in 1999: "We had got our first encore ever and we went backstage and agreed that we were going to play this song and he [Lars] went into something else which we hadn't rehearsed in months and months. I didn't know the lyrics, so we just muddled our way through it and after he got up from his drum riser I just slugged him really hard in the stomach and said 'Don't ever fucking do that again!' There have been a few times where I have felt like using my size against him, but he gets the picture most of the time".

Hetfield effectively chose the band over his childhood friend, McGovney. "I don't think at the time it had anything to do with my musicianship because I was basically playing what they asked me to play", McGovney later confessed to *Shockwaves'* Pat O'Connor in 1997. "James showed me what to play and I played it. I understood the camaraderie between James and Lars as far as writing goes and I didn't want to infiltrate that".

However, after initially declining to join this thirsty young metal band, Burton had a change of heart and offered them one stipulation at the end of 1982: that they move to El Cerrito in the San Francisco Bay Area, Burton's home town. Burton wanted nothing to do with the superficial LA scene and he was growing tired of Trauma and wanted a change. "They were starting to adopt these attitudes about".

Burton reflected in February, 1986. "Well, it was starting to get a little commercial in different ways, just different general musical attitudes that I found annoying".

Cliff Burton was born on February 10, 1962, in Castro Valley, California. He was close to his parents Jan and Ray and to his elder brother Scott and sister Connie. Though he was initially being given piano lessons after being introduced to classical music by his father, Burton picked up a bass aged thirteen and his interest in rock and heavy metal deepened. This came after the early death of his brother.

His mother, Jan Burton, said: "He said to a couple of people, 'I'm gonna be the best bassist for my brother'. We didn't think he had too much talent at all (*laughs*); we had no idea! We just thought he'd plunk, plunk along, which he did at first; it was really not easy for him at first. Then, about six months into the lessons, it started to come together. I thought, 'This kid's got real potential', and I was totally amazed 'cause none of the kids in our family had any musical talent! He took lessons on the boulevard for about a year, and then he totally outgrew him [the teacher] and went to another place for a couple of years and outgrew him, too. Then he went to the school and took lessons from a very good jazz bassist, a very fine musician. He was the one who made Cliff take Bach and Beethoven and Baroque [music,] and made him learn to read music and stuff like that. He was with him for a long time, and then he really outgrew him, too".

Burton's influences ranged from Geddy Lee of Rush to Black Sabbath's Geezer Butler to Phil Lynott of Thin Lizzy and the jazz musician Stanley Clarke. Certainly the way Lemmy of Motörhead use(d) distortion had an effect on Burton. Burton practiced for hours each day aspiring to be like his idols.

Burton formed his first outfit EZ-Street during his tenure as a student at Castro Valley High School. EZ-Street had a couple of players who would later go on to have notable careers of their own: drummer Mike Bordin from Faith Known More and Ozzy Osbourne's solo band and "Big" Jim Martin, also from Faith No More. The name EZ-Street derived from a topless bar in the Bay Area. Burton and his buddy Martin formed a second band together called Agents Of Misfortune whilst studying at Chabot College in Hayward, California. They entered a 'Battle Of The Bands' contest at the Hayward Area Recreation Department which was filmed on video tape. The video in question contains Burton's riffs for what would become Metallica's '(Anesthesia) Pulling Teeth' and 'For Whom The Bells Toll'.

In 1982, Burton became a member of Trauma who later

contributed a track called 'Such A Shame' to the *Metal Massacre, Vol 2* compilation. Trauma were especially keen on Iron Maiden and Montrose, the hard rock band fronted by Sammy Hagar who later found fame as David Lee Roth's replacement in the Californian rock band Van Halen. Hagar would become one of the most iconic frontmen in American rock.

Burton's last appearance with Metallica onstage was at the Solnahallen Arena in Stockholm, Sweden on September 26 whilst it was also Hetfield's first show playing guitar since his accident. Burton was cremated on October 7, 1986 and his ashes were spread at Maxwell Ranch. Perhaps the most well-known tribute to Metallica comes from Megadeth. Dave Mustaine penned 'In My Darkest Hour' which features on *So Far, So Good... So What!* released 1988.

Burton's premature and tragic death created an obviously huge void within the realms of the band and it wasn't a case of replacing him – because that would have been impossible given his talent and importance in the early years of Metallica; his bass literally shaped the sound of the band – but about finding a different type of bassist. In other words that particular sound on the first three Metallica albums died with him.

C

CHIRAZI, STEFFAN

Steffan Chirazi is currently the Editor of the Metallica fanclub magazine *So What*. A freelancer, he has also contributed to a number of esteemed publications, including *Sounds*, *Village Voice*, *Spin* and *Q*. Chirazi is also a published author having penned a biography of Faith No More (*The Real Story*) and he is also the Editor of the Metallica fanclub collection *So What!: The Good, The Mad, And The Ugly*. Here is an interview the author from 2009.

Can you give me a brief history of your writing career?

I've written for *Sounds*, *Kerrang!*, *RIP*, *Bam*, the *San Francisco Chronicle*, the *Village Voice*, *Penthouse*, *Spin*, *Salon.com*, *Bikini*, *Ray Gun*, *Q* magazine, *Soma* magazine, numerous foreign language publications, including *Rock Hard* in Germany, various other syndicated outlets; plenty of online stuff, including *Amazon.com* and *Launch.com* (which has probably become something else by now). Oh yes, a parenting magazine who's name I can't remember. I'm probably forgetting a wedding menu I scribed in Cleethorpes too, so excuse me for that omission!

What was your first paid article?

The first paid article? That would be a *Sounds* review of *Ride The Lightning* by Metallica, followed very closely by a live review of someone I cannot remember for a free paper called *Soundcheck*; that could've been Manowar. The gig review was written first but the album review ran first. That was in 1984 and I was seventeen years-old. But I'd interned at *Sounds* a year earlier and written a Motörhead story in the summer of '83, which was why *Sounds* came back in the middle of '84 to see if I wanted to cover rock and metal for them.

Did you always want to write about rock and metal music?

Honestly, I found myself doing it. I loved writing and I also loved acting. I got a chance to audition for the National Youth Theatre, but Thatcher was chopping the grant money so I knew there would have to be a "job" involved to support myself too, it was around the time *Sounds* came in and offered me the opportunity to regularly freelance and before I knew it, I was on a plane to do my first assignment, writing about a band I loved. It seemed too easy. Plus I was going to go to university for journalism and would've ended up doing work experience on a music paper at twenty-one with a degree. I'd had the work experience when I was fifteen/sixteen via my own bullshitting, so there could be no turning back in all reality.

Who was the first rock star you interviewed?

Lemmy. Spring of 1983 for my school newspaper *Hollyvine*. What a gent. What an absolute winner of a human being. There I was, all fifteen going close to sixteen years of me, sitting there with my tape-recorder and stapled together A4 school rag and he treated me like I was from *Rolling Stone*. A man of such enormous integrity that I was fooled into thinking all rock stars were like him. They aren't. The man should be fucking knighted.

Which artist gave you the best interview?

Well, it's hard to beat that "first time" because I was young, naïve, a Motörheadbanger who literally sprinted home and made his parents listen to the entire interview! But I have to say that David Bowie has twice been responsible for fantastic interviews, really great moments in time. It would be unfair to mention Lars Ulrich or James Hetfield in here as I suspect the question is more based on "one-offs" than the nature of what I do with those guys, which is far more of a rolling chronicle; because there have been some pretty heavy interviews with each of them too. I also felt I had a couple of really strong ones from

Kurt Cobain…

And who was the least enjoyable interviewee?

Earl Slick. He was old and jaded, I was young and naïve, one of my first trips to Hollywood (via Sixth Form English and a "pass from class!") and the assignment was tacked on the end of something bigger. He was such a total dick, and I was so completely bamboozled by his dickishness, that I stood outside his Hollywood Hills house, looked at the tape I'd just run, took it out of the recorder and dropped down a drain by his drive. I told my Editor he'd been a bit of a dick and fortunately, my Editor agreed. It was an out-of-character thing for me to ditch the tape…the only time I ever did anything like that.

When did you become the Editor of the Metallica fan club magazine So What?

I officially became Editor in 1999, but I'd been doing the bulk of editorial feature work since it started, so I suppose it was a logical progression although I was delighted when I was offered the chance to take it on.

What does the job involve? Do you travel much?

I creatively oversee four issues of the magazine every year for the Metclubbers. I see it now as a rolling chronicle of their lives and career, a living encyclopedia of sorts. I travel when I need to; obviously there are home commitments to consider, but even without them I wouldn't be on the road all the time because it would simply not be necessary. I think it's very important to know when you need to be out there. I go when I have work to do directly with the guys, or there's a story I need to get. For example, as much as I'd love to go to the next Moscow show with them, I cannot justify a report written by me about going to the Moscow show with them because I've written many reports like that. Now, let's say they were to go to a country they'd never played before…there's a story and a reason. I mean, this job is basically a dream job, and the band give me full creative license to do it. When I sit back and think about the fact that they have a salaried Editor and a proper full-colour magazine, and then I think about the freedom I have to produce it and the access I get, it's extraordinary. I feel I have enormous privilege with them in this regard, because they basically let me go where and when I please; it's a trust that's come with many years of knowing each other. They know I wouldn't take advantage of that because ultimately, it would cheapen me in a professional sense…*wow, did I just tangent there?*

Can you tell me about the Metallica book So What!: The Good, The Mad, And The Ugly, *it must have been a tough book to compile?*

It was a lovely challenge. Four months to put that book together, and to be fair, once I'd worked out how I wanted to break it down, it was easy enough; it just became a race against time. What gratitude I have for my designer Mark Abramson for being ready to go with me every step and meet the challenges I threw down. I am very, very proud of that book. Cliff Burnstein (QPrime, Metallica manager with Peter Mensch) was the man who suggested I do it, he was extremely supportive. Amidst a few conversations we had, and he reiterated a truth: he said that the most important thing was to make sure I liked the book I made. Very wise. And you'd be a fool not to listen to Cliff when he offers you advice. It reinforced what I knew was important. And it's why I can look at the book today one hundred per cent regret-free.

What is your most memorable Metallica moment?

This is the first one which leaps out, so I'll throw it down: 1988, Monsters Of Rock, Pontiac Silverdome, Detroit. Metallica, second from bottom on the bill, but sixty thousand people inside. For them. James asks to see the hands out there as 'For Whom The Bells Toll' starts, literally sixty thousand pairs of hands clapping, me on Kirk's side of the stage, Kirk looking over his shoulder, closing his eyes, screaming and grinning before yelling at me *"Can you Fucking see that!"* Magical. But so many moments, seriously…that's a very pure, raw, instantly relatable one, I think.

How do you approach research for a book? Did you book on Faith No More present any difficulties?

Well to be fair, the FNM book was written with real passion, deep knowledge, a ton of what I would call "grit" research (i.e. there was no *Wikipedia* then baby!) and piles of heart. When it was printed, someone had swapped out the proofed copy with the unproofed one. That book was printed with the wrong word file. My friends and family popped champagne corks for me but I was actually distraught.

How does Kerrang!, Metal Hammer *and* Classic Rock et al *compare with the rock/metal magazines of the eighties?*

Can I be honest and say I don't read them that much? The main difference in music magazine publishing is as much societal as anything else. Everything is short-attention span, you know, *"hit them with a nugget of gossip"* or *"spin a piece of filth and controversy"*, it's a shame. I feel sorry for the great young writers there must be out there, because I don't see where their supported voice is going to be given expression, although to be fair to *Kerrang!* they work very hard to give the young writer room and scope, Paul Brannigan's a proper metal man from the street himself and he understands how important that is. But magazines today are run by figures, and figures dictate editorial format. It's sadly the way of life. And as such, you won't see the same level of feature writing because people don't want to spend that long reading (they have the Internet to waste time on). Plus, PRs have got more protective, managements are less gung-ho and the whole thing is just a little less "fast and loose", so I will always maintain that our era of rock writing and magazines was better. Then again, I just went to an Andy Warhol retrospective, and I saw people in their sixties, who you could tell had seen their daze! I'm sure they feel everything from The Factory pisses on anything from the eighties. It's generational in the end, isn't it...though I wish people would read more!

Do you have any entertaining anecdotes from your times as a freelancer in the eighties on magazines like Kerrang!?
I won't get into the back-story; needless to say I heard that Axl Rose had, at the 1991 Rock In Rio, refused to allow Rob Halford to ride his

bike onstage. I thought it was such a joke that I left the gig and reviewed their set from my hotel room, telling the readers I'd done that (and pissing off my Editor at the time). About a month later, my phone rang. When I asked who it was, the voice said, *"Axl"*. I replied, *"Fuck off Lars!"* because I was convinced it was Lars winding me up. The phone rang again. It was Axl. I asked him how he got my number, and it was via a mutual friend of ours Del James. So he got very, very angry for fifteen minutes, culminating in asking me why I hadn't found him to confirm that he's said that about Halford's bike because he said he hadn't. I laughed and asked him if he'd tried finding himself recently, explaining how hard it was to know he was really there, let alone speak to him without signing your life away. There was a pause and then he agreed, said I had a point, he was sorry for how things had become and we ended up talking for over an hour about all sorts of stuff that had never come up anywhere. I didn't tape the call because I would never pull a stunt like that. It was dynamite "material" but it was a conversation we were having, and that's what it remained. He invited me as a special guest to review their warm-up show in San Francisco the following year and to hear a preview of the album on the condition I did not write a word for *Kerrang!* I told him that was impossible as *Kerrang!* was over half my living at that time and it would've been dishonourable. He said he'd have to revoke his invitation, I said I understood but thanks, and that was that. In that hour of unfettered, unscheduled conversation, he struck me as someone who when you stripped away the bullshit, was a really good-hearted, decent guy that wanted to do the best he could in as many ways as could be done. But surround any rock star with sales and sycophants, well, you'll never really know them and if they're lucky, they'll hang onto themselves by the coat-tails long enough to re-visit when the lights fade away. I hope he hung on, I'd imagine he has. Who knows. It's a lot to speculate on an hour.

Do you prefer to research for an article/book via use of the Internet or magazines and books?

All sorts. I'll go wherever, but ultimately, I'm happiest finding old articles via hard copies, but given the technology, I'm not proud.

Who are your favourite rock scribes?

Rock scribes...Sylvie Simmons has always been a great writer, at her best when she gets a little lyrical and almost "dreamy" in tone. David Fricke is top class too; he blends authority with a humanity all-too-lacking in rock writing. I think Ian Winwood is a top incendiary read when he wants to be, and when Paul Elliott's given the space to fly, properly fly; he has a wonderful way of wrapping you up on his journey.

From the old school days I loved the likes of Sandy Robertson and Robbi Millar at *Sounds* (solid, decent people who gave me great advice too once I became a writer for them and not just a reader of theirs), but the favourites it would have to be Garry Bushell and Geoff Barton. Barton was a great lover of alliterative writing, good old fashioned fun-style grab your reader by the knackers stuff, and something (frankly) we could do with more of *if* we want to get people interested in reading the rock press again. Bushell was fantastic, a proper geezer who wrote what he felt. He's also an extremely misunderstood person; he's been miscast as something he's not thanks to his like of skinhead music back in the day. He chose to turn that rancour to his advantage and good for him! I'll tell you this, he's the man who got me a journalists visa which allowed me to move six thousand miles at the age of eighteen and escape one of the nastiest, most spiteful, hateful and miserable bastards I've ever known; he was an 'Editor' of mine for a period at *Sounds* and he knows who he is. That "man" (I use the term loosely) tried to destroy me, but I wouldn't let him. In '83 when I had that first internship with *Sounds* it has been

Bushell who'd given me the page space, and here he was again, in the spring of '86, meeting me at Charing Cross Station, one week after starting at *The Sun* and putting his name to a visa request for me to be in the US as a reporter. There was no obligation to necessarily write for him, he was doing me a firm favour. I'd sit there in *Sounds* editorials and listen to some of the old steam heads moaning and whinging about Garry, but all of them secretly wished they were him, had his courage, his ability to not give a fuck and know who he was despite what the *NME* said. Bushell was one of the reasons I was a *Sounds* reader (I was also an Anti-Nazi League member so anyone who thinks I was naive is ignorant, I was a very political youth) which is why I can comfortably say that at heart, in his actions and gestures, Garry Bushell has always been a socialist-minded person. It makes me angry to this day when I hear someone ignorantly slag him off. I was not the only working class kid he helped, trust me, and *none* of his detractors helped me one bit.

And what are your favourite books on rock and metal?
Psychotic Reactions And Carburetor Dung by Lester Bangs is near-impossible to beat. *Lords Of Chaos: The Bloody Rise Of The Satanic Metal Underground* by Michael Monyihan is another good read. *The*

Dirt by Mötley Crüe /Neil Strauss is superb, a fine read, as is his book with Marilyn Manson which was thoroughly entertaining. *The Dark Stuff* by Nick Kent is required reading too, a great collection. And for raw tragedy, *Touching From A Distance* by Deborah Curtis is tough to beat.

Are you a full-time writer? What is your daily routine?

I am, combined with another freelance gig in creative consultancy. Schedule? I write for at least ninety minutes a day, five days a week but again, sometimes loads more, sometimes less...

What advice would you give to aspiring rock scribes?

To be a critic/reviewer...start by reviewing local shows for yourself or a free paper. Always be prepared to give something for nothing at the start, but never be afraid to ask your worth once the ball is rolling. Never ever think you're a "proper" writer because there's no such thing. You'll never stop learning. Always write *exactly* as *you* want to "read" in the beginning...if you're going to screw up, screw up on your own terms, that way you can blame no-one else and you will really learn something. Never ever miss a deadline. Ever. Always qualify a criticism...if someone reminded you of a retarded chicken, explain why.

Always be passionate; never try to be too clever. Always enjoy your writing. Always take the best bits of advice from every Editor you get advice from...and always be aware of the Editors who are frustrated writers and not Editors.

Can you recall some of the best gigs you've been to over the years?
Again, so many (and I won't include Metallica). I'll offer a few: Ministry in 1989/90 in San Francisco at The Warfield (amazing); Nirvana, 1993 in Atlanta – the most "perfect" show I saw them play from all perspectives; Nirvana, 1989 at the Kennel Club in San Francisco, knowing this band was different and very exciting; Faith No More, The Ritz in New York, 1988 because they were so great; FNM again in 1991 at Rock In Rio because they were just so explosively potent that night...there are so many more, I've been blessed...

Besides Metallica who are your favourite metal bands?
It changes, but the mainstays for a while have been (and this is metal, I listen to a lot of stuff but I'm keeping to sort-of metal here) Motörhead, Slayer, Ministry, Prong, Minor Threat (we can go punk to, right?), Bad Brains, High On Fire, Big Business and Torche.

Are you working on any new projects?

I've got a bunch of fiction I need to get courageous enough to inflict upon people, I'm constantly wondering if the world needs, or wants, another "rock hack's" book, but the solid project I've been working on for a while is not music related at all. It's about the reality of being the father of a teenager and a pre-schooler. It's a column I post at *www.iamfather.wordpress.com.* I've kept the readership to an invited list for a long time, only recently opening it up more. I want to make a book from these columns and some yet to have been written. I think that not only could they raise a giggle as you take that quick ten minute dump, they might also raise feelings of empathy and joy at the fact that it isn't *"just you who experiences/ feels like that"* sometimes. Check it out and let me know...

CLIFF 'EM ALL

Metallica released *Cliff 'Em All*, a video collection in memory of the deceased bassist. The title of the VHS collection is an obvious homage to Metallica's classic debut album, *Kill 'Em All*. The collection consists of bootleg videos, TV appearances and some professional shit footage of Burton's three and a half years in Metallica. Metal anoraks were also pleased to see footage of Dave Mustaine's stint in Metallica; shot on

March 19, 1983 shortly before he was ousted from the band. The video contains performances of: 'Creeping Death', 'Am I Evil?', 'Damage, Inc'., 'Master Of Puppets', '(Anesthesia) Pulling Teeth', 'Whiplash', 'The Four Horsemen', 'Fade To Black', 'Seek & Destroy', 'Welcome Home (Sanitarium)', 'For Whom The Bells Toll', 'No Remorse' and 'Metal Militia'. There's some footage of one of Burton's famed bass solos while there are also narrations from Ulrich, Hetfield and Hammett. The rare VHS gives fans an interesting glimpse into the inner world of Metallica during the early Cliff Burton years.

COAL CHAMBER

One of the better known nu-metal bands, Coal Chamber released their self-titled debut album through Roadrunner Records in 1997. Renowned video director Nathan "Karma" Cox directed Coal Chamber's debut video 'Loco'. Coal Chamber was formed in 1994 in Los Angeles by former She's In Pain members Dez Fafara and Meegs Rascon (Mike Cox, who replaced John Thor, joined as drummer and Rayna Foss as bassist thereafter). Similarly to nu-metal band Linkin Park, Coal Chamber played a number of high-profile music venues in the LA area such as the iconic The Roxy Theatre and the Whisky A Go-Go. After playing Ozzfest in 1996 the band were signed to Sharon

Osbourne's management; they played Ozzfest's in 1997 and 1998. However, they parted company not long after the release of their breakthrough album *Chamber Music* in 1999. Apparently due to inner band conflicts, Coal Chamber split up after the release of their third opus *Dark Days* in 2002. What usually spells the end of a band's career, a *Best Of* album was released in 2004.

CRAZY TOWN

Crazy Town's 1999 debut album *The Gift Of Game* spawned the Number 1 *Billboard* Hot 100 single 'Butterfly'. However, that particular song would cause fans at the 2001 Ozzfest to mock them during their set, shouting "The Butterfly Boys". The song featured the Red Hot Chili Peppers whom Crazy Town had supported on a tour immediately after the release of their debut album. The band was formed in 1995 in Los Angeles by Epic (Bret) Mazur and Shifty Shellshock and gigged hard and fast in the LA area until a record deal was signed with Columbia for their first CD. Crazy Town played on the Main Stage on the 2001 Ozzfest, but their success would not last. They had fallen victim to the fickle nature of the nu-metal trend and called it a day in 2003 after the disappointing sales of their second album *Dark House*. However, the band reformed in 2007 but broke up again in

2011, then reformed and finally released a new album, *The Brimstone Sluggers*, in 2015.

CREEPING DEATH

'Creeping Death' was the only single released from Metallica's second album *Ride The Lightning*. It is one of the band's most performed songs.

CUNNING STUNTS

A live video released by Metallica in 1998. The DVD features live footage as well as a documentary and band interviews.

CYANIDE

The third single released by Metallica from their album, *Death Magnetic*.

D

DAMAGE INC. TOUR

Metallica commenced the Damage, Inc.Tour on March 27 by supporting Ozzy Osbourne throughout most of the USA dates leading up to the final show in the States on August 3. Ozzy was promoting his *Bark At The Moon* album at the time. It would be Metallica's last support slot before they became headliners themselves.

James Hetfield recalled Ozzy's hospitality to *Metal Hammer* in 1999: "We went out and did *Master Of Puppets.* He gave us full reign on the stage and sound checks every night; we got our backdrop and little crosses up behind us. We would get up and play Black Sabbath songs and hope he would get up and jam with us, but we knew it wasn't going to happen. He thought we were taking the piss when in fact we were honouring him".

The road jaunt would not go without its troubles. Whilst on tour frontman James Hetfield broke his wrist during a skateboarding accident which prevented him from playing guitar; he continued to sing whilst his guitar tech James Marshall played guitar. John Marshall later became a member of the band, Metal Church. This would not be the first incident on the Damage, Inc. Tour; things would only get worse...

The band flew over the Atlantic for the European leg of the tour, beginning on September 10 with support from Anthrax. "We tour because it's fun and because that's what we know and that's what we do best, I think", explained Hetfield in 1996.

Speaking to the author of this book, Brian Tatler of Diamond Head remembered an anecdote from said tour: "On September 20, Lars called me and to say that Metallica (supported by Anthrax) were playing that night at the Birmingham Odeon and would I like to come along. So I caught the Number 9 bus to Birmingham, got my backstage pass and a crew guy took me to see Lars. It was the first time we had met up since 1981, and boy, how times had changed! Lars introduced me to James Hetfield, Kirk Hammett and Cliff Burton, we chatted and Lars suggested I play 'Am I Evil?' onstage with them. Well, why not? Lars said they would be playing it in the encore and suggested that I go and watch the show but come back towards the end of the set. They opened with 'Battery' and I could not get over the energy coming from the band and the enthusiasm of the audience, I had played this venue myself but this crowd was definitely crazier than a Diamond Head audience. This was the *Master Of Puppets* [Damage, Inc.] Tour. I thought that Metallica were still quite small, but this night changed all that. I didn't know any of the songs and my first thoughts were that it was terrifically fast and complicated (Lars had sent me a cassette of the new album but I hadn't got into it at that point). They were all so much in synch, I remember thinking that if one of them were to leave, how on earth would the remaining members be able to replace him. After about an hour I went backstage – still wondering how Lars could play that fast – where the guitar tech strapped James's white Flying V onto me and then I was being introduced as 'The guy who wrote this next song'. The five of us played 'Am I Evil?' up to the fast section, at which point Metallica went into 'Damage Inc'. and I scampered offstage".

Tragedy would hit the band on September 27. During the European leg of the Damage, Inc. Tour, members of the band drew cards to see which bunk in the tour bus they would sleep on because they were frustrated with their own bunks, which were presumably uncomfortable. Bassist Cliff Burton chose to sleep in Kirk Hammett's bunk as he won the game with an Ace Of Spades. In Ljungby Municipalityn, near Dörarp in Sweden, the driver of the tour bus lost control in the early hours of the morning just before 7a.m. and the bus skidded several times causing it to successively flip over. While Ulrich, Hetfield and Hammett escaped with minor cuts and bruises, Cliff

Burton was killed. Burton was thrown outside of the bus, which landed on top of him. Fate had quite literally dealt Burton a shitty card. Hammett on the other hand was a lucky man. Very lucky.

Following the North American and European legs with the late Cliff Burton, the final leg of the Damage, Inc. Tour consisted of world dates and this is when James Newsted was introduced to Metallica's metal crazy fans. Newsted had played his first gigs in Metallica at the Country Club in Reseda, CA and on the following night at Jezebel's in Anaheim.

The world tour leg lasted from September 8, 1987 to February 13, 1988 and included the band's first visit to Japan for five sold out shows in November. Looking back at Metallica's first experience in Japan, Lars Ulrich said to *MF* in 1989 on the band's second visit: "…we went out there and done our shit and they just sat there through the whole show and clapping politely, and we thought 'What the fuck is going on here?!' We thought they didn't like it or something, but then you talk to them after the show and you find out that it's like the best gig they've seen in their life! So they have a really different way of showing emotion up here, they're just so subdued, but after a while you realise that they're into it as much as the kids in Bradford or Dallas, Texas or wherever".

In the United States, Metallica was supported by Metal Church. However, during the following month after the tour, James Hetfield broke his wrist (again) during another skateboarding accident.

The famed artist Pushead (aka Brian Schroeder) said to *Transworld Skateboarding*, 2002: "It was their first time skating an empty pool – James was really excited and asked me a lot of questions. I showed him some lines, and soon he was ripping it up – he was hitting tiles and going for coping. Then it happened. James somehow lost his balance coming down off the transition into the flat around the drain and fell backward. His wrist snapped and the bone was protruding out from his wrist brace. That basically ended James' skating career, since it affected his main career. The first Metallica skateboard design was done in 1986 – the 'Pirate'".

DAMAGED JUSTICE TOUR

Metallica kicked off the Damaged Justice Tour on September 11, 1988 which would take them right through to the winter. The Damaged Justice Tour was the fourth headlining tour by Metallica following the Kill 'Em All For One, Bang That Head That Doesn't Bang, *Ride The Lightning* and Damage, Inc. Tours. The European leg ran from

September 11 to November 5, 1988; followed by the rest of the world from November 15 to October 8 of the following year.

Exciter's John Ricci remembers seeing the band in concert in his home town of Ottawa, Canada as he told the author in 2011: "They played a huge arena where they had a dynamic stage show which was a far departure from the time at the Marquee Club [in London, 1984.] Again they performed an over the top show and the crowd went wild".

The tour included to date Metallica's only every performance in Delaware. It consisted of over 270 shows with around four million people worldwide in attendance. Metallica had become a metal juggernaut.

Kirk Hammett (Pushead interview, *Thrasher Magazine*, 1986): "When you go out there and bash it out it brings up a rush of adrenaline. Adrenaline is flowing and along with that is a touch of nervous energy. The adrenaline like totally takes over when you get up on stage and start playing and having a lot of fun. Then you forget the nervous energy. But I get nervous".

DARRELL, DIMEBAG

Dimebag Darrell, the now iconic guitarist was born Darrell Lance Abbott on August 20, 1966 in Ennis, Texas to parents Carolyn and

Jerry Abbott. Darrell grew up in a musical family as his father Jerry was a country musician and producer and at aged twelve, which is relatively late compared to other famed guitarists, Darrell picked up a Hondo Les Paul with a small Pignose amp and started to play. The story goes that one Christmas, Darrell was asked by his dad if he wanted a BMX bike or a guitar; Darrell surprisingly chose the former. However, after hearing a Black Sabbath album for the first time and discovering KISS guitarist Ace Frehley he asked his old man if he could trade in the BMX for said Les Paul. Darrell's fate was sealed. However, perhaps Darrell's dad wasn't entirely keen on his son pursuing a career in rock 'n' roll knowing full well about the hedonistic lifestyle that the music world entails.

    Darrell later told *Guitar World*'s Brad Tolinski: "Initially, I just used the guitar as a prop. I'd pose with it in front of a mirror in my KISS makeup when I was skipping school".

    After learning Ace Frehley's moves and licks Darrell then mastered the lead riff to Deep Purple's hard rock monster, "Some on the Water" from 1972's *Machine Head*. Jerry showed his son how to play barre chords and the next minute Darrell's playing gets heavier and heavier and with an Electro-Harmonix Big Muff Fuzz he discovered feedback distortion. It was a revelation for the young amateur guitarist.

Indeed, the impact of KISS and specifically original guitarist Ace Frehley on Darrell cannot be overstated. Darrell would dress up as Ace Frehley complete with the KISS make-up and stand in front of the mirror with his fake starburst orange pink Les Paul guitar posing as his rock idol; imagining himself as an extrovert rock star. He was originally nicknamed Diamond Darrell in tribute to KISS ('Black Diamond').

Pantera was a very image conscious band and believed – rightly or wrongly – that in order to make the kind of music they wanted to make they had to dress like all the other bands. "I've got pictures of James Hetfield [of Metallica] wearing spandex", said Vinnie Paul to *Electronic Musician*'s Jeff Periah years later. "We were young kids when we started. We emulated our favorite bands, like Judas Priest, KISS, and Van Halen".

Until James Hetfield met Danish born drummer Lars Ulrich, he was into the same kinds of bands as Diamond Darrell: Van Halen, Aerosmith, KISS, Ted Nugent, Queen and Peter Frampton. Ulrich introduced Hetfield to the New Wave of British Heavy Metal bands that sprung up around the U.K. between 1979 and 1981.

Metallica rolled into Texas in mid-1985 and everyone at

Savvy's in Fort Worth got to see Metallica and Darrell Abbott and Rex Brown play onstage together for three or four dollars a ticket. There were only about thirty people at the gig but it didn't matter because it was such an historic event. Nobody told Rick Perry of Texan metal band Gammacide about the gig because he was going out with Rita Haney at the time. It was completely unrehearsed and unannounced gig. They had such a blast that they played the next night.

During Metallica's stay in Texas, frontman/guitarist James Hetfield and drummer Lars Ulrich went over to Darrell's to jam in his garage after one of Metallica's shows. Ulrich didn't jam; he just hung out. Hetfield and Darrell played mostly Metallica songs and riffed all night long. They swapped licks and a few techniques. It was from this jam that rumours began to circulate that Hetfield borrowed some of Darrell's licks and vice versa. Hetfield and Ulrich were blown away by how good Darrell could play Metallica songs. He knew them all and excelled during his take on "Damage, Inc". The trio became friends and admired each others work, tremendously. It was because of Metallica that Pantera began to appreciate and understand the heavier regions of metal.

Still working under the glam-tinged moniker of Diamond Darrell, the guitarist attended an audition for the unoccupied guitarist slot in the Dave Mustaine fronted thrash outfit, Megadeth. Pantera had drifted from view. However, Diamond Darrell offered one stipulation when he passed the audition and was given the vacant slot: he wanted to bring his brother Vinnie along with him even though Megadeth already had a fine drummer in Nick Menza. This caused Diamond Darrell to decline the invitation and Mustaine then recruited guitarist Marty Friedman. It was a blessing in disguise; however, as the Abbott brothers from Texas focused all their time and energy on recharging Pantera.

"Not saying we've always had the greatest relationship with Megadeth", Phil Anselmo later told *MMN*'s Kenny Herzog. "It's hot and cold. One second, Dave Mustaine can be ragging on ya, and the next second he can come out and say the most unbelievably nice thing in the world about you".

Panter's major label debut, after four self-released albums, was *Cowboys From Hell*. However, the title-track has a slightly convoluted past as Walter Trachsler explains: "It was a Metallica song. One hundred percent. James Hetfield came up with that. It had nothing to do with Texas. Nothing to do with cowboys. What happened was it was one of those times they came to the fucking house to hang out… there's a picture on my Facebook of James Hetfield playing one of Darrell's guitars and he's sittin' on a couch. When this picture was taken James was playin' me that fuckin' song. We're hanging out in the front room with James playing guitar and I said, 'Hey dude, you're gonna come up with any new Metallica stuff?' He said, 'Yes, as a matter of fact [I'm finishing this off] wanna hear it?' I said, 'Yeah'. Well, back then, all we tried to do was play fast stuff. Everything was a million miles an hour. He starts playin' and it was a fuckin' slow song. He played all the way through and it was a slow song. I was like, 'Dude, what the fuck? What's that called?' He said, 'Cowboys from Hell'. They never put it out so Rotting Corpse – six maybe, seven years later – we went and did a song that was as much as I could remember that song called 'Cowboys From Hell' and everything we recorded we recorded at Pantego Sounds with Vince so he heard everything we did. He goes, 'Hey man, that was kinda fucking cool? What was that song called?' That was the only one that he ever said **anything** about... Dude it [the song] came from San Francisco".

He was killed onstage Alrosa Villa in Columbus, Ohio by a crazed fan on December 8, 2004.

Tributes were made from some of the most iconic names in metal throughout the coming weeks. Scott Ian from Anthrax, Megadeth's Dave Mustaine, Zakk Wyle and Jonathan Davis of Korn spoke to *Rolling Stone* about Dimebag and his senseless murder.

On Saturday, August 9, 2008 an all-metal star tribute was paid to Dimebag Darrell at the one day Ozzfest held at Dallas' Pizza Hut Park. The super-jam featured Kerry King of Slayer, Scott Ian from Anthrax, Max Cavalera formally of Sepultura, King Diamond, Hatebreed's Jamey Jasta, Alice in Chains' Jerry Cantrell, Hellyeah/Mudvayne singer Chad Gray and Metallica's Lars Ulrich as well as bassist Mike Inez and singer Pearl Aday were in attendance. Perhaps the most memorable tribute of the night was a cover of Pink Floyd's 'Wish You Where Here'.

DAY THAT NEVER COMES, THE

This was the first single from Metallica's *Death Magnetic* album. It was released in August 2008.

DEATH ANGEL

Death Angel formed in Concord, California in 1982 but the first phase of their career would only last until 1991 although they resumed work in 2001. Prior to releasing their first major label album on Geffen in 1990 with *Act III*, they had independently released two albums: 1987's *The Ultra-Violence* and 1988s *Frolic Through The Park*. There have been many amendments to the band's line-up throughout their history with guitarist Rob Cavestany as the only constant member.

Their best known albums are *Frolic Through The Park* (1988), *Act III* (1990) and *The Art Of Dying* (2004).

DEATH MAGNETIC

Between May, 2007, and April of the following year, Metallica worked on their ninth studio album with producer Rick Rubin. The band had opted out of working with Bob Rock who they had collaborated with on every album since 1991s *Metallica*. It was a bold attempt to go back to their thrash metal roots with long and technically accomplished solos and thrash metal riffs whereas *St. Anger* contained no solos, minimal production and a modern sound. The album was recorded at three studios on the East Coast: Sound City Studios in Van Nuys, California, Shangri La Studios in Malibu, California, and HQ in San Rafael, California. *Death Magnetic* was also their first album to be released via Universal. It was released in September, 2008 and hit Number 1 in the United States making it their fifth album to do so. In just its first three days of release, *Death Magnetic* sold almost half-a-million copies and peaked at Number 1 in 34 countries, including the UK. It received four Grammy Award nominations and was in many end of year polls, including ones printed by *Q*, *Uncut*, *TIME*, *Revolver*, *Rolling Stone*, *Metal Edge*, *Metal Hammer*, *Metal Maniacs* and *Kerrang!*. By mid-2010, *Death Magnetic* had sold 4.5 million copies worldwide.

John Doran wrote a lengthy review on the highly-influential website *The Quietus* where he enthused: "Initially though the first thing that strikes you is how expensive this album sounds compared to the last effort [*St. Anger.*] By comparison this sounds like it was recorded on a space ship. Or at the very least it sounds like it was recorded on instruments in a studio rather than on bales of hay in a shed".

Doran continued: "At five minutes the first of Kirk Hammett's shredding hoves into view. It pretty much just lunges out of the speakers at you, like he's been coiled like a spring waiting for this moment for nearly the last decade".

Andrew Perry wrote in the UK's *Daily Telegraph*: "In terms of regaining their primacy, *Death Magnetic* is every inch the record they needed to make: a more wisely chosen mentor, producer Rick Rubin, has them exploding anew with the battle-rabid, flat-out thrash-metal of their late-eighties heyday".

Writing in the UK board sheet *The Guardian*, Emma Johnston said: "As bright young things fall in and out of fashion, it's a joy to have these gnarled veterans back to reinforce the sheer visceral thrill of timeless heavy metal".

Indeed, *Death Magnetic* was a major triumphant for the band and while it may not be as groundbreaking or masterful as one of those albums from the 1980s, it was nevertheless a significant step in the right direction after the abysmal *St. Anger*.

DEEP PURPLE

Purple were a huge influence on Ulrich and Hetfield in particular though every rock and metal band probably owes some sort of debut to Deep Purple. The band shifted towards a hard rock sound in 1970 and have released such albums as *In Rock* and *Machine head*, two extraordinary hard rock opuses. Of course they are also known as a stellar live band as evidence on *Made In Japan*. In the 1970s they were declared the loudest band on earth. There have been various line-up changes but the most common eras are the 1968–1976 line-ups which are labelled Mark I, II, III and IV. Their second and most commercially successful line-up featured Ian Gillan (vocals), Jon Lord (organ), Roger Glover (bass), Ian Paice (drums), and Ritchie Blackmore (guitar) which lasted between 1969 to 1973, and was revived from 1984 to 1989, and again from 1992 to 1993. Between 1974 and 1976 (Tommy Bolin replacing Blackmore in 1975) with the line-up including David Coverdale (vocals) and Glenn Hughes (bass, vocals). Ian Gillan is today the only original member of the band. They continue to record and tour.

DEF JAM

A record label that was founded by producer Rick Rubin in his dormitory at New York University. Their first and only thrash metal signing was Slayer in 1986 with their third album which was distributed through Geffen Records.

DEFIANCE

Formed in Oakland, California in 1985, Defiance is an obscure thrash metal band but they are known by thrash metal enthusiasts for their technical brilliance and for their exhilarating live shows. The first phase of the band's career lasted until 1994. After a couple of demos their debut album, *Product Of Society* was released in 1989 with their most recent album being 2009's *The Prophecy*.

Some of their best music is *Product Of Society* (1989), *Void Terra Firma* (1990) and *Beyond Recognition* (1992).

DEFTONES

Deftones are an alternative metal band from Southern California that influenced many of the nu-metal bands of the late 1990s. Their debut album *Adrenaline* was released in 1995 (via Maverick and Warner's) and was produced by Ross Robinson who throughout his career has worked with Limp Bizkit, Machine Head and Slipknot. The band toured rigorously throughout the nineties and worked hard on the festival circuit, as well as doing the usual rounds with the media. *Around The Fur* was released in 1997 and was a top 30 hit in the States. It recognised the band as significant players in the metal world. The more experimental album *White Pony* (2000) peaked at Number 3 in the *Billboard* 200 and Number 13 in the UK. A self-titled album was released in 2003, *Saturday Night Wrist* came out in 2006 and in 2009 the band promised to release their sixth album *Eros* which actually turned out to be called Diamond Eyes and was released in 2010. *Koi No Yokan* was issued two years later. Within their music you can hear progressive rock, heavy metal, grunge and avant-garde rock.

DIAMOND HEAD

Diamond Head was formed in 1976 by high school mates Brian Tatler (guitars) and Duncan Scott (drums). Singer Sean Harris soon joined and the band had adopted the name of Diamond Head derived from the 1975 Phil Manzanera album. The band eventually recruited bassist Colin Kimberley and they began playing shows. Their sets consisted mostly of cover versions though they did pen their own material. They self-released a bunch of demos and even supported AC/DC and Iron Maiden. Diamond Head's influences included Black Sabbath and Judas Priest. With the New Wave Of British Heavy Metal in full swing and no sign of getting signed to a major record label, they founded their own label, Happy Face Records and released the single 'Shoot Out The Lights' with the B-side 'Helpless' in 1980. Their now legendary debut *Lightning To The Nations* was initially released via Happy Face in 1980 and was only available via mail order for £3.50. The album includes such popular tracks as 'Am I Evil?'. 'It's Electric' and 'Helpless'.

Brian Tatler said to the author in 2009: "The first album *Lightning To The Nations* is always the one people want to get hold of, it still pops up on eBay occasionally for £70 or sometimes more. There were two thousand copies of that pressed and sold. The early singles are quite rare, and the *Diamond Lights EP* because they all had a limited number of pressings, usually a thousand copies".

With the success of their debut album they signed to MCA Records in 1981 and released the *Four Cuts* EP and they played at the

1982 Reading Festival. Their first MCA released album was 1982's *Borrowed Time* which included artwork by the revered fantasy artist Rodney Matthews known for his work with Birmingham pomp rockers, Magnum. It hit Number 24 in the UK charts and the band launched a UK road trek in support of the acclaimed album. Those two albums plus the demos and singles releases were not only a major source of inspiration to Lars Ulrich and the rest of Metallica but also other metal bands on the West Coast scene.

Despite the blatant influence Diamond Head and their NWOBHM ilk had on Metallica and *Kill 'Em All,* the album slipped of Brian Tatler's radar for quite some time. He explained to the author in 2011: "I did not hear *Kill 'Em All* till about 2005. Lars had sent me several Metallica albums over the years including *Puppets, Justice* and *The Black Album* [*Metallica*] but I never had the first album. James vocal style owes a debt to Sean Harris on that record and it reminds me of Diamond Head in places but having said that, it is uniquely their own".

Tatler continued: "I am constantly amazed at their incredible success and their longevity. If I had heard *Kill 'Em All* in 1983 I would not have put money on them becoming the biggest metal band of all time, who would? They have worked extremely hard for it though; this kind of success is not easily achieved".

DIE DIE MY DARLING

Metallica covered this Misfits song on their *Garage Inc* covers album and released it as a single.

DISTURBED

The band we now know as Disturbed has been in action since 1996, previously they were called Brawl. Disturbed's debut album *The Sickness* was released in 2000 on Giant Records. An immediate success with the alternative rock/nu-metal crowd, Disturbed played on the 2001 Ozzfest with Linkin Park and Coal Chamber, amongst many other bands. Furthermore their sophomore release *Believe* (Reprise) was a number one hit in the US *Billboard* 200. Their third album *Ten Thousand Fists* (Reprise) was also a number one hit. The band issued their third studio opus *Indestructible* in 2008. There's been little controversy in their career; the most high-profiled piece of news was when the video for the single 'Prayer' was banned from many TV stations because of its vivid imagery, which is similar to the September 11 (2001) attacks in America. *Indestructible* is by far the most sombre and menacing album to date. They released a new album called *Immortalized* in 2015.

DOE, BERNARD

Bernard Doe who co-founded and edited the UK magazine *Metal Forces* told the author about his relationship with Ulrich: "The first time I met and interviewed Lars Ulrich was the day after he arrived in the UK ahead off the band's first European tour with Venom in 1984, and over the next ten years I interviewed him several times for *Metal Forces*. I remember after each interview in those early days Lars would nearly always call me at home a couple of days later and ask me to change or leave some comments out that he had made about an individual or another band. Lars was very conscious of trying to remain diplomatic and not upset anyone back then. I've always got on well with Lars and I think that we had a mutual respect for one another. He spent a lot of time in Europe, and in particular London, when Metallica were not touring. There were many drunken nights out on the town, and I have the photos to prove it! Back then he never seem to pay for anything. I guess with Metallica's fast growing popularity he didn't have to, but I never ever saw him once buy a drink!"

Doe continued: "Lars also had a habit of turning up in Shades record store in London just as they were about to close so he could blag some free records. He was always asking about my New Wave Of British Heavy Metal record collection. I remember he was after a copy of the Trespass 'One Of These Days' 7" single. It wasn't a particular rare record, but I had a copy with a picture sleeve which he didn't have. Lars actually agreed to trade an official Metallica RIAA Gold Album Award for my copy of that Trespass single! A great deal as far as I was concerned... except Lars never did fulfil his side of the bargain!!"

DOME, MALCOLM

Malcolm Dome is a highly-respected rock journalist, author and broadcaster. Along with the likes of Mick Wall and Geoff Barton, Malcolm was one of the original writers at *Kerrang!* in the eighties. He worked there from 1982 to 1987 before he joined *Metal Hammer*. He then co-founded *RAW* before going back to *Kerrang!* as a freelancer in the early 1990s. He also a broadcaster on *Total Rock Radio* and regularly contributes to *Classic Rock* and *Metal Hammer*. His sleeve notes include releases by Motörhead, Judas Priest, Black Sabbath and Saxon. He has written books on AC/DC, Aerosmith, Mötley Crüe and Metallica; and he also penned the official Bon Jovi book *Faith & Glory:*

The Official Story. He has co-penned A-Z encyclopaedias on Metallica and AC/DC. Here is an interview with the author from 2009.

Can you give me a brief history of your writing career?

Career? When did it become that – ahem! Well, I started writing about music in 1979 for *Record Mirror* – now defunct – taking over from a guy called Steve Gett in terms of being their 'specialist' rock/metal scribe. I fell into that situation through a happy accident. From there, I became Editor of *Metal Mania*, which was a poster-oriented monthly that emerged around the same time as *Kerrang!* and then onto *Kerrang!* where I was very fortunate to spend an amazing five years. I would regard that as a truly special time.

The decision to leave *Kerrang!* in 1987 was wrapped up in a lot of soul-searching (well, a bit!) before throwing in my lot with *Metal Hammer*, along with a number of *Kerrang!*sters. We were given the indication at the time by the German owners that they were keen to make an impact in the UK. As such, many promises were made and subsequently broken. So, the core of *Hammer* then quit and started *RAW* magazine, with considerable help from one Pete Winkelman, now chairman of MK Dons FC. And Jonathan King played his part as well.

Good grief, I've only got up to 1988 so far! Well, from then on it was a case of writing for various magazines, until getting the chance to do my own radio show with *Rock Radio Network*, which is now *Total Rock*. Radio and writing are almost equal now in terms of time and commitment, plus being interviewed for DVDs and TV shows, Oh, and the occasional book...talking of which...

Your latest book is on Metallica with Jerry Ewing; what can you tell me about it?

It's an A-Z reference work on Metallica. We like to think it's exhaustive. What makes it different is that this is a reference book, not a biography as such. We've just had one published on AC/DC as well.

There are numerous books on Metallica. Are there any you'd recommend?

Mark Putterford and Xavier Russell wrote an excellent one in the early 1990s. Not sure if that's still in print, though. It was published by Omnibus Press. Well worth hunting down, even via eBay.

What is your opinion of Death Magnetic?

It's no more than average. I really believe that is the first time in their career that Metallica have made an album by asking themselves, "What *do the fans want?"*. In that respect, it's a compromise. Metallica made their name by being their own people, standing (or falling) on their own terms. Much as I believe *St. Anger* is awful, it is their own work – it's what they wanted to do. But *Death Magnetic* isn't totally down to what the four wanted to achieve. I believe those who have been acclaiming this as a special album are deceiving themselves. Just because it is an attempt to return to the 1980s values doesn't make it a good record.

Compared to the eighties, how does rock writing differ?

I think there's a lot more attention paid to reader, industry and audience viewpoints now that was the case in the 1980s. Back then, we followed our instincts. Now, there's more awareness of the bigger picture. Is it any better or worse now? Just different, I feel. But still exciting.

What books have you written?

Lots, from *Encyclopedia Metallica* in 1980 to *AC/DC – The Encyclopedia* in 2008. Along the way, I've done books on Bon Jovi (including an official one), Van Halen and Mötley Crüe.

Of all the interviews you've done, who has given you the most enjoyable interview?

Almost everyone has an enjoyable angle somewhere. It's always great to talk to people who are articulate and have an opinion. Take a bow Bruce Dickinson, Lemmy and Ronnie James Dio, among many.

And the least?

The least enjoyable ones tend to be on the phone with people I don't know. They're difficult, because it's tough to get any sort of rapport going. Nobody's fault but the situation.

What are your favourite rock books?

I love Mark Blake's exhaustive book on Pink Floyd [*Pigs Might Fly*] – well researched and superbly written. The same goes for Dave Ling's excellent story of Uriah Heep. And let's not forget Mötley's *The Dirt* and [Led Zeppelin's] *Hammer Of The Gods*.

Who are your favourite artists?

So, so many. Led Zeppelin, though, will always top the pile. As for the rest, a huge list from AC/DC to ZZ Top.

What are the most memorable gigs you've been to?

Gawd, again so many. I feel privileged to have seen AC/DC's first ever UK show at the Red Cow in London, the same goes for Metallica at The Marquee. Guns N' Roses in Pasadena at Christmas 1987 springs to mind. Led Zeppelin at Earl's Court, 1975. Sabbath at The Marquee. Mastodon at The Underworld. Baroness at the Borderline (both in London). Soulfly at the Astoria (again in London). U2 at the Electric Ballroom in London in 1979 – third on the bill! Maiden at The Marquee in 1979 (my first ever live review)...and there are lots of others.

What can you tell me about your next book on AC/DC?

It's a reference work like the Metallica book. Jerry Ewing and I have chronicled their career in an A-Z format. Again, encyclopaedic.

Do you think Black Ice will be their last album and tour?

Personal opinion? Yes. I've now heard the whole album, and it is superb. If this is farewell...what a way to go out. On top of their game.

Can you fill me in on the history of Total Rock?

Well, *Total Rock* started out as *Rock Radio Network*, run by rock enthusiasts from the front room of a house in Finchley, North London.

That was in 1997. In 2000, with funding, *RRN* became *Total Rock*, operating from studios purpose built in Fulham, West London. Sadly, a combination of circumstances (from which we've never fully recovered) undermined the station, but we're still going (albeit only broadcasting on the Internet at *www.totalrock.com*), and have a base in Central London.

How does rock/metal writing of today compare to the eighties?
I believe that I the 1980s there was more freedom of expression. So many media outlets now are tied in to festivals, tours and even labels, which is inevitably restrictive. But there are talented writers around. It is interesting to note those who have lasted the course – all too often writers appear and disappear within a matter of a couple of years. Also, rock/metal is perceived now as appealing to such a broad spectrum of age groups. In the eighties, it was still about youth culture.

Do you have any interesting anecdotes from the years spent working on Kerrang! *and* Metal Hammer *in the eighties?*
Yes. But I shall protect the ignorant by keeping those to myself. You know who you are – cash (used notes) in a brown paper bag under the third bush from the left will keep these secret! There is the well-

known musician who once played me his whole album – and the tape was blank. Except he didn't realise it was blank, even when the thing was playing! Or the bassist who constantly borrowed a fiver or a tenner off you…and never paid you back!

What is your opinion of the modern-day Kerrang!?
I wish them well, but it has little connection to my era. *Kerrang!* seems to be trend driven these days, and as such hasn't the drive or enthusiasm of old. It's more a brand name than a professional fanzine (which is what we were).

Which rock/metal writers did you admire back in the eighties?
Pete Makowski, Mick Wall, Geoff Barton, Sylvie Simmons, Dave Ling, Phil Alexander, Mark Putterford…a lot of people I was eventually privileged with work with, in one guise or another.

How did the nineties impact on the likes of Kerrang!, Metal Hammer and the short-lived RAW?
It undermined a lot of what we championed. And it also meant these magazines had to adapt. *Kerrang!* did it well, under the guidance of Phil Alexander. *Metal Hammer* eventually found its niche, *RAW* was so

badly handled that it disappeared. *RAW*'s demise is still disappointing. We created a classy, intelligent yet passionate magazine in 1988, only to then stand on the sidelines and watch it being run into the ground.

Are there any contemporary rock/metal magazines/fanzines which you admire?

Well, *Metal Hammer, Classic Rock, Classic Rock Presents Prog* all spring to mind. But I admire and respect *Terrorizer* and *Rock Sound* as well.

What's next?

A trip to the Crobar for some well-earned drinks – arf! I think part of the beauty of the last thirty years or so for me is that what happens tends to veer away from cunning plans.

DON'T TREAD ON ME

A promo single released from Metallica's *The Black Album*.

DROWNING POOL

Formed in the country music lovin' city of Dallas in Texas, Drowning Pool like peers Linkin Park their music has evolved from nu-metal to a more alternative rock/metal sound. They played on the 2001 Ozzfest to promote their debut album *Sinner*. But on August 14 of that year lead singer Dave Williams died in his sleep due to an alleged defective heart muscle, possibly caused by a disease. Singer Jason 'Gong' Jones joined the band in 2003 for their second album *Desensitized* (2004). However, Jones soon left the band and was replaced by former SOiL singer Ryan McCombs who was first heard on 2007's *Full Circle*. Disturbed are still working on new music and released their fifth studio opus *Resilience* in 2013 with plans for a follow-up 2016 release. Their first live album *Loudest Common Denominator* was released in 2009. While many of their nu-metal peers have descended into oblivion, Disturbed have done well to continue their careers.

E

EGLINTON, MARK

Mark Eglinton is the author of the first James Hetfield biography, *The Wolf At Metallica's Door* which was published early 2010 by IMP Books. Based in Edinburgh, Mark is a contributor to *The Quietus.com* as well as a number of rock and metal magazines. His website is http://meglinton.com. Additionally, Mark is the Overseas Executive Producer for a film making company in Arizona called www.killingtimeproductions, with his colleague Eric Braverman. Here is an interview the author did with Eglinton in 2010.

How did The Wolf At Metallica's Door *come about?*

Not conventionally. I had been proposing several book ideas for most of early 2009, and in all truth, had not settled on my best idea. I had, and still have two official band biographies in the discussion stage, but these things move at speeds best described as glacial. I was approached, on the recommendation of a friend, to write the book on a short deadline. I was a fan, so it was an opportunity I simply couldn't turn down, although I knew time was short.

What did you learn about James Hetfield the "person" as opposed to James Hetfield the "international rock star"?

I already had a good idea of how I thought he was, but I made a decision to not rely on his peers' testimony when attempting to demystify his personality, simply because these perspectives are completely skewed and therefore not easily related to by 'normal' people. With that in mind, I contacted people who have known him who are not rock stars, to get that crucial perspective. Worth mentioning too, is the fact that despite rehab, etc., Hetfield is every bit as controlling within his and Metallica's sphere as he ever was – maybe even more so in some ways...

What sort of research did you undertake?

I already had a good idea of the Metallica story generally, but I wanted to make the viewpoint specific to Hetfield himself. Consequently, I tracked down key people from his past, particularly his early days, in order to uncover some fresh information. Strangely, I used very little web research. I feel that too many books out there rely too heavily on web-sourced information and I wanted to do the opposite where possible.

Who did you interview for the project?

I had several key interviews for each era. Hugh Tanner was vital, as he was a friend from Hetfield's youth who had never discussed the subject previously. His role is more significant than he is given credit for. Interestingly, Hetfield and Hugh Tanner have reconnected after many years, largely to do with Hugh's involvement with my book, and that feels good to know.

Eric Braverman was important too, mainly because he had been around Hetfield and the band for years, and was able to give that crucial 'non rock star' view that I needed. All the other interviews were of my own doing – many as a result of Facebook approaches. In a lot of cases, one interview often led to a few others, and I can only thank all the people who were kind enough to give time and knowledge over the months I conducted the interviews.

How did you go about writing the book? (For example, did you write a timeline of events in Hetfield's life, etc?)

No. I did it in sections according to who I had spoken to, and then built the book from there. That did present some continuity challenges later on, but it was enjoyable to see all the gaps being filled. It wasn't as simple as just using a Metallica timeline, because there are events which are huge in Metallica's story which aren't necessarily as significant in Hetfield's, Napster being one.

How long did it take you to research and write the whole book?
The entire project probably took me three months, of which six weeks was solid writing. The remainder was interviewing (mostly in the dead of night), transcribing and of course structuring the material. I speeded the process up a little too by doing some editing as I wrote, simply because I didn't like the thought of a mass of typos/errors in my slipstream!

It is an unofficial book. Do you think unofficial books are unkindly treated by the more enthusiastic fans and critics?
I think that many read the word unofficial and think 'scandal', and that is just not fair, particularly with the current privacy laws which suffocate the life out of these kinds of books. As I said earlier, the days of mashing together a book of Internet sourced quotes are long gone, simply because fans and critics demand much more than that nowadays. That said, by sourcing new first-hand material, you become a victim of your own success, because it opens up a whole new legal issue which just isn't a factor with previously published quotes etc. I

don't always think that official books are any better than their grittier (generally) unauthorised counterparts.

There have been a number of Metallica's books published over the years. Can you name some of the more worthwhile ones?

I actually think that given Metallica's huge brand, there are far less books on the subject than you might expect, and I think that says a lot about the attitude of those surrounding the band about unofficial publications. I don't blame them for that however, and in some ways believe that because they have been so well managed over the years, they have been even more successful. If I was forced to choose, I really enjoyed photographer Bill Hale's *Metallica: The Club Dayz 1982-1984* with text by my friend Bob Nalbandian. It's a light read, with some fabulous pictures from the LA and SF club days. Both Joel McIver's Metallica books are great of course, but personally his Cliff Burton biography really hit the mark for me.

What other books on rock and metal would you recommend?

Quite honestly, I don't really explore everything that is out there as much as I should. On balance, I probably read more sport orientated book and of those, John Feinstein has the most incredible ability to evoke emotion from human stories within the game of golf.

Which publications do you write for (and have written for in the past)?

Very few. A lot of my work is for a brilliant music website called www.thequietus.com and they are very kind to me by letting me do whatever I want basically. I also do some work for a magazine in California called *Outburn* which is a very good general rock and metal magazine. Most of my time is taken up with the documentary and book writing side of things.

Do you have any favourite rock scribes and who are your literary influences?

There are very few rock scribes who have prompted laugh out loud, spit coffee across the room hilarity for me, but John Doran, editor of *The Quietus* and writer for *Metal Hammer*, *NME* and others, is definitely one – brilliant. Another guy I enjoy is Keith Bergman who writes for *Blabbermouth* on the web. As far as influences are concerned, I have never really thought about it. I try to write in a very direct way, with little wastage of words where possible though which isn't ideal when you are trying to hit your word count!

What is your music collection like?

Bizarre. I have bought and re-bought loads of things over the years, but the focus is on 1980s thrash, with emphasis on some of the lesser known bands. I have a huge selection of metal from over the years generally, with a few more sensible artists sprinkled in there too.

Do you have any more book projects in the works?

Yes I do. I'm currently working on co-writing the biography of a very significant 1990s metal artist, and it is certain to be a fantastic process which could take most of 2010. Additionally, I'm still discussing two official band biographies; one of them East Coast, the other West Coast!

EL ARSENAL COMPLETO / THE FULL ARSENAL

A Metallica tour of North America from July to August 2012. Some shows were recorded for the band's movie *Through The Never*.

ELLEFSON, DAVID

Bassist and founding member of Megadeth, Dave Ellefson is a thrash metal hero. His side-projects include Temple Of Brutality, F5 and Killing Machine. He released his autobiography *My Life With Deth* in

2013 with co-author Joel McIver.

ENTER SANDMAN

'Enter Sandman' was the first single for Metallica's self-titled album also dubbed *The Black Album*.

EPIDEMIC

This Bay Area thrash band also crossed over into the death metal genre and formed in 1985 but later disbanded in 1995. The band's name is derived from a Slayer song and they released their debut *The Truth Of What Will Be* in 1990. Two more albums followed but the band folded after their third release and some internal differences and record company issues. They were not a prolific band but made a reputation as a furious live band particularly on the 1993 tour with Cannibal Corpse and Unleashed.

Some of their most acclaimed albums are *The Truth Of What Will Be* (1990), *Decameron* (1992) and *Exit Paradise* (1994).

ESCAPE FROM THE STUDIO '95

A Metallica tour from August to December 1995. It included a performance at the Monsters Of Rock at Donington.

ESCAPE FROM THE STUDIO TOUR '06

To celebrate 20th Anniversary of *Master Of Puppets* in 2006, the band played the album in its entirety at several shows during the Escape From The Studio Tour. They even played a complete performance of the instrumental 'Orion' for the first time which was dedicated to Cliff Burton. Needless to say at those shows the audiences went wild! The tour was March to August 2006.

2008 EUROPEAN VACATION TOUR

A Metallica tour from May to August 2003 which included their first spot at Ozzfest headlining the tour.

2012 EUROPEAN BLACK ALBUM TOUR

A Metallica tour of European festivals as a late celebration of the 20th anniversary of *The Black Album*.

EXODUS

Formed in Richmond, California in 1980, Exodus may never have received the high reverence and commercial success of Metallica and their ilk but they remain one of the genre's key bands. The very first line-up of Exodus consisted of guitarists Kirk Hammett and Tim

Agnello, drummer Tom Hunting, bassist Carlton Melson and singer Keith Stewart. Their debut *Bonded By Blood* was released in 1984. The band has undergone several line-up changes and there was in a period in the 1990s when they remained inactive but resumed work in 2001. Between 1984 and 2010 they released ten studio albums; they continue to tour regularly.

Their best known albums are *Pleasures Of The Flesh* (1987), *Fabulous Disaster* (1988) and *Impact Is Imminent* (1990).

F

FADE TO BLACK

A promo single released by Metallica from their second album *Ride The Lightning*.

FERRIS, DAVE

David "D.X". Ferris is a staff writer for the Cleveland Scene and his freelance credits include the revered US publications *Alternative Press* and *Decibel*. His book on the making of Slayer's legendary thrash metal opus *Reign In Blood* is out now via Continuum Books as part of their excellent 33 1/3 series. Here is an interview the author did with Ferris about his career in 2008.

Can you tell me about your writing career so far?
I've been writing full-time, mostly about music, for nine years. Technically, 2008 marks my twenty-third year in the metal press – if you want to count my letter *Hit Parader* published in fall 1985. I graduated with a journalism degree in 1995 and pretty much wiped my ass with it. Then I spent a few years doing different work from suit jobs to bartending.

Went back to school in 1998, then again in 1999. I've always been a music guy, and once I went back to school, after years and years of being burned by bad record reviews, I figured I could do the job at least as poorly as most critics. I've been writing steady since 1999, and being paid for it since 2001. Mostly about music and entertainment, but I've done a few stints for daily newspapers – beat reporting, covering municipal meetings, education, that kind of stuff. I spend some time hanging out in clubs, but I also take the occasional walk to the courthouse to search public records.

My current gig: I work for *Cleveland Scene*, a weekly newspaper in the metal-heavy city of Cleveland. I've been here six years. Until recently, I was Clubs Editor/de facto Assistant Music Editor. I recently made the leap to Staff Writer, where I still cover music, but do more feature writing and reporting. I consider myself more a reporter than a critic – not that there's anything wrong with being a critic. I just try to tell you what's happening and what artists have to say – as opposed to telling you what I think. I don't think "my favourite" is synonymous with "the best". And that's one of the reasons I interviewed so many people for the Slayer book. Of course, I like *Reign In Blood*. But I think Matt Pike's opinion carries some weight, too. I freelance for *Alternative Press*, and *Decibel* was kind enough to run a leftover chapter from the

Slayer book.

What made you want to write a book on Slayer's Reign In Blood?
'Cuz... as they say: *"Fuckin' Slayer",* you know? The book is part of Continuum Books' *33 1/3* series, a pretty prestigious collection of sixty (and growing) books about classic albums, from the Beach Boys to the Beastie Boys. I wanted to be a part of the series, and when I looked down the list, the lack of metal was a glaring omission. And if you're going to start with one metal album, what better than *Reign In Blood*?

What's the best Slayer gig you've been to?
The *South Of Heaven* tour was just the most crushing thing I've ever witnessed – musically, physically, everything. Goddamn, were they tight. Looking back, it's hard to imagine that it was four guys making that kind of full-on assault. It in a roller-skating rink, just packed to the gills. Total madness. I still can't believe how loud Slayer's 2007 tour with Marilyn Manson was. In Cleveland, at least.

In your opinion, how has Slayer's music changed over the years?
It has, and it hasn't. That's part-and-parcel with their greatness. The music is much the same: straight-up thrash, no clean vocals, no

acoustic bits, unconventional solos, no sissy melodies. The content has shifted from fantastic demons-and-Satan-and-vampires fare to more fuck-you-and-your-god realism.

One of the great musical issues I can never really resolve is this: what's worse – a band that stubbornly records and re-records essentially the same record, or band that refuses to record and re-record essentially the same record? I don't think that's exactly what Slayer does. Mötörhead, I think you can argue the point. With the Red Hot Chili Peppers, I liked *BloodSugarSexMagic* better the first time they made it.

Did the band cooperate?

The band did cooperate with the book. I interviewed all of them, in a few different sessions between the summer and fall of 2007. I also interviewed Rick Rubin, who produced the record – it was his first rock record. Also Andy Wallace, who mixed it, and went on to produce Jeff Buckley and mix Nirvana. Also, the band's manager. Also, Russell Simmons – the disc was first released on Def Jam. And many more. So, yeah, I got some good input.

Do you know if any of them have read your book yet?

I'm not sure. They all have copies of the book. And the manager requested more copies, so as far as I can tell, they're not unhappy with it.

How long did it take you to write the book?

It took about nine months to put together. About six of that was doing research – I conducted about eighty original interviews for the book, in addition to digging up archives, crawling through the Internet, etc. Then writing it took about three months. I wound up with a lot more than what fit into the book, basically a short biography of the band. But the assignment was to write a book about the record.

What other bands do you like?

A lot. I'm a metal guy, but I'm a music person. I never did decide whether I liked Anthrax's *Among The Living* or *Spreading The Disease* better, but I think I'd take *Spreading The Disease* on a dessert island. *High On Fire* kills. A local band called Fistula; their 2006 EP was my favourite record of that year. Tori Amos. Amy Winehouse. 16, Mastodon. The classic-rock canon. If there were a church of Johnny Cash, I'd go to it.

I'm not a big tattoo guy, but I'd be comfortable with a tattoo from any of Danzig's bands or the Dropkick Murphys. I'm always surprised when I realise how much white rap and rap-rock I have. I listened to a lot of John Coltrane and PJ Harvey while writing the book – when I write, I usually need mellow stuff in the background that isn't too distracting

What are you favourite rock books?
Steven Blush's *American Hardcore* is tremendous, a staggering piece of work. The way he talked to everybody who's anybody for that is amazing, and I admire how he lets people talk and stays out of the way. I hate rock books where you learn more about the author than the band. That said, I think Chuck Klosterman's *Fargo Rock City* is great; like Hunter S. Thompson, he's the one person in a generation who can write about himself and make it about something bigger. Dan LeRoy's *33 1/3* book about the Beasties' *Paul's Boutique* is superb, also; I think he really set the bar for really getting inside the creation of an album, and making it a lively story. And Jim DeRogatis' *Milk*; it is a great companion reader for the nineties alt-rock era.

Are there any books written specifically on metal which you like?

David Konow's *Bang Your Head* is something I've read a dozen times, but I always find something new in. Killer research in it, too. Really nails the golden age from the eighties and nineties. Klosterman's *Fargo Rock City*. Albert Mudrian's *Choosing Death*. Mick Wall's *Iron Maiden: Run To The Hills* is nice.

Which rock/metal magazines do you read?

Decibel's the best for metal. I think most of it will age far better than *RIP* has. Times are so weird now; it's a real bloodbath. *Metal Maniacs* is gone, *Metal Edge*. Rest in peace, gentlemen. In terms of well-written music content, *Blender* was by far the best of the big three – with *Rolling Stone* and *Spin*. I read *Rolling Stone*, more for stylistic notes than substance. Say what you will about *Alternative Press*, but nobody's broken more popular music over the last... hell, couple decades. They were there before alternative broke, and they own the *Warped Generation*. That is music journalism.

Who are your favourite metal scribes?

Ian Christe, Martin Popoff, they've turned metal writing into real respectable careers. A couple good guys that I've been able to work with and learn from, Aaron Burgess and Jason Bracelin, are metal guys who write intelligently, passionately, and well about any kind of music and pop culture. And I guess *Decibel* Editor Albert Mudrian is pretty much the dean of the school at this point.

Do you have any favourite periods in the history of metal?
I'm partial to eighties metal. Everything had its own sound. Metal's bigger than ever now, but to me, everyone's doing essentially a variation on one of, like, seven established sounds or genres. Even the production is pretty standard.

What is the current state of metal journalism like in North America?
Aside from half the quality magazines going tits-up, it's good. Metal is here for good, and you don't have to fight for attention as much. That said, it will always be a fight. Metal scares people. If you cover it a little, your Editors inevitably think you're covering it a lot, maybe too much.

In a town like Cleveland – where metal, punk, and hardcore are the city's real bumper crop – you often have to explain that you're not just covering your favourite music; you're covering the local scene, which happens to have a lot of extreme music.

And then, writers in general lose their minds when it comes to entertainment, whether they're just writing a record review or covering *Wire* creator David Simon for a highbrow magazine like *The Atlantic*. Even professionals fail to recognize entertainment reporting as a form of beat reporting, with certain rules and guidelines to observe.

If I run two items in two months about major local acts like Chimaira, Tim "Ripper" Owens, or Mushroomhead, I'll have to justify my choice – even though they're busy, internationally respected bands with a big following. I don't think the Sports Editor of the local newspaper tells his sports reporters, *"Come on, guys, you wrote about the [local American football team] the Browns last week. Let's get some variety in here".* The team did something last week, it played a different game this week, somebody got hurt – you report it all. But with music, somehow there should be a different standard? I don't think so.

My former Music Editor, the kick-ass Jason Bracelin, said that metal is like horror movies for most people: they get a little taste, and they're good for a year. And if somehow more than one makes it onto their radar, they think the goddamned apocalypse is nigh.

Do you have any other writing projects lined up?

I'm idly gathering material for a second music book as we speak. Aside from that, just week-to-week stuff at my job – writing feature stories, covering the local music scene, freelancing when the bigger outlets will have me. Branching out into sports writing a little; it's a much more disciplined field. I'll write more books, at least one music one.

What's been the highlight of your career so far?
Depends what you mean by highlight. Writing the first English Slayer book is my distinction. That's the feather in my cap. An assignment for *RollingStone.com* is as far as I've made it up the ladder.

Personally, I'm geeked by a bunch of various things. Watching the Dropkick Murphys from backstage at a European festival. Talking to Tori Amos about her whole catalogue in fifteen minutes, and fans saying it was a good, distinct interview. I'm glad I got to talk to Kevin DuBrow before he died. Contributing a little piece of information or perspective in the ongoing saga of the Misfits, which is maybe the best band ever.

Things like having the opportunity to interview Mike McColgan about the fourth Street Dogs album, which I love more every time I listen to it. Or talking to Marc Avsec – the songwriting partner and producer of Donnie Iris, one of the great under-heralded album-rock artists – as a source for a story about entertainment law. Those are my *SportsCenter* moments. None of them are industry-changers, but they're good work if you can get it.

$5.98 EP: GARAGE DAYS REVISITED, THE

As a kind of therapy after the death of Cliff Burton and to welcome Newsted into the band as well as to test out their new rehearsal space, Metallica released the covers collection *The $5.98 EP: Garage Days Revisited* in August, which they'd mostly recorded at the Conway in LA. Kirk Hammett commented to *Guitar World* in 1998: "Our older covers definitely have a certain rough charm because we didn't put them under a microscope or record them as anally as we would normally record our own songs".

The covers were largely recorded at Ulrich's garage but latter re-recorded when the band bought a new studio. This now ultra-rare collector's item features the following tracks: 'Helpless' (Diamond Head), 'The Small Hours' (Holocaust), 'The Wait' (Killing Joke), 'Crash Course In Brain Surgery' (Budgie) and 'Last Caress/Green Hell' (Misfits). The EP is now out of print but those cover versions along with some others were included on the 1998 double CD set, *Garage Inc*. The EP peaked at Number 27 in the UK.

Lars Ulrich said in 1998: "It's definitely easier to work with other people's material. We like to turn them into something very Metallica, different than how the original artist did it. You don't get so fucking anal about it, and you can bang these covers out in like five minutes".

"Cover songs are a part of our history, and fans know that", he continued. "We have just put them all in a nice little package for easy listening... We don't sit and analyse things on a sales level... there are people who'll get off on hearing what we do to a Thin Lizzy track".

There were various reasons behind the recording of *The $5.98 EP: Garage Days Revisited.* Kirk Hammett explained in 1998 to *Guitar World*: "Doing that album was also a good way for us to break Jason in to the public and give our audience a preview of what was to come. We needed to buy some time, because we really weren't ready to record another full-length album yet. We didn't have anything new written. So it was a good way for us to put some product out there and take our time before getting ready".

FOR WHOM THE BELL TOLLS

The second promo single released from Metallica's second album *Ride*

The Lightning.

FORBIDDEN

This Bay Area thrash band was initially formed in 1985 drummer Jim Pittman and guitarist Robb Flynn under the moniker Forbidden Evil before they shortened it. Their debut *Forbidden Evil* was released in 1988. They have broken up a couple of times but are still active in the 2010s. They remain one of the most influential Bay Area thrash bands of all time. However, they have struggled on a commercial level to gain higher prominence outside of the genre where they remain unknown. Nevertheless, they were an important band in the beginnings of the Bay Area thrash scene in Northern California.

Have a listen to *Forbidden Evil* (1988), *Twisted Into Form* (1990) and *Green* (1997).

FRANCAIS POUR UNE NUIT (FRENCH FOR ONE NIGHT)

A live DVD from Metallica released only in France and recorded in Nimes on July 7, 2009.

FRANTIC

This was released as a single by Metallica from their *St. Anger* album.

FRIEDMAN, MARTY

His stint in Megadeth last nearly a decade as the band's lead guitarist throughout the 1990s. He is generally regarded as one of the band's most popular former members. He lives in Tokyo and is the presenter of *Rock Fujiyama* and *Jukebox English*.

FUEL

The third single from Metallica's *ReLoad*. It was nominated for a Grammy for 'Best Hard Rock Performance' in 1999.

G

GARAGE INC

In November, 1998, Metallica released the double CD covers collection *Garage Inc.* which contained the whole of the previously out of print *The $5.98 EP: Garage Days Revisited* as well as new covers that had been recorded at The Plant Studios between September and October of 1998. Many of the songs featured were NWOBHM bands that had inspired Metallica in the first place. The success of the album (over two million copies sold worldwide) meant that the artists covered would receive not only a higher degree of recognition but also royalties. The artists covered include Diamond Head, Holocaust, Killing Joke, Budgie, Misfits, Blitzkrieg, Queen, Anti-Nowhere League, Sweet Savage and Motörhead. Reviews of the double album were pretty good.

Entertainment Weekly enthused: "We'll have to wait until Metallica's next 'proper' album to find out if this trip to the garage recharges their batteries. Still, all things considered, *Garage Inc.* is an intermittently exhilarating joyride".

The album peaked at Number 2 in the United States and the following singles were released: 'Turn The Page', 'Die, Die My Darling' and 'Whiskey In The Jar'. The latter won the band a Grammy Award for

'Best Metal Performance'.

GARAGE INC PROMO TOUR

Metallica played promo shows in November 1998 in support of *Garage Inc*.

GARAGE REMAINS THE SAME TOUR

From April to December 1999 Metallica were on the road supporting *Garage Inc*.

GODSMACK

Godsmack are another band that are not, strictly speaking, nu-metal but after touring on Ozzfest and with the success of their second album *Awake* in 2000 the band were often lumped in the nu-metal genre. Touring with Limp Bizkit in Europe certainly didn't help them move away from that generic tag which critics love to use. The band formed in 1995 in Boston and rose to fame during their late 1990s. Their independently released debut album *All Wound Up* was remastered and re-released in 1998 through Universal/Republic Records. *Faceless* and *IV* followed in 2003 and 2006, respectively. There's been some line-up changes after guitarist Lee Richards and drummer Joe D'acro both left in '97 and then drummer Tommy Stewart left, came back again and then left again. But for some time now the line-up has been steady with Sully Erna on vocals, Tony Rombola on lead guitar, Robbie Merrill on bass guitar and Shannon Larkin on drums. After a lengthy break Godsmack announced plans for a brand new studio album to be released in 2010 which was called *The Oracle*. It was followed by *1000hp* in 2014.

GOOD, THE BAND & THE LIVE, THE

An LP box set from Metallica that was released in 1990. It contains four singles and two EPs.

GRUNGE

Grunge music had a lot to do with the shape, sound and ultimately, the downfall of hard rock and heavy metal in the 1990s though bands like Metallica, Megadeth, Slayer, Anthrax, Pantera and Guns N' Roses had survived the movement remarkably well, which was somewhat reminiscent of the way Queen had endured the punk era back in the mid to late 1970s, a lot of lesser-known rock and metal bands lost record deals and ticket sales dropped, alarmingly. Hard rock and heavy metal didn't completely disappear; it just went underground and dropped out of the public's consciousness until a time came when it would become fashionable again which is the way trends and tastes work. Everything goes around in circles. Nothing is new.

Grunge was like punk in that it was anti-establishment and anti-authoritarian and whereas punk was an obvious reaction to prog rock, grunge was a reaction to pampered poodle-haired LA metal. Seattle shaped the sound of American music in the late 1980s and early 1990s and non-grunge bands that were still in the same depressive, alternative rock-vibe like REM, were also becoming extremely popular. Those guys wore flannel shirts and ripped jeans; they looked like the kind of youths that alternative dorky-lookin' students would buy drugs from at college campuses whilst chatting about Nietzsche's philosophy and Nicolas Roeg films. At least that's the impression they gave.

The biggest bands of the grunge scene included Nirvana, Pearl Jam (who were big fans of English hard rockers UFO), Soundgarden and Alice In Chains. The latter two bands were certainly heavy enough to appeal to metal fans and even some of their influences were metal, notably the Godfathers of the genre, Black Sabbath. However, grunge, just like all music movements, came to an abrupt end. Nirvana's tormented frontman Kurt Cobain killed himself in April, 1994.

Metallica and their fellow Big Four bands were enclosed in a self-contained bubble with all the various musical trends passing them by while they did their own thing and their hardened fanbase followed their every move.

There were some metal achievements in the early nineties primarily thrash bands like Metallica and Slayer who had huge success with album sales and concert attendances. Metallica had the biggest album of their career in 1991 with their self-titled album (often referred to as 'The Black Album') and quite possibly turned them into the biggest band in America. Guns 'N' Roses and The Black Crowes also had albums high in the charts. To some observers, heavy metal and hard rock was losing its fans during the grunge years yet there were some successes for what are commonly referred to as 'old school' bands. Def Leppard's classic 1992 album *Adrenalize* was a huge hit instigated by its fabulous lead single 'Let's Get Rocked'. Led by the death of Freddie Mercury in November 1991 (from what was actually bronchial pneumonia caused by Aids), Queen had enormous success with their second greatest hits album and a raft of reissues in the early nineties.

Metal wasn't dead in the '90s, it just went out of mainstream consciousness.

GUNS 'N ROSES

It can be argued that Guns 'N Roses are the most overrated band of the past 20 years. But on the other side of the coin it can be claimed that they are the most influential band of the modern era. Their debut album *Appetite For Destruction* set a new benchmark for hard rock. The punk aggression and classic rock riffs gave them a huge audience and significant mainstream exposure. The band did not shy away from controversy especially with an erratic yet venerable frontman like Axl Rose and an arrogant yet hugely talented guitarist like Slash. After the release of the massively overblown albums *Use Your Illusion I* and *II* in 1991, the band's creative output has been patchy and there have been a number of line-up changes. Ex-members have always denied a reunion but considering the amount of money they could make mssers Rose, Slash, Duff McKagan, Izzy Stradlin and Steve Adler are bound to reform at some point in the future. The Guns N' Roses/Metallica Stadium Tour was staged during 1992.

GUNS N' ROSES/METALLICA STADIUM TOUR

July to October 1992. The tour ran into both Metallica's Whereever We May Roam Tour and Guns N' Roses *Use Your Illusion* Tour. Hetfield suffered serious facial burns during a gig in Montreal so his tech James

Marshall filled in on guitar for the remaining dates.

H

HALE, BILL

Bill Hale is a renowned photographer who worked with bands such as Metallica and Megadeth in the 1980s. He has also published photography books on both bands. Here is an interview the author did with Hale in 2011. Check out *photosbybillhale.blogspot.com*

When was the first time you shot Metallica?

That would be September 18, 1982 at the Stone in San Francisco. That would also be the band's first gig in the Bay Area. We (John Strednansky – editor and chief – *Metal Rendezvous* magazine) knew Lars before he had started the band! Lars and Stred met up and Lars would call us at the MRV offices… We heard 'Hit The Lights' as it was coming together, over the phone!!

What do you remember about those early days?

We were all just trying to live the metal dream. The Bay Area had a great scene already. Think '60s and the '70s, so the clubs where there, the press was there and when my generation came of age… we just inherited this huge musical legacy… Ya know Quintana had his mag going we were right behind him... there was a ton of fucking cool record shops and fans, fans who dug metal! There was a big thing going on when Metallica happened up the state from LA. They really just found a home here but you have to keep in mind, there was a ton of bands! Metallica just played harder, faster and louder!

What did you first think of Dave Mustaine?

HA! Mustaine was cool! Where James was shy and did not talk much, Dave was a RIOT...

I went on to photograph Dave for most of the '80s. We got to be good friends. Ya know, Dave really took a bad rap from Lars. They all drank, we all drank. Lars got in his fair share of trouble but Metallica was his band so...

What were your impressions of Lars Ulrich?

Lars Ulrich had a plan! And that was to make Metallica the biggest band on the planet! Lars knew what he wanted, who he wanted to work with and how to get it. Lars and I were never that close...

Did you think they'd become so popular?

Metallica had "IT"! Whatever it was, but they had it! Metallica was just the band for and of its time. They started out as four friends in a band; had a few lineup changes; toured their asses off but they never forgot their fans or where they came from and that is why they are still going strong after all these years!

Why are those first four albums so important?

I would say the first three albums – never heard the fourth. The fans over here wanted/needed to have a band all their own. Yeah we all dug Motörhead, Diamond Head, Maiden, Angel Witch... But they were not one of us – Metallica was! Four they unlikely friends in a band annd being his band Lars of course had big plans. Ron was the first to go followed by Mustaine. Musically, the band was straight from the gut – no filler, no fluff just pure young angry metal riffs. Oh yeah, they "borrowed" from the British bands but the sound that they made was all their own!

What do you remember about Cliff Burton?

I meet Cliff way before the band played up here. Even saw Trauma once! Cliff was anything you ever read about him. Cliff was cool, Cliff dug music, Cliff was Cliff! Right around the release of *Ride* our friendship started to get strained a bit. We both started to get some success but *MRV* had not done a proper article on Metallica. Also I had not shot the band since '83 and at first it was just playful posturing, but then it got more aggressive we would almost come to blows! This went on for a while, but hey that's life…

So Megadeth rolls into town and is opening for King Diamond at The Stone (8/12/86). I'm finishing up my photo session with Megadeth when I see Cliff walk in. Oh great I tell myself, and get ready for round 25 with Cliff but he comes up to me and gives me a big bear hug and tells me how great it was to see me?! I get some pix with him and Dave hanging out with the King Diamond guys. On the way home I'm thinking what was up with Cliff? A few short weeks later, Cliff saw DEAD! As I recall Cliff was the first one of us to pass on!

The next time I saw Lars and James was at a Megadeth gig a few weeks after Cliff passed Lars was ok BUT James was a mess. Talked to Dave and he was pissed off. Life as we (the Bay Area) would never be the same again…

Anything else?
Way before Metallica and Megadeth came along, the Bay Area had some great bands already, Vicious Rumors, Exodus, Trauma, Griffin, Anvil Chorus, Death Angel, Testament, Lääz Rockit, Heathen,

Forbidden, Blind Illusion, Ruffians, Vio-lence, Possessed, just to name a few...

But somehow Metallica rose to the top of the "Thrash Metal Heap". The Bay Area has always been a hot bed for music. The 1980s was just the "Heavy Metal" chapter!

HALFIN, ROSS

Undoubtedly one of the most successful photographers in the music business, Ross Halfin has photographed some of the biggest bands in the world including Led Zeppelin, The Who, Guns N' Roses, Iron Maiden, The Police, Rush and KISS. He started working for *Sounds* in the '70s on a freelance basis and moved on to other publications, including *Kerrang!, Mojo, Q* and *Classic Rock*. Halfin also has quite a few pictorial books to his name, notably on Metallica, The Who, Def Leppard and Iron Maiden. He has collaborated extensively with Metallica over the years. His website is *www.rosshalfin.com*.

HALFORD, ROB

The Metal God was born Robert John Arthur Halford in Sutton Coldfield in Birmingham on Saturday August 25, 1951. He spent his childhood growing up on Lichfield Street in Walsall, Staffordshire, which is to the north west of Birmingham. The Beechdale Estate in Walsall was a tough working class environment, which was at odds with the young Halford who knew he was different from every other boy in the area.

Coincidently the Metal God shares his birthday with KISS front man and money spinner Gene Simmons who was born Chaim Whitz in Israel in 1949 while Def Leppard guitarist Vivian Campbell was also born on the same date in 1962 in Belfast. Queen bassist John Deacon was born several days before Halford on August 19, 1951. It was quite a rock 'n' roll month, all round.

He joined Judas Priest in 1973, and they became one of the most influential metal bands in the world (Slayer even started out as a Judas Priest tribute band!) but left in 1992 to pursue a solo career.

Halford spent the early months of 1992 with younger bands, bands he influenced who in turn would influence his next career making decision. *Painkiller* was – and indeed still is – a harsh album but Halford expressed in interviews that he wanted to go even harder and faster, and it was those aforementioned bands that helped him achieve his goal. The Big Four bands influenced Halford as much as he influenced them.

Halford was invited to join Pantera on stage in California in March, 1992. They ripped through classics 'Grinder' and 'Metal Gods' from the *British Steel* album. Not only was it an exhilarating moment for the ageing Halford but a lifelong ambition come true for guitarist Dimebag Darrell (RIP), a Priest fan since youth. Halford and Pantera also had time to record a song for the *Buffy The Vampire Slayer* movie. The song 'Light Comes Out Of Black' was a key track on the movie soundtrack. Halford launched the short-lived metal band Fight whose debut *War Of Words* remains a lost masterpiece. Yet the failure of Fight's second album A *Small Deadly Space* to capture the minds and wallets of heavy metal fans and critics, and the failure to attract a big crowd of their own making did little to boost Halford's confidence. After a tour of the USA (they played support to Metallica and Anthrax) in the summer of 1995, having played just 38 live shows in their career, the end seemed near for Fight.

Rob Halford's solo career was literally going into the pit. At the end of 1997, Halford told Gerri Miller, the former editor at *Metal Edge*, that "metal is dead and I am done with it".

Obviously it came as a major shock to heavy metal fans. In April, 2000, he told *Rock Hard*: "I think I didn't express myself quite clearly then. What I meant – and I pointed that out a little later – was that in the metal genre, big changes aren't possible. Classic metal has defined itself in the '70s and '80s and I didn't see any outstanding new bands. Look at the bands on the cover of your magazine: Metallica, Thin Lizzy, Running Wild, all bands that exist for many years. Of course metal isn't really dead, I'm not so stupid that I would really claim something like that, but I don't expect in the near future some mega-bands will appear. And I can't imagine that a young musician will create something really new out of the old influences, which has the same musical meaning. Maybe I'm wrong and there is somewhere a 16-year-old new Randy Rhoads genius who proves me to be wrong. I hope so. I wish nothing more than to see the new Sabbath, Priest, Maiden or Metallica – a bunch of kids who blow everything away – very young bands who have the characteristics of classic metal in them".

Of course, since that famous quote Halford has tried to defend himself, saying it was a silly mistake. He told *Launch* in August, 2000: "I tried to fudge my way out of that by saying, 'I didn't mean really that', what I meant was the metal where I came from, bands like Priest and stuff, there's no more bands like that. When in reality, there are bands of that ilk from Europe. I think that just went to prove my emotional state of mind at that time. I remember I was sitting on the bus with Gerri Miller, I was just so frustrated and not settled, and I made that ridiculous statement that metal is dead, which is a fucking stupid thing to do.

"I've been confronted all over Europe by that statement, and I've just been making amends by saying that I was off my John Rocker. It was a stupid thing to say, and you've got to be able to admit your mistakes, and that was a big mistake on my part.

"Metal fans are extremely loyal, devoted people, and if you rub them up the wrong way, like I did, you've got to step up to the plate and put your hands up and go, 'I'm sorry'".

He then hooked up with Trent Reznor for the failed Two project resulting in one album called *Voyeurs*. Halford relaunched his career with *Resurrection* in 2000 before re-joining Judas Priest. Still in his rightful place, outside of Priest he continues to indulge in a sporadic solo career with 2010's *Made Of Metal* being his latest release.

HAMMETT, KIRK

On April 1, 1983, Ulrich and Hetfield hired guitarist Kirk Hammett from the thrash metal band Exodus that had previously supported Metallica. Metallica's soundman was the manager of Exodus at the time and introduced the band to Hammett. Was this fate? "I remember the first time I heard Kirk", enthused Ulrich to *Guitar World* in 1991. "He had a feel that very few young players have – very rooted in European metal. It was really nice to hear an American guy who didn't play like Eddie Van Halen".

Metallica's first show with their new lead guitarist Kirk Hammett was at The Showcase in Drover, New Jersey on April 16, just a few days after Mustaine left for LA. Hammett learned the Metallica setlist in just four days. It would change the landscape of the band's sound but Hammett's skill on the fretboard was immediately apparent to even the most enthusiastic of Metallica fans. Ulrich and Hetfield knew right away that they had made the right choice in hiring Hammett who was not only a very professional player but also supremely talented. They hit it off right away. Hammett brought a new aspect to the band's sound.

Kirk Hammett was born on November 18, 1962, in San Francisco. Hammett is of both Filipina (from his mother) and Irish (from his father) descent. Hammett went to De Anza High School in Richmond, California where he made friends with Les Claypool, later of Primus fame. Such as Hammett's dedication to playing the guitar he took a soul-destroying job at Burger King where he saved up enough cash to buy a Marshall Amp, needless to say he quit the poorly paid vocation once he bought his cherished item. Some of his earliest guitars included a copy of a 1978 Fender Stratocaster and a 1974 Gibson Flying V. Growing up in Northern California; Hammett adored KISS, Aerosmith, Led Zeppelin and Jimi Hendrix. He was into bands were there was a distinctive guitar edge to their sound. He loved to hear the crazy fretboard wizardry of Hendrix at his most raw or Jimmy Page's wild solos especially on live bootlegs.

In 1980, Kirk Hammett formed Exodus, one of the most important and influential thrash metal bands of the Bay Area, with singer Paul Baloff. They both met at a house party in North Berkeley. Initially they got together with guitarist Tim Agnello, bassist Carlton Melson and drummer Tom Hunting. However, once the band had been christened Exodus, there would be some changes to the line-up: Hammett's guitar tech Gary Holt replaced Agnello and bassist Jeff Andrews took over from Melson. The band would merge their punk and metal influences together creating one furious melting pot of aggressive riffs and fierce vocals. The only recording Hammett made whilst in Exodus was a 1982 demo tape. Hammett would be replaced by Rick Hunolt.

Metallica was a name that could not be avoided in the Bay

Area. Kirk Hammett told rock writer Jaan Uhelszki of *Music Radar* in 2008: "I was familiar with their music before I joined the band. Exodus played with Metallica quite a bit, so I knew the songs. I had the *No Life 'Til Leather* demo and listened to it quite a bit. It was what everyone in the San Francisco underground metal scene was listening to in 1982".

When Hammett joined Metallica he was taking guitar lessons from the fretboard wizard Joe Satriani. Hammett first visited Satriani at his music store in Berkeley called Secondhand Guitars. Friends of Hammett immediately picked up on the difference in Hammett's playing since he had been taking guitar lessons. Hammett had learned more about technique and style and discovered how not to compromise sound but to embrace experiment and innovation. Satriani liked Hammett from the get-go and whereas he'd spend approximately half-an-hour with other students he'd spend a little longer with Hammett simply because he enjoyed playing the guitar with him. Hammett had a totally different approach to playing the guitar than Satriani's other students because Hammett's influences were intricate European players like Uli Jon Roth and Michael Schenker, both of whom are German.

Hammett confessed to *Guitar Magazine* in 1996: "Joe was a big influence back then…but not so much these days. He showed me how to use modes, and he showed me a lot of theory – like what chords to play over what scales, and vice versa. I learned a lot of finger exercises, as well. I had lessons from 1983 'till, like '87, on and off – maybe four lessons a year, sometimes. I never had enough time 'cause I was always touring! And then when he hit big with *Surfing With The Alien* he didn't have time either. In fact, I think I was probably his last student".

The former Exodus guitarist also shared similar musical influences with members of Metallica. He enthused to *About.com*'s Ryan Cooper in 2009: "We've toured with a lot of these bands, and a lot are inspirations... Like Judas Priest, huge inspiration... Lynyrd Skynyrd is a huge inspiration, Mercyful Fate is a huge inspiration..."

Hammett first met Ulrich and Hetfield during his tenure in Metallica and liked them both; especially Hetfield as they both played the guitar and had similar backgrounds and influences. It took Hammett some time to warm to Ulrich's eccentric European traits. "The first time I spoke to him was when Exodus played with Metallica", Hammett informed Jaan Uhelszki of *Music Radar* in 2008. "They had just finished their set and as I was talking to him, he started taking his stage clothes off, and before I knew it he was completely naked in front of me. I was just shocked".

HANNEMAN, JEFF

The late Jeff Hanneman was a founding member and guitars of Slayer. He wrote such tracks as 'Raining Blood', 'Wear Ensemble' and 'South Of Heaven'. He died on May 2, 2013.

HARVESTER OF SORROW

'Harvester Of Sorrow' was the first single from their first album recorded after the passing of Cliff Burton, ...*And Justice For All*. The band played it live for the first time at the 1988 Monsters Of Rock Tour.

HEATHEN

Formed in the Bay Area in 1984 by guitarist Lee Atlus and drummer Carl Sacco, Heathen released the *Pray For Death* demo in 1986 and two full-length albums before they broke up in 1993 only to reform in 2002 and release the *Recovered* EP a year later and then *The Evolution Of Chaos* in 2010. Like Metallica, Heathen have a strong NWOBHM influence in their sound; certainly on their earlier work before they began to develop their own musical identity.

Their most popular albums are *Breaking The Silence* (1987), *Victims Of Deception* (1991) and *The Evolution Of Chaos* (2010).

HERO OF THE DAY

This was the first song recorded by Metallica for their album *Load*. It was recorded in December 1995, the album was released in 1996. It was the second single from said album.

HETFIELD, JAMES

James Hetfield was born in Downey, California on August 3, 1963 to amateur Opera singer Cynthia and blue collar truck driver Virgil. Hetfield's siblings were from his mother's first marriage; two elder brothers and a younger sister. However, Hetfield's father left the family when he was young and Cynthia and Virgil divorced in 1976. Hetfield's parents were both devoted Christian Scientists and did not believe in medicine or any form of conventional or unconventional medicinal practices even when Hetfield's mother was dying of cancer. They believed that things happened as a consequence of God's will. They did not want any king of scientific intervention in their lives regardless of what the outcome might be. Consequently, aged sixteen, James Hetfield's mother died in 1979 and he moved to his brother's house in Brea some twenty minutes' drive from his home but he went back at weekends to jam with his buddies. (Virgil Hetfield died in 1996 during Metallica's *Load* Tour). Hetfield was a keen music fan and had begun playing the piano around aged seven before he picked up some drum sticks. He soon started to play the drums using one of his brother's drum kits before he finally picked up a guitar aged fourteen. His fate was sealed.

As an adult, James Hetfield spoke about his classical musical lessons to *Virginmega* in 1999: "I did [take lessons] when I was about six or seven years-old. My mother saw me banging on the piano once and mistakenly thought I was the next child prodigy, so she put me in some old lady's house after school to learn. It really stunk. It's one of those things when you blurt out, 'Hey lady, your house smells funny'. I would have rather been out playing football with my buddies, but now I thank her every day for that because it developed my ear, and she made me sing at rehearsals as well, so I had to sing in public. I did read music for a while, but as time goes on, you forget things you don't use. I wish I had kept up with it, but it's not really necessary for us. It's all by ear. That's how I learned to play guitar, off playing records".

Hetfield was a huge fan of hard rock music particularly Aerosmith, Thin Lizzy, Deep Purple, AC/DC, Black Sabbath, Ted Nugent and KISS. He was a huge fan of Steve Tyler, Aerosmith's iconic frontman. A couple of his earlier bands included Obsession (with guitarist/singer Jim Arnold, bassist/singer Ron Valoz and his brother

Rich Valoz on drums) that churned out Sabbath, Zeppelin, Deep Purple and UFO covers while his next band Phantom Lord was formed with Hugh Tanner at Brea Olinda High School. They jammed and played covers but they did not play any gigs, ever. Hetfield recruited Ron McGovney to play bass even though he hadn't a clue how to do it but Hetfield taught him. However, it is Leather Charm that is best known by Metallica fans...

HIT THE LIGHTS

'Hit The Lights' was recorded for the *Metal Massacre* collection – the first Metallica recording – with Hetfield also taking on bass duties while local player Lloyd Grant also played a guitar lead but on later pressings all the guitars were played by Mustaine.

"'Hit The Lights' was composed by James and one of his friends. I remember the day I went over to Lars' house, he said, 'Check out this song' and he played me 'Hit The Lights'", Grant told metal fan and writer Bob Nalbandian in 1997. "We were both into that heavy kind of shit. He wanted me to play some guitar leads on it but I couldn't make it over to Ron McGovney's house to do the recording so James and Lars brought the four-track over to my apartment and I did the solo on a little Montgomery Ward amp".

HOOBASTANK

Formed in 1994 in Agoura Hills, sunny California, some of the original band members went to Agoura High School which was also attended by Linkin Park's Mike Shinoda, Rob Bourdon and Brad Delson.

Hoobastank have gone through several members over the years; the most current line-up is: Doug Robb (vocals/rhythm guitar), Dan Estrin (lead guitar), Chris Hesse (drums/percussion) and Jesse Charland (bass). They released their debut and sophomore albums, *Muffins* and *They Sure Don't Make Basketball Shorts Like They Used To*, (both self-produced) in 1997 and 1998, respectively. Their third self-produced album went unreleased and they finally made it in 2001 with their self-titled album which was released through island and hit Number 25 in the US *Billboard* 200. They have a small but loyal following in the UK. Their latest album was 2009's *For(N)ever*, which peaked at Number 26 in the *Billboard* 200.

Hoobastank supported Linkin Park (along with P.O.D. and Story Of The Year) around North America in early 2004. Previously, both Hoobastank and Linkin Park had played the famous Colbalt Café where Incubus and Avenged Sevenfold also started their careers.

They look likely to always be on the fringes of mainstream popularity although the support of a label like Island will certainly aid their career. They're sold around five million albums with five studio albums under their belt. *Fight Or Flight* was released in 2012.

I

I DISAPPEAR

This single does not appear on any of Metallica's albums. It was recorded for the *Mission: Impossible II* soundtrack and released in 2000 as a single. It is the last single to feature James Newsted.

IAN, SCOTT

The only remaining original member of Anthrax, Scott Ian is rhythm guitarist, bassist and backing singer. He is also a member of the metal supergroup The Damned Things and founder of the Stormtroopers Of Metal. The author spoke to Ian about his love of his metal heroes Judas Priest in 2006 during Anthrax's US tour with Rob Zombie.

What's your first memory of hearing Judas Priest?

My first memory of hearing Judas Priest...that's a good question, it's a long time ago. It was way before the *Hell Bent For Leather* album. It was probably *Stained Class* but definitely one of the earlier albums. I'm a huge fan.

What is it about the music that appeals to you?

They're just a great metal band, you know. They play great and make great songs. They created the template for mostly everything that came after them. All that music that they created still holds up well today; they're just awesome songs. The stuff that they were creating in the seventies and early eighties; it always sounds like Priest. Nobody else sounds like them; few metal bands are as good as they are. I mean twenty years later, even thirty years later, and nobody at all sounds like them. They're the original metal band.

They were the first metal band?

I mean Sabbath were the ones that started it all but Priest took it to another level. Sabbath and Priest, to me anyway, are the two metal bands that there's really not much of a touch stone before them to hear were they came from, exactly. They didn't really sound like any bands that came before them. Those bands, to me, really came out of nowhere. Whereas with most other bands, you can see the influences more directly. You can see it direct or listen to it direct. I mean I love Iron Maiden but you can hear them in Wishbone Ash and Thin Lizzy. Without Thin Lizzy there's no Iron Maiden. Whereas for me with Priest, I don't hear the bands that came before them or any other bands in their sound. It's just Priest, man.

You've toured with Priest on two occasions – Demolition *and* Angel Of Retribution *U.S. tours. How did that start?*

When we got asked to go out it was originally in 2001. We were supposed to do that *Demolition* tour in 2001 but then 9/11 happened so it got postponed for a couple of months. Amongst all that insanity of 9/11 one of our stresses was 'oh no, is the Priest tour gonna get cancelled? And how are we not gonna get to tour with Judas Priest now'. Of course that was a very, very minor thing of everything else going on in the world but in our little small world of Anthrax we were like 'oh shit! We still wanna tour with Priest!" When they told us that is was gonna happen a couple of months later we were really excited. It was fucking awesome man! They treated us amazingly and it was great to get to see them every night, you know, with 'Ripper' and then a couple of years later we got ask again to go back out with them with Rob back in the band. It was like a dream come true...we never got to play with them, you know, back in the early eighties, so it's just one of those bands were you always wish 'God, I hope someday I get to tour with those guys'. And now we have...twice!

Did you play with them onstage?

No...but, of course, if they would ask me, yeah definitely. Of course, I would (laughs).

Did you go out with the band at any point on the tour?

We went out for dinner a few times and we would hang out quite a bit after the shows but more so on the *Demolition* tour than the last one we did with them. Glenn even told me on the last run that it was like the end of the cycle for them. They were all just pretty tired and really looking to be done and just get home but they weren't really hanging out too much after the shows. It was right at the end, the last week or so when we started hanging out and that's when Glenn told us 'I apologise, please don't think anything bad…we're all just tired and we all just wanna get home. We've been out for a year'. So that was really sincere.

What about 'Ripper'?

He's got the voice. He's got the uncanny metal voice I've ever heard. He's incredible. They couldn't have gotten anybody better to follow Rob Halford. There's no one out there that could have done the job that he did. You're talking about the biggest shows in the world to fill and his story's been told a million times, just from a personal and professional level I don't think no one could have done a better job than Tim. He was just so professional about the whole situation and coming in and knowing who's shoes he was filling, and just going in and doing the best job he could as a fan of Judas Priest and not wanting to disappoint anyone and just being the up-most professional and a gentleman when Rob came back, you know, I think Tim is amazing.

Quotes From The Interview:

"The VH1 Rock Honours in Vegas was awesome…I got to play in the KISS tribute".

"I was walking around the place and thinking I knew all these guys".

"I didn't really see a difference in sound with those albums (*Jugulator* and *Demolition*). It just sounded like Priest to me. Tim's voice was amazing on those albums".

"I love all that old artwork on those early albums like *Hell Bent For Leather*".

"I spoke to Glenn (Tipton) in Vegas about the *Nostradamus* album. He said they're going to try and play the whole album live…something that's never been done before".

"I would definitely tour with them again. They're just a group of great guys".

ILL NINO

Founded in 1998 in New Jersey, the Latin-American nu-metal outfit Ill Nino released their debut album *Revolution Revolucion* in 2001 via Roadrunner Records. It was a success in the United States shifting over a quarter of a million units. In between albums there was some notable changes in the line-up (guitarist Marc Rizzo and percussionist Roger Vasquez moved on) so by the time their second album *Confession* (2003) was released former Machine Head guitarist Ahrue Luster has joined the fold. *Confession* was not as commercially successful as its predecessor but it was more critically acclaimed. As nu-metal started to lose its appeal, bands like Ill Nino suffered from significantly poorer sales than seen in previous years. Their third opus *One Nation Underground* was a commercial flop (it peaked at Number 101 in the US *Billboard* 200) and the band left Roadrunner to join a new label. A *Best Of* collection was issued in 2006. Yet the band keeps going: they released a new studio album in 2007 called *Enigma*. It was far from being a commercial success. It was followed by 2010's *Dead New World*, 2012's *Epidemia* and 2014's *Till Death, La Familia*.

IRON MAIDEN

With over 85 million albums sold, countless awards, including an Ivor Novello and even a BRIT Award, 2000 concerts played to millions of people around the world and an induction onto the Hollywood RockWalk, Iron Maiden's legacy is evidently assured for quite some time.

The band formed in London in 1975 and after several line-up changes they cemented their status as pioneers of the now legendary New Wave Of British Heavy Metal movement that lasted from around 1979 to about 1981. The NWOBHM was just a short period of time but it spawned many bands which will be documented in this book.

While Maiden's first two albums – *Iron Maiden* and *Killers* – are iconic in their own way it was not until former Samson singer Bruce Dickinson replaced Paul Di'Anno in 1981 that Maiden's flight to success properly took off. The trilogy of *The Number Of The Beast* (1982), *Piece Of Mind* (1983) and *Powerslave* (1984) gave the band worldwide fame and success in the USA. Those three albums are often included in 'greatest heavy metal albums' polls and they have lost none of their appeal over 20 years later. 1988's *Seventh Son Of A Seventh Son* was also a masterpiece after the somewhat experimental *Somewhere In Time* in 1986.

While the band suffered from a downward slide in the mid-nineties after the departure of Bruce Dickinson and the hiring of ex Wolfsbane Blaze Bayley, Maiden steadily made a comeback beginning with 2000s "reunion" album *Brave New World,* and indeed right up to the end of the decade the band began re-building their career. In 2011, they are quite simply a force to be reckoned with.

Iron Maiden are a very British band; their working class mentality has never diminished and their Britishness is widely known yet they are extremely popular elsewhere, especially in the USA and parts of Europe, South America and heavy metal lovin' Japan. Their appeal in the USA while sometimes tumultuous has not been lost amongst the countless bands that followed in their wake. Indeed, the whole Bay Area thrash metal scene of the eighties continues to owe a massive debt to Maiden as do all the other thrash metal bands that formed not just on the West Coast but elsewhere in the States during the eighties. It's a lengthy list which includes such high-profile players as Metallica, Megadeth, Slayer, Anthrax, Annihilator and Exodus et al.

To have influenced an entire movement of bands is simply incredible. Of course Maiden were not the only band to have made an indelible impression on the thrash scene but they certainly made a big enough splash. There are several big named metal bands from the 1990s onwards such as Marilyn Manson, InFlames and Trivium that have been greatly inspired by Iron Maiden.

How many so called celebrity "It girls" and socialites do you see wearing Iron Maiden t-shirts? For them it may not be about the music but it does show that Maiden have touched many corners of pop culture. There are all kinds of Maiden related multimedia devices, applications and of course, there's all the merchandise too. Iron Maiden are more well-known than their peers and it is mostly because they've made more right decisions than wrong.

The band's first two albums – *Iron Maiden* and *Killers* – saw them fronted by Paul Di'Annno.

Slayer author D.X. Ferris: "Those albums nourished the next generation of bands – Slayer covered 'Phantom' in early sets, and that wave of groups brought the mosh into metal. So that's why I think Di'Anno-era Maiden gets the punk tag: It took metal to a whole new space, physically, mentally, and musically. It was so tough, you didn't know how else to describe it".

"When we got signed and the whole New Wave Of British Heavy Metal started, or the NWOBHM, the newohbam ha ha, that's what really kicked off what we have today". Di'Anno reaffirmed to the Australian entertainment website *Spotlight Report* in 2012. "If it wasn't for Maiden and bands like Saxon, Motörhead, etc you would never of had bands like Metallica, Slayer, Megadeth and Anthrax, if you didn't have those bands you would never of had Sepultura, Morbid Angel, and then Pantera etc, so at the time they were just bloody good albums, but in the history of things, they really kicked off what started for anything today that has heavy guitar and yeah they are timeless, those albums still sell millions, you don't see the crap that was around then still selling shit, like Shaking Stevens or Spandau Ballet do ya?"

Maiden have a number of classic albums to their name such as *The Number Of The Beast* and *Piece Of Mind* as well as the stellar live opus *Live After Death*.

The Number Of The Beast was the first album fronted by Bruce Dickinson.

In an article called '10 Great Duel Lead Guitar Albums' by Russell Hall of *Gibson.com*, *The Number Of The Beast* is listed alongside Television's *Marquee Moon*, Thin Lizzy's *Jailbreak*, Sonic Youth's *Daydream Nation*, Derek And The Dominos' *Layla And Other Assorted*

Love Songs, Lynyrd Skynyrd's *Second Helping*, Wishbone Ash's *Argus*, Neil Young And Crazy Horse's *Zuma*, Lou Reed's *Rock And Roll Animal* and The Allman Brothers' *At Fillmore East*. Hall wrote: "Like their peers Judas Priest, Iron Maiden injected a darker element into the twin-guitar approach pioneered by Thin Lizzy and Wishbone Ash. The band's masterpiece, *Number Of The Beast*, was propelled by Bruce Dickinson's operatic vocals and the dynamic, blistering two-guitar swirl of Dave Murray and Adrian Smith. A host of bands, from Metallica to the Red Hot Chili Peppers, were profoundly influenced by the group's ferocious melodicism".

Brian Slagel: "My friend Lars (that drummer in that metal band, Metallica) and I often listened to this album [*The Number Of The Beast*] over and over. To say it was an influence on me and the metal scene is just not strong enough. This changed my life... The inspiration they provided and especially this album, really forged the US scene. Bands like Metallica, Slayer, Megadeth, Anthrax, etc... never would have happened without Maiden. The chance to be heard on a bigger level really gave us all inspiration".

Ulrich spoke to *Rhythm* magazine in 2011 about Iron Maiden's impact on Metallica which he recalled during the making of 1987's *The $5.98 E.P.: Garage Days Re-Revisited*. "We've always been around

English people", said. "In those years all our tour managers, our minders, our crew guys were all Brits and so there was always a very strong sense of English cynicism and sarcasm and a bit of twisted humour. We all incredible Maiden fans, obviously, and I don't think Metallica would be where Metallica is today if it wasn't for Iron Maiden, not only paving the way but also for just inspiring me in 1981 to form a band. We were sitting there recording the *Garage* thing in LA and it was a pretty loosey-goosey set of sessions and one day we started going into 'Run To The Hills' which is one of those things that anybody could attempt at any time

The Number Of The Beast was the last album featuring drummer Clive Burr. Clive Burr sadly died of MS on March 12, 2013.

Charlie Benante of Anthrax: "It was 1981. I was hanging with friends in the back of the Palladium in New York City. Judas Priest and Iron Maiden were playing. Two taxis pull up and Maiden get out. Steve and Clive hang and talk for a bit. Clive at the time was an up-and-coming drummer that I thought played with a style all his own. The drumming on *Killers* inspired me to kick it up a notch and I did. I spoke with him and asked him for a pair of sticks. When he was done signing things, he went into the venue and ten minutes later came out with a pair of sticks for me. I still have those sticks. RIP Clive – you have influenced so many, and to this day nobody plays like you".

Dave Lombardo of Slayer: "Sadness overcame my morning when I heard this news. His style was inspiring and the albums he recorded with Iron Maiden are touchstones of my music education. He played with a particular energy which bought edge and excitement to the Maiden classics. I never got to meet him, but I wish did".

Burr was replaced by Nicko McBrain. Ulrich spoke to *Rhythm* in 2011 about McBrain's influence as a metal drummer. "Nicko was always great and obviously still is great because he has personality and there is an approachability about him", Ulrich enthused. "People really felt that he was enjoying himself and there was something slightly nutty about him but never Keith Moon level, it was never scary. He just really enjoyed what he was doing. I've always really enjoyed playing. People talk to me about, 'Why do you stick your tongue out while you're playing?' I don't have an answer for that, it just happens. I'm the one that has to sit and look at the pictures, I know it looks ridiculous, it just happens. I turn into this little gremlin. There is no cosmic thought or premeditated thing".

Ulrich continued to explain McBrain's impact: "Being around creative people is inspiring to me and I love to try to understand what their inspirations are. I'm very interested in musical lineage and history. I'll sit and talk with Nicko about when he did that with Trust or when he did this with so-and-so. Every time I've even looked at his drum kit, it's so overwhelming and frightening. He's got one of the biggest set ups in rock 'n' roll – I try to be a little more low-profile – but I've never done any of the technical wizardry stuff with them".

Released in April '88, *Seventh Son Of A Seventh Son* was a Number 1 hit for the band in the UK and it peaked at Number 12 in the USA. It was a huge worldwide hit and proved that after the experimentation of *Somewhere In Time* the band had not lost touch with their fanbase or their heavy metal roots. While bands like Metallica and Megadeth were setting the metal scene on fire with a new breed of razor sharp metal, Maiden were still hot contenders and originators. Though Metallica and their ilk made a different sort of metal from the traditional style that Maiden pioneered, and were very popular with the metal youth, Maiden were still at the top of their game and the metal scene as a whole.

The band launched the successful 7th Tour Of A 7th Tour in Cologne, Germany in April and finished in December of the same year. On 20th August Eddie and Maiden made their first headlining appearance at the famed Monsters Of Rock festival in Donington, England. They were supported by a number of bands throughout the entire tour: David Lee Roth, Metallica, Anthrax, Megadeth, Guns N' Roses, W.A.S.P., Helloween, Killer Dwarfs, Ossian, Trust, Great White, L.A. Guns, Backstreet Girls and Ace Frehley's Comet

Maiden first headlined Monsters Of Rock on August 20, 1988 on a bill that also saw performances from KISS, David Lee Roth, Megadeth, Guns N' Roses and Helloween. Their fiery performance can be found in the *BBC Archives* collection.

Twenty years later and in 2008, the band released the famed *Live After Death* performance on DVD and to coincide with its release Maiden launched the celebratory *Somewhere Back In Time* World Tour on February 1 in Mumbai, India. The highly-publicised tour lasted over a year and was divided in to four legs. They were supported by a number of artists namely, Agora, Anthrax, Atreyu, Avenged Sevenfold, Behind Crimson Eyes, Lauren Harris, IRA, Kamelot, Made Of Hate, M.A.S.A.C.R.E., Morbid Angel, Parikrama, Salamandra, Slayer, Tainted Carcass, Trivium, Trooper, Vanishing Point, Witchblade and Within Temptation.

"You've just got to have a sense of fearlessness", Dickinson said to *Metal Hammer* in 2011. "I got into trouble for saying that we're better than Metallica... and, it's true! They might be bigger than us and they might sell more tickets than us and they might get more gold-plated middle-class bourgeoisie turning up to their shows but they're not Maiden. I did say it's a bit of a wind-up. I thought, if I'm going to turn into an (expletive), I might as well, you know, go for it!"

They released the Number 1 critically revered *The Book Of Souls* in 2015. Maiden are as relevant as ever.

J

JUDAS KISS, THE

The fourth single released by Metallica from their album *Death Magnetic*.

JUDAS PRIEST

Legendary heavy metal band from the English West Midlands. Their most iconic albums include *British Steel*, *Screaming For Vengeance* and *Painkiller*. The most famous line-up of the band is: singer Rob Halford, guitarists K.K. Downing and Glenn Tipton and bassist Ian Hill. They still tour and record minus K.K. Downing in the fold and with long-term drummer Scott Travis. They are the second originators of heavy metal after Godfathers, Black Sabbath.

1982's *Screaming For Vengeance* would quickly become one of the decade's most defining albums, influencing bands such as Slayer and Metallica. German metal singer Doro is a huge fan of the early 1980s Priest albums.

The San Francisco Bay area – had become a force to be reckoned with. Metallica's masterful 1983 album *Kill 'Em All* led a new type of metal with sonic riffs, fluid bursts of electric energy, harsh vocals and many sporadic bouts of aggression.

From around the time of Priest's 1984 underrated opus *Defenders Of The Faith* to the end of the decade, thrash metal reigned supreme on the metal circuit both with album sales and touring. Other important bands and early albums of the time, which also spearheaded the way for this new sub-genre of heavy metal, included such titans as Anthrax with *Fistful Of Metal*, Slayer with *Show No Mercy*, Megadeth with *Killing Is My Business...And Business is Good!* and Exodus with Bonded By Blood. Metal Church, Testament, Watchtower and Voivod were also founding fathers of the genre. Like its parent genre, the origins and influences of thrash are often debated but one thing is for sure Judas Priest can lay a claim to its influence with the remarkable kick-drum speediness of 'Exciter' from the *Stained Class* album and the blood-drenched ferocity of 'Riding On The Wind' on *Screaming For Vengeance*. But what did Rob Halford, self-proclaimed Metal God, think of the thrash metal scene?

He told *Kerrang! Mega Metal*: "I mean, if you listen to some of the so-called thrash metal, you can hear a bit of the old, frantic Priest guitars in there, the stuff we used to do more in our early days. It's good".

Anthrax's Scott Ian, a committed Priest fan, said to the author: "My first memory of hearing Judas Priest...it's a long time ago. It was way before the *Hell Bent For Leather* album. It was probably *Stained Class* but definitely one of the earlier albums. I'm a huge fan.

He continued: "They're just a great metal band. They play great and make great songs. They created the template for mostly everything that came after them. All that music that they created still holds up well today…they're just awesome songs. The stuff that they were creating in the seventies and early eighties…It always sounds like Priest. Nobody else sounds like them…few metal bands are as good as they are. I mean twenty years later, even thirty years later, and nobody at all sounds like them. They're the original metal band!"

Other significant early examples of thrash metal including Black Sabbath's 'Symptom Of The Universe', Motörhead's 'Overkill' and surprisingly, Queen with the ultra-fast duo 'Sheer Heart Attack' and 'Stone Cold Crazy' (Metallica covered the latter on *Garage Inc*).

Thrash also inherits traits from the punk rock genre primarily from the musically talented skills and fast aggression of Iggy Pop and the Stooges and the NYC punk band the Ramones.

Priest got wind of this burgeoning scene on the West Coast of the USA. So with this new kind of faster, more forceful and aggressive style of modern metal, they really had to prove that they could compete with the bands they influenced without moving away from their own style and melody. Halford told *Kerrang!* in the mid-eighties: "...I wouldn't say that we ignore the state of the music scene, we always look at it from year to year...we do seem to follow our own path!"

There's no question that the American metal bands had an influence on 1990's *Painkiller* opus; which was also a means for the band to vent their frustrations over the famed court case involving two young men who attempted suicide in Reno, Nevada after listening to Priest's cover of the Spooky Tooth number 'Better By You, Better Than Me', which the prosecutors alleged was the subject of subliminal messaging and prompted the two men to attempt to kill themselves. *Painkiller* is a heavy, angry album.

The immense *Painkiller* tour began in Canada on October 18 and shifted to the USA on November 1 with Testament and Megadeth as support. This time the centre piece of the stage show (designed by Tom McPhillips) was the great futuristic creation known as the Metallion, which the band lovingly referred to as 'Metal Mickey'.

Pantera and Annihilator supported Judas Priest on a European tour in 1991. Some of Priest's road crew were really generous towards both support bands; one such dude was K.K. Downing's guitar tech Andy Battye who had been James Hetfield's for a number of years, and was on tour with Priest while Metallica were working on their self-titled album (aka *The Black Album*), released in August 1991. Battye knew that Annihilator and Pantera couldn't afford a hotel room, but whenever they had days off Battye would let them hang in his hotel room rather than the tour bus. Battye saw that they were good guys and musicians. He would get beers from Darrell and Waters, and they'd sit back and chat about metal.

No other metal band on the planet whether it be Black Sabbath, Iron Maiden or Metallica has fought for the growth and prosperity of heavy metal more than Judas Priest. Judas Priest was born to be a heavy metal band. Even when Halford famously proclaimed the death of metal he returned to the genre (not that he ever left, mind you) with the stunning 2000 release, *Resurrection* before joining Priest.

Of course Judas Priest have had their ups and downs like any band, there was a tumultuous period with Tim "Ripper" Owens which resulted in two albums, *Jugulator* and *Demolition.*

After Europe in 1998 in support of *Jugulator*, the band toured Japan in May and played a couple of dates in Mexico on September 17 and 19 before a second American tour in September and October with Megadeth as support. The tour resulted in a terrific live album called *'98 Live Metal Meltdown*, which hardly made an impact in the charts compared to previous lives albums *Unleashed In The East* and *Priest...Live!* However, the sheer power of Owens' vocals and the band themselves is incredible and well worth mentioning. The setlist is a treat. Inevitably, there are some new songs in the mix but the most tinkling songs in the setlist are the old classics such as 'The Ripper', 'The Sentinel' and 'Grinder'. 'Rapid Fire' is dynamite and proves that Owens can indeed give Halford a run for his money in terms of live performances.

In 2001 after a European leg in support of *Demolition* there was a quick tour of South America in September but a US tour (with Anthrax and Iced Earth planned as support) due to begin in LA on September 14 was cancelled after the terrorist attacks on New York's World Trade Centre on that day that is implanted in everybody's mind as 9/11. The US tour was wisely re-arranged for 2002.

Scott Ian of Anthrax recalls, "When we got asked to go out it was originally in 2001...we were supposed to do that *Demolition* tour in 2001 but then 9/11 happened so it got postponed for a couple of months. Amongst all that insanity of 9/11 one of our stresses was 'Oh no, is the Priest tour gonna get cancelled? And how are we gonna get to tour with Judas Priest now?' Of course, that was a very, very minor thing of everything else going on in the world but in our little small world of Anthrax, we were like 'Oh shit! We still wanna tour with Priest!' When they told us that is was gonna happen a couple of months later we were really excited. It was fucking awesome man! They treated us amazingly and it was great to get to see them every night, you know, with Ripper and then a couple of years later we got ask again to go back out with them with Rob back in the band. It was like a dream come true...We never got to play with them back in the early eighties...so it's just one of those bands were you always wish 'God, I hope someday I get to tour with those guys'. And now we have...twice!"

In 2002, Priest began their re-arranged tour of the USA and Canada with Anthrax on January 17 in Las Vegas and finished on February 19. As a committed Judas Priest fan, Scott Ian was overjoyed that Anthrax was given an opportunity to tour with his metal heroes. Ian has nothing but praise from Halford replacement Tim Owens.

Scott Ian: "He's got the voice. He's got the most uncanny metal voice I've ever heard. He's incredible...really they couldn't have gotten anybody better to follow Rob Halford. There's no one out there that could have done the job that he did. You're talking about the biggest shoes in the world to fill...and his story [has] been told a million times, just from a personal and professional level I don't think...[any] one could have done a better job than Tim. He was just so professional about the whole situation and coming in and knowing who's shoes he was filling and just going in and doing the best job he could as a fan of Judas Priest and not wanting to disappoint anyone...and just being the up-most professional and a gentleman when Rob came back - I think Tim is amazing".

The second leg of the 2005 North American tour began on September 23 and finished in Texas on November 1 with special guests Anthrax and Hatebreed. Although a special one-off gig called, 'Priest Feast' was held in San Diego, California on October 30 with Rob Zombie and Anthrax as support. Another band that took part in the show was Hoax UK – a band (made up of high school children) that was formed by Gene Simmons on his TV show *Rock School*.

By this point, fatigue was kicking in amongst members of the band and after two solid years of hard work, they were really looking forward to a holiday but there was still a few months left on the tour. Scott Ian of Anthrax said: "We went out for dinner a few times and we would hang out quite a bit after the shows...but more so on the *Demolition* tour than the last one we did with them. Glenn even told me on the last run that it was like the end of the cycle for them. They were all just pretty tired and really looking...to be done and just getting home but they weren't really hanging out too much after the shows. It was right at the end, the last week or so when we started hanging out and that's when Glenn told us, 'I apologise, please don't think anything bad...we're all just tired and we all just wanna get home. We've been out for a year.'. So that was really sincere".

Regardless of whatever fickle styles of music or image is in vogue, Priest has nevertheless persevered in their convictions. They have raised the flag for heavy metal and carried it around the world with aplomb. Rob Halford told *Kerrang!* in January, 1982: "We represent British heavy metal and we want to take it around the world".

In Las Vegas in May, 2006 Judas Priest along with Queen, Def Leppard and KISS were honoured at the initial *VH1 Rock Honours* awards ceremony, which was televised around the globe. Bands such as the Anthrax and The All-American Rejects paid homage to their childhood idols.

There are far too many connections between Priest and the Big Four bands to name them all. Another little facto is that Slayer covered 'Dissident Aggressor' on their 1988 album *South Of Heaven.*

Suffice it to say that Judas Priest were of enormous influence on Metallica, Slayer, Anthrax and Megadeth.

JUMP IN THE FIRE

'Jump In The Fire' was the second and last single from *Kill 'Em All*, Metallica's debut. It was one of the band's first original songs.

K

KILL 'EM ALL

After Ulrich, Hetfield and Mustaine moved to sound engineer Mark Whitaker's house at 3132 Carlson Boulevard in El Cerrito in February, the first time the newly amended line-up of the band played together in front of an audience was on March 5, 1983 at a club called The Stone while in the same month they recorded their first demo – *Megaforce* – with their recently acquired bassist, Cliff Burton.

Indeed, with their live reputation growing with each gig, they were eager to begin work on their first album but Metal Blade Records were not a position to finance it. "…Rocshire [Records] brought us in to record an EP during the summer of [19]82 but just two days before we were about to sign the contract to release the EP we changed our mind because we had been playing that tape to some different people and the response we had got was so overwhelming that we decided to wait and see what could happen", Lars Ulrich told *Metal Forces'* Bernard Doe. "Anyway the people at Rocshire didn't really know too much about what was going on with HM [heavy metal.] So we shopped around and talked to Firesign, the people that handle Riot, Mike Varney at Shrapnel and Brian Slegal's Metal Blade".

However, help was just around the corner. Johny "Z" Zazula, a concert promoter, had heard the demo tape *No Life 'Til Leather* and tried to help Metallica get a deal with some New York labels rather than the LA area. Cliff Burton is credited on *No Life Til Leather* but he did not actually play on the demo. Unable to get a deal, Zazula got some cash together to found the album himself and consequently signed Metallica to his own label Megaforce Records which he founded specifically for Metallica's release(s). Zazula was also the owner of New Jersey's famed record store Rock 'N' Roll Heaven where they would import many foreign metal releases, mostly European. He was a fundamental figure in the East Coast metal scene. Metallica relocated to The Old Bridge in New Jersey. They slept in their rehearsal area at a place called the Music Building and members of the thrash band Anthrax gave them a toaster and a refrigerator. Where Metallica slept was basically a dingy storage area. Times were hard.

Mustaine was soon replaced by Kirk Hammett and thus Ulrich/Hetfield/Hammett/Burton began work on what would become Metallica's debut album.

In May, 1983, Metallica with their new guitarist Kirk Hammett – who had barely been in the band a month – ventured to Music America in Rochester, New York to begin work on their debut album to be called *Metal Up Your Ass*. Hammett learned Mustaine's chords surprisingly quick and given the short amount of time he had to get used to Metallica's music he did a superlative job. With every show he got better and better and though he wasn't keen on playing Mustaine's solos he didn't want to cause any contention within the band; after all he was the newbie. He did adapt the solos by using the first four bars of Mustaine's solos and then changing them. The band liked what he did.

The recording sessions for the first album lasted between May 10 and 27. Obviously Dave Mustaine wasn't too pleased to hear about Kirk Hammett. In 1984, he told metal writer and fan Bob Nalbandian who witnessed the genesis and rise of Metallica: "Kirk is a 'Yes' man.... 'Yes, Lars, I'll do Dave's leads;' 'Yes, James, I'll play this'... James played all the rhythm on that album and Cliff wrote all Kirk's leads – so it shows you they're having a lot of trouble with this 'New Guitar God!'"

Though Mustaine was no longer in the band his contributions to the album were still valid: four of the Metallica's songs feature co-writing credits from Mustaine. 'The Four Horsemen', which was originally titled 'The Mechanix', is probably the most notable example. It was an early staple in Metallica's setlist although after Mustaine's departure the band added a melodic middle-section that differed from

Mustaine's original, faster tempo version. 'Phantom Lord' and 'Metal Militia' were Mustaine's other songwriting contributions. As with 'The Four Horsemen', the lyrics for 'Jump In The Fire' were reworked by Hetfield though Mustaine kept a co-credit. Hetfield is solely credited with having penned 'Motorbreath' and Burton for the bass solo '(Anesthesia) Pulling Teeth'. Many of the songs had already been created in one way or another prior to the recording of *Kill 'Em All*. George Marino who is a well-known name is rock and metal circles would master later reissues of the album.

Indeed, the album title was not the only problem the band's label took a well-known issue to; they also took objection to the original album cover. Just as self-proclaimed Metal Gods Judas Priest had problems with the artwork for *British Steel*, their 1980 classic which has a razor blade on the cover, Metallica's original idea for the *Kill 'Em All* artwork was a hand emerging from a toilet with a dagger like some cheesy B-movie horror from the 1940s; a special area of interest for Kirk Hammett who collects horror memorabilia and comics. The band were told by their management to use photographer Gary L. Heard to shoot the back cover band shot but he wanted direct ideas for the front cover artwork from the band. "Cliff Burton mentioned something about wanting there to be a bloody hammer on the cover – but then Cliff carried a hammer with him everywhere he went", Hammett told writer Jaan Uhelszki of *Music Radar* in 2008. "He always had a hammer in his luggage, and he would take it out occasionally and start destroying things".

The officially released album cover features the shadow of a hand letting go of a hammer with blood dripping from it. It was in many ways the personification of a rebellious band. "When Metallica started we were the outlaws, the rebels", Kirk Hammett admitted of Therese Owen of *Tonight* newspaper. "No one wanted to have anything to do with us. We were too harsh and thought of as the lowliest of the low. All those beginning years we thought we were never getting anywhere or making an impact. Then one day we woke up and it was like, 'Oh my God – we're famous; everyone knows us".

Metallica's debut album was released via Megaforce Records in the States in June 1983 and through Music For Nations in Europe the following month. It peaked at Number 155 in the *Billboard* 200 album charts in 1986 but did not chart, initially. When it was released by Elektra in 1988 it peaked at Number 120. While in the UK it did not chart either on its initial release .Though the album was not a great commercial success it did increase the band's fanbase and cement their new line-up: drummer Lars Ulrich, guitarists James Hetfield and

Kirk Hammett and bassist Cliff Burton. Their debut album spawned the singles 'Whiplash', 'Jump In The Fire' and 'Seek & Destroy'. All of them classics in their own right although it must be pointed out here that 'Whiplash' actually won Motörhead their first and so far only Grammy Award for 'Best Metal Performance' in 2005 from the Metallica tribute album, *Metallic Attack: The Ultimate Tribute*. It was especially ironic because Metallica were – and still are – hugely influenced by Motörhead so for the British band to win a Grammy for covering one of Metallica's songs was an odd turnaround of events but it certainly helped raise Motörhead's profile.

"This release pretty much set the whole speed/thrash metal ball rolling, and for that reason alone *Kill 'Em All* is a crucial album", commented *Metal Forces'* Bernard Doe to the author in 2011. "There was already a huge buzz surrounding the band thanks to the tape trading scene, and *Kill 'Em All* was also probably the most anticipated debut release ever from an underground metal band. Of course, Metallica would go on to write better material, but even now it's still a great album and to me 'Whiplash' remains an anthem that epitomises that whole era".

In September, 2007, Dave Grohl of the Foo Fighters confessed to *Kerrang!* In 2007: "I still listen to *Kill 'Em All* once a week and there's a part of me that will never lose the love of riffs. That's where a song like this comes in. As a drummer and a guitar player, the rhythmic quality of a decent riff is like a cannon to me. I can write riffs all day long because I look at the guitar like a drum set. So, just as I'll sit at a drum kit and play beats, I sit with a guitar and try the same thing".

Anthrax's Scott Ian has rated it as one of his Top 10 thrash metal albums of all time amongst Slayer's *Reign In Blood*, Suicidal Tendencies self-titled opus, Exodus' *Bonded By Blood*, Venom's *Welcome To Hell*, Raven's *Rock Until You Drop*, Anvil's *Metal On Metal*, Mercyful Fate's self-titled EP, Pantera's *Vulgar Display Of Power* and Megadeth's *Killing Is My Business...And Business Is Good!*. He said to Jon Wiederhorn of *Noisecreep*: "We were listening to them so much back at that time, and I couldn't listen to that more than I was back then when it first came out. That EP was a huge influence on everything that was to come. The playing, riff wise, that thrash element is certainly there in the guitars".

Bob Nalbandian wrote in his *Headbanger* fanzine: "*Kill 'Em All* displays OTT, ultra-fast, riff-orientated metal... And to think that I had doubts when drummer Lars Ulrich once told me a couple of years ago that he was gonna form the heaviest metal band in the U.S.! Anyhow,

Kill 'Em All delivers 100% Power Metal, not advised to be purchased by those with weak hearts".

On future reissues, publications would rave over the album. Here's what the rock and metal scribes said in the noughties:

Rolling Stone said: "It contains the first great Metallica standard, 'Seek & Destroy', not to mention the instrumental '(Anesthesia) Pulling Teeth', which features the late Cliff Burton delivering the greatest metal bass solo ever, for what it's worth. But the remainder of the album reflects the cover photo of four zitty teenagers trying to look tough".

Punks News declared: "The guitars are the highlight of this album. All the main riffs are memorable and even a lot of the secondary ones are as well. Kirk Hammett's lead work is frantic (no pun) and energetic, and several of the solos on this album rank among his best... Lars is a terrible drummer, but he clearly did his best to hide it on this album. Every song on this album is unique and contributes something to the album in total".

Metal Storm enthused: "The history of the best metal band began with this CD. In this album the bases of the thrash metal appeared for first time. By this time Metallica was surely the fastest band of the world, even faster than Venom [precursors of black metal style.] In this CD Metallica finds an own style which some years later will bring them to the top of metal".

Metal Observer said: "That time, they had the Hetfield/Ulrich/Mustaine/Burton line-up and the young band from the Bay Area created a true speed/thrash metal highlight. Raw, fast and crude, the band thrashes through true speed metal shells like 'Whiplash', 'Motorbreath' or 'Phantomlord' [*sic*.] Though the sound isn't as pressuring as on later releases, you can still listen to it harmlessly today. Maybe, it's because of this sound, that mangily, that spirit of *Kill 'Em All*, which makes this album so irresistibly. Every guitar solo, every punch on the drums is on the right place".

Steve Huey of *All Music* stated: "The true birth of thrash. On *Kill 'Em All*, Metallica fuses the intricate riffing of New Wave Of British Heavy Metal bands like Judas Priest, Iron Maiden, and Diamond Head with the velocity of Motörhead and hardcore punk... Frightening, awe-inspiring, and absolutely relentless, *Kill 'Em All* is pure destructive power, executed with jaw-dropping levels of scientific precision".

Suite101 expressed keenness for the album and its historical appeal: "*Kill 'Em All* was a great catalyst for Metallica. They were also playing live shows, building their reputation and gaining followers with their type of music. With the record, they were testing the waters for recognition. With the technical structuring of the songs outdoing the lyrics by quite a margin, Metallica still had a long way to go in being an accomplished, polished band. As a debut album, it didn't quite set the world on fire, but instead stirred and created interest. The world would follow soon after".

The Canadian metal historian and author Martin Popoff examines the album's strengths and weaknesses as he says to the author of this book in 2011: "My impressions upon hearing *Kill 'Em All* for the first time haven't really changed much. There was always one thing that kept it from being an absolute masterpiece, and that's this idea that it seems to be an album that is all about riff and very little else. It's almost like all other performances gather around and marvel at these amazing riffs, and they are amazing, but really every song seemed to be built and focused purely on riff. Part of this has to do with the production. It's a good, fierce, alcoholic production job, but there is a separation that also makes you compartmentalise, simplify, focus on rhythm guitar, with everybody else just supporting. Even James – when it comes to the vocals, it sounds like they are there to react to and support the riff as well, to egg on the riffs. Still, there was something new and nasty about the record. Obviously, almost all of the important NWOBHM albums had come and gone, and this seemed to be a band that was netting out the pure bleached heaviness from all of that and focusing purely on that, providing the Coles notes, the greatest hits of the NWOBHM. That's what I took away from that album and still take away from that album, a fierceness and nastiness, an even greater understanding of heavy metal that began with the NWOBHM, those British bands being the first that sort of put the message out there that we could be proud of metal".

KILL 'EM ALL FOR ONE TOUR

Metallica begun their first ever tour – the Kill 'Em All For One Tour – on July 27 1983 which would run for dozens of shows until July 20, 1984 with the NWOBHM band Raven.

James Hetfield said to *Metal Hammer* in 1999: "There were really horrible smells on that bus as there was a lot of drinking, puking and fucking going on. You would have to get drunk to actually fall asleep on that thing as it was so horrible. We would always fight for the top bunk. The air conditioner broke down somewhere in Texas, so it was about 200 degrees when you woke up. Raven weren't really the drinkers, but we got their drummer drunk on the last show and he went completely nuclear and started smashing up the place".

The tour was financed by Megaforce while the band's setlist mostly consisted of songs from their upcoming debut and leftover material that would later be used on their second studio release. Their regular setlist ran as follows: 'Hit The Lights', 'The Four Horsemen', 'Jump In The Fire', 'Fight Fire With Fire', 'Ride The Lightning', 'Phantom Lord', 'The Call Of Ktulu', 'No Remorse', 'Seek & Destroy', '(Anesthesia) Pulling Teeth', 'Whiplash', 'Creeping Death' and 'Metal Militia'.

James Hetfield to *Metal Hammer*: "That was where we cut our teeth on the road. We actually got to do one show with Motörhead, Raven and us. Getting out there playing fields in the middle of Arkansas to your dumpy little club called the rat in Chicago was great. We made a lot of friends on that tour. It was also pretty amazing to find out how our demo tape had gotten across the country and taken a hold on a lot of the young, angry youth of America".

By this point, Metallica were building up a reputation as a powerful live act. They continued to play some cover versions and alternate the selection of other artists' songs with each gig but they also played a significant amount of their own material. They were faithful to the original songs. "I think a lot of that, particularly with the older covers, was because we really didn't know that we had our own style", Hetfield admitted to *Guitar World* in 1998. "We were inspired by those songs, so we played them like the original versions". Metallica never did shy away from paying tributes to their heroes and they had fun doing it.

They were becoming tauter, leaner and better rehearsed with each gig. Cliff Burton said in February, 1986: "Different shows have different good points and it's really great to do a big show in front of the home town. But there's also other gigs, like when things are really, really happening. There's been a few of those. There's different things that make different shows memorable. I couldn't pinpoint one as being my favourite".

After initially wanting to have a frontman James Hetfield was coming out of his shell and transforming himself into a powerful onstage force gig after gig. He was learning how to talk to a crowd, how to control them and how to get them to work with the music. Initially, he didn't sing and play at the same time but he soon learn how to do both tasks. It was a challenge but singing and playing together soon became natural for him.

Over a decade later, James Hetfield confessed in 1996: "Maybe some of that singing/playing thing started when I was forced to take piano lessons as a kid. Doing the two-hand thing gets your brain thinking a couple different things at once. In the early days, singing was just something that I had to do, because I couldn't let all those lame guys sing for us. I'm gonna do it. But then that guy's not playing the riff right – give me the guitar back!"

He continued: "It was a battle for which thing I wanted to do. People would say, 'Your band's not going to do shit unless you have a frontman. You've got to have a singer out there who's got his hands free to do stuff', to throw the fucking sign or whatever".

They had a little bit more material to play onstage than the previous year but they still covered other bands songs but it was becoming easy for them to play a full set of originals. "Like any other band starting out, we would cover material because we needed to have enough songs to fill up the set when we played live", Hetfield said to *Guitar World* in 1998. "We had 'Hit The Lights', 'The Four Horsemen' and a few others, but not enough originals to do a full set. And since we were covering songs by these British heavy metal bands, people thought they were our own songs".

KILLING IS MY BUSINESS...AND BUSINESS IS GOOD!

Debut solo album from Megadeth that was released via Combact

Records in 1985. The band were given just $8000 to make their first full length studio album. The album suffers from poor production but is still regarded as a milestone release in the annals of metal. It contains a version of 'These Boots Are Made For Walkin' and the song 'Mechanix' which Mustaine wrote during his tenure in Metallica. A remixed version of the album was issued in 2002.

KING, KERRY

Guitarist and co-founder of Slayer with the later Jeff Hanneman. He was also the lead guitarist in Megadeth in 1984.

KING NOTHING

The fourth and final single released from Metallica's 1996 album *Load*.

KISS

From New York City, KISS are one of the most successful American rock bands of all time with sales of over 100 million albums. Known for their shock rock image and electrifying stage performances that feature elaborate stage designs and props such as fire breathing, blood spitting, smoking guitars, shooting rockets, glitzy drum kits that levitate, pyro and smoke and all manner of other stage effects, KISS are truly unique. Some of their classic songs include 'Cold Gin', 'Deuce', 'Detroit Rock City', 'Shout It Out Loud' and the ballad 'Beth'. They are one of the most entertaining live bands in the world. KISS are an influence on each of the Big Four bands.

L

LÄÄZ ROCKIT

Lääz Rockit began life as a power metal band before they began to introduce thrash metal riffs into their music. Though they remain an obscure name, each album is highly thought of by aficionados and critics of the genre. Their debut *City's Gonna Burn* was released in 1984 but they later broke up in 1992. Some former members created the groove metal outfit Gack. They reformed in 2005 and released *Left For Dead* in 2008.

For evidence of their kick-ass metal check out *City's Gonna Burn* (1984), *No Stranger To Danger* (1985) and *Know Your Enemy* (1987).

LOLLAPALOOZA NO.6

Metallica headlined the festival tour in 1996.

LOMBARDO, DAVE

Lombardo is one of the most influential drummers in metal. He has performed on nine Slayer albums including their seminal release

Reign In Blood.

LEATHER CHARM

Leather Charm was formed in June, 1981. The initial line-up featured singer James Hetfield, drummer Jim Mulligan, guitarist Hugh Tanner (who was later replaced by Troy James) and bassist Ron McGovney. They churned out covers by many of their favourite bands, including legendry British hard rockers Deep Purple whose album *Machine Head* was a major source of inspiration for most aspiring rock bands of the 1970s and 1980s regardless of nationality. Purple was formed in 1968 and while the band has had various line-ups over the years (even prior to the formation of Leather Charm) the most revered and commercially successful was undoubtedly singer Ian Gillan, guitarist Ritchie Blackmore, bassist Roger Glover, drummer Ian Paice and organist Jon lord. This, the Mark II line-up, created arguably some of the most famous and enduring hard rock albums of all time: *In Rock* (1970), *Fireball* (1971) and *Machine Head* (1972). The latter certainly had a major impact on the evolution of metal with the classic songs 'Highway Star', 'Smoke On The Water' and 'Space Truckin''.

Leather Charm created an original song called 'Hit The Lights' but the outfit folded just months after it was formed. They also penned a couple of other tracks; one was called 'Handsome Ransom' and the other was named 'Let's Go Rock 'N' Roll'. 'Let's Go Rock 'N' Roll' later became the Metallica track 'No Remorse'.

Rob McGovney speaking to Pat O'Connor of *Shockwaves* in 1997: "We were doing kind of a glam thing, like, Sweet, and this British band called Girl (which featured Phil Lewis and Phil Colin), we did that song 'Hollywood Tease'. We did a bunch of covers as well like 'Pictured Life' from Scorpions, 'Wrathchild' and 'Remember Tomorrow' from Iron Maiden and 'Slick Black Cadillac' from Quiet Riot (the Randy Rhoads era)".

LEMMY

Ian Fraser "Lemmy" Kilmister is one of the most iconic rock stars ever. He was a member of Hawkwind before being fired from the band which led him to form Motörhead, named after a Hawkwind song. He is a pop culture iconic, and the lead singer/bassist/songwriter behind Motörhead. He is good friends with each of the Big Four bands and has toured and/or played on the same bill as all four bands. In October 2009 Lemmy performed vocals and bass on a cover of 'Stand By Me' with Dave Lombardo of Slayer on drums. Lemmy has appeared onstage with Metallica several times over the years. Metallica even performed as Hey, Hey, We're The Lemmys as a tribute to Lemmy's 50th birthday at the Whiskey in Los Angeles, CA on December 14, 1995. He died December 28, 2015 aged 70. RIP.

LIMITED EDITION VINYL BOX SET

A limited edition box set from Metallica that was released in 2004 and contains four studio albums, an EP and picture disc single.

LIMP BIZKIT

Of all the nu-metal bands Limp Bizkit was by far the most high-profiled and also the most heavily mocked (mostly due to the arrogant nature of lead singer Fred Durst). The band was formed in 1995 in Florida and released their debut CD two years later: *Three Dollar Bill, Yall$* was not a success. Limp Bizkit made themselves stand out from other bands of their ilk through their showmanship and individual personalities. Their breakthrough came with the Number 1 US album *Significant Other* in 1999 and followed it up with *Chocolate Starfish And The Hot Dog Flavoured Water* which sold millions. *Results May Vary* (the first album not to feature guitarist Wes Borland) was self-explanatory; critics offered mixed opinions as did the band's fans. An EP (*The Unquestionable Truth: Part 1*) was released which saw the return of Wes Borland but then, after some live dates, the band laid low. Guitarist Wes Borland left the band again but returned in 2009 for what was heavily promoted as a "comeback" for the band. Whereas, say, peers Linkin Park, have sort of become accepted by the music critical establishment and have a degree of reverence, Limp Bizkit seemed to be the complete opposite. It seems that after the nu-metal phase was over the band lost their appeal. At the time of writing in 2015 they are recording their seventh album *Stampede Of The Disco Elephants* which follows 2011's *Gold Cobra*.

LIVE AT GRIMEY'S

A Metallica live EP recorded at The Basement, a venue beneath Grimey's New & Preloved Music in Nashville. It was recorded on June 12, 2008.

LIVE SHIT: BINGE & PURGE

In November, 1993, Metallica released their first ever live album *Live Shit: Binge & Purge*. The original release contained three CDs and three video tapes with concerts recorded in Mexico City on the Nowhere Else To Roam Tour while the more recent collection houses two DVDs with concerts recorded in San Diego on Nowhere Else To Roam Tour and Seattle from the Damaged Justice Tour. It peaked at Number 26 in the United States. Live albums are rarely big success stories.

LOAD

The controversial (amongst fans, anyway) sixth album *Load*, was recorded at The Plant Studio in Sausalito, California over the course of several months between May, 1995 and February, 1996. They had around thirty demos to worth with. Again with producer Bob Rock, the sound of the album was markedly different from *Metallica* and especially their first four albums. *Load* was far removed from the traditional American thrash sound with heavy blues influences and a mainstream heavy metal sound. It remains their longest studio release. Released in June, 1996, almost a full five years since *Metallica,* the album hit Number 1 in the United States and sold over half-a-million copies in its first week of release in the United States alone and has gone on to sell a staggering five million worldwide. However, despite *Load* being one of the luke-warmly received albums by fans, many critics did appreciate the band's shift in sound.

Q magazine exclaimed: "These boys set up their tents in the darkest place of all, in the naked horror of their own heads... Metallica make existential metal and they've never needed the props... Metallica are still awesome... What is new is streamlined attack, the focus and, yes, the tunes".

While *Melody Maker* said: "A Metallica album is traditionally an exhausting event. It should rock you to exhaustion, leave you brutalised and drained. This one is no exception. It is, however, the first Metallica album to make me wonder at any point, 'What the fuck was that?' It's as if the jackboot grinding the human face were to take occasional breaks for a pedicure". Six singles were released from the album: 'Until It Sleeps', 'Ain't My Bitch', 'Hero Of The Day', 'Mama Said', 'King Nothing' and 'Bleeding Me'.

LULU

In October, 2011, Metallica released their collaborative album with Lou Reed, formally of the legendary New York band, The Velvet Underground. The album was rather bizarrely named *Lulu*. The roots of the collaboration went back to the 2009 Rock And Roll Hall Of Fame's 25th Anniversary Concert where they both performed. They began working together two years later. Recording had been completed in June, 2011 and released at the tail-end of October. One of America's top rock writers, David Fricke of *Rolling Stone,* had been privileged enough to hear a couple of tracks from the album prior to its release and compared it to a combination of Reed's 1973 *Berlin* and Metallica's 1986 *Master Of Puppets*. How wrong was he!

M

M2K MINI TOUR

A short tour of the states for Metallica from December 28 1999 to January 10 2000.

MADLY IN ANGER WITH THE WORLD TOUR

Another Metallica tour in support of *St. Anger*. This was a long jaunt from November 2003 to November 2004.

MAMA SAID

'Mama Said' was the third single released from Metallica's 1996 album *Load*.

MASTER OF PUPPETS (ALBUM)

Again, they'd hooked up with producer Flemming Rasmussen with the legendary Michael Wagener mixing. However, the band had initially wanted Rasmussen to mix the album but because they ran over schedule and on the penultimate day of recording on December 26 they still hadn't mixed the album so when it came to mixing it in January, after playing a low-key warm-up gig in preparation for the forthcoming tour with Y&T and Armored Saint, Rasmussen had moved on to other projects so they recruited Wagener.

"Cliff Bernstein from Q-Prime management contacted me and asked if I was interested, I was", said Wagener to the author in 2011. "If I remember it right about two weeks, normal time for an album mix... They knew exactly what they wanted to hear. The whole session went pretty easy, no major problems... At the time this was the heaviest album I had done. We had a lot of fun during the process. I am very happy that it went so well for them".

Even though Hetfield had another outlet for his talents, Metallica had spent longer working on *Master Of Puppets* than they had on their first two albums which resulted in a longer wait between releases. Fans were eager, Lars Ulrich explained after the album's release in an interview with *Metal Forces*: "I mean a lot of bands go into the studio; find the right guitar or drum sound and then bash it out, particularly with the first album. But if you listen to *Master Of Puppets* you can hear a lot of different moods and feels, so sometimes we would work for maybe one or two days on just getting the right guitar sound for a specific part of a song".

Master Of Puppets was released in March, 1986. It peaked at Number 29 in the American *Billboard* 200 album charts but like most classic albums sales kept steady over the years. The album sold 300,000 copies in its first four weeks of release and it spent a lengthy 72 weeks in the charts in the United States. It would become one of the band's most enduring albums. *Master Of Puppets* was certified Gold in November, 1986 and it was certified Platinum six times in 2003. It peaked at Number 41 in the UK. The band were slowly climbing the charts with each subsequent release. Metallica unleashed 'Master Of Puppets', 'Battery' and 'Welcome Home (Sanitarium)' as singles. Yet despite their success they had not yet made a music video nor would any radio station play their music. To many people, Metallica was a scary creation. The band liked being outsiders, lone wolves of the music world. Like many of their idols, they craved a cult underground status rather than worldwide mainstream adulation. They were a metal band through and through. Would that kid of appeal and image it last?

Critical opinion was high. Suffice it to say *Master Of Puppets* remains Metallica's most accomplished work; at least that is the general consensus of Metallica fans and metal followers in general. However, Metallica were not concerned with the critics or even their own fanbase. Ulrich said in 1986 to *Metal Forces*: "...I don't know if people will believe this or not but we write and play for ourselves, we're really not consciously trying to please anyone else, we just go about pleasing ourselves and it just seems that we have a tendency to please other people as well".

"*Master Of Puppets* is an absolute classic album which really put Metallica in a league of their own in terms of the whole thrash movement that was booming at the time", *Metal Forces*' Bernard Doe told the author in 2011. "The material was generally more complex and more varied, but the songs retained that 'crunching' heaviness that had become Metallica's trademark. Also, the album saw James Hetfield develop into a more confident vocalist".

On subsequent reissues, the albums still garners high praise and suffice it to say its position in the pantheon of metal albums is more than assured. The album's legacy will outlive the band for sure. The success and reverence bestowed upon the album has meant the band has achieved immortality; as long as metal lasts, this album will be remembered.

Here's what the rock and metal scribes said in the noughties:

Metal Archives said: "Very few albums can stand the test of time like this album does. People have a very biased opinion on Metallica but let's forget all that. This was before the *St. Anger* abomination and well before they sued Napster or headlined

Lollapalooza and toured with Limp Bizkit and Linkin Park. This was Metallica, the young band who were hungry and produced a truly remarkable, timeless album for generations to come".

Metal Storm enthused: "From the intro of 'Battery' to the last guitar riff of 'Damage, Inc.'. The CD is just perfect, incredible and all the adjectives you want. In this album Metallica composed the song of songs: 'Master Of Puppets', astonishing. Eight minutes 38 seconds of pure metal. The virtuosity on composing of Metallica appears clearly in that song. In *Master Of Puppets* (maybe influenced by Black Sabbath) some songs are really dark and paranoid like 'The Thing That Should Not Be".

Steve Huey of *All Music* stated: "...by bookending the album with two slices of thrash mayhem ('Battery' and 'Damage, Inc'.), the band reigns triumphant through sheer force – of sound, of will, of malice. The arrangements are thick and muscular, and the material varies enough in texture and tempo to hold interest through all its twists and turns. Some critics have called *Master Of Puppets* the best heavy metal album ever recorded; if it isn't, it certainly comes close".

BBC.co.uk pointed out some of the album's themes: "It's hard, fast, rock with substance that doesn't require the listener to wear eyeliner or big fire-hazard hair to enjoy. It also features more serious themes (albeit expressed in a particularly aggressive and direct way) and more complex arrangements than similar acts of the same era".

The revered and prolific Canadian metal writer Martin Popoff gives the author of this book his take on the band's third mighty opus: "I did a book called *The Top 500 Heavy Metal Albums Of All Time*, and the ranking was purely something that fell out of a poll. This album took Number 1. Obviously, amazing album, but I remember feeling at the time, and still feeling, being I guess old school and maybe even a little jaded by 1986, that *Master Of Puppets*, great album that it is, was really just a refinement or a tuning up over *Ride The Lightning*. As one is wont to do as a kid, Metallica made it easy to order one's universe, instrumental against instrumental, the fast, punky, irreverent ones, the catchy mid-paced ones, the epic with vocals. There was almost a complete album to album match-up of the songs on this 'new and improved' Metallica album, over the last one. I dunno, there was a vague more of the same, but yeah, two *Ride The Lightning* was better than almost anything else, than one and something else, so no complaints! So I think the second album is way more of a groundbreaker, but *Master Of Puppets* is killer way-great in its own way, highly utilitarian. Perhaps the production is a shade better, more bite, maybe even a little more obstinate and underground, but I love both knob jobs. Another impression I do take away is that this record's tour was the first time I saw Metallica live, with Metal Church backing up, and it was one of the most ferocious, face-flung live performances I can recall (Jason was on bass). And much to one's amazement, flying the flag for metal all these years, here is a band that was actually headlining hockey barns, although not nearly full ones, with the big stage show, with pretty darn extreme music. It was a musing like an early version of the marvel at seeing Pantera, Slayer and Slipknot so high in the charts, or selling lots of records".

It was their first major label release so it got more of a promotional plug than *Kill 'Em All* and *Ride The Lightning*. It was their first album to be awarded Gold status having sold over half a million copies. In the States it was awarded Platinum status six times and five times Platinum in Canada.

The fact that *Master Of Puppets* is so highly revered and spoken about in metal circles means it has quite a legacy. It has given the band a lot of mainstream attention over the years. *TIME Magazine* in the States listed it in 'The All-TIME 100 Albums' poll in 2006 while *Q Magazine* and the acclaimed reference book *1001 Albums You Must Hear Before You Die* also gave it a lot of coverage. *IGN* went so far as to place it at Number 1 in their list of 'Top 25 Metal Albums' in 2007 and

Rolling Stone also placed it (at Number 157) in their poll, 'The 500 Greatest Albums Of All Time'. Other polls the album has featured in include *Guitar World*'s 'The Greatest Guitar Solos' where they positioned the title track at Number 51 while said magazine also positioned the album at Number 4 in a poll of great guitar albums. *Total Guitar* magazine has also rated the album highly in polls dedicated to great riffs. In 2006, *Kerrang!* magazine even so far as to dedicated a special issue of the magazine to *Master Of Puppets* called *A 20th Anniversary Tribute , Kerrang! Presents Remastered: Metallica's Master Of Puppets Revisited*. The editors of the magazine got various artists to review each track on the album; those artists included, Machine Head, Trivium, Mendeed, Bullet For My Valentine, Chimaira, Fightstar, Mastodon, and Funeral For A Friend. The lists could go on and on but basically, the album's quality has guaranteed it an enduring and lengthy legacy and not just within the confines of metal.

Songs from the album have also been covered by an array of artists, including, but not limited to, the following: Machine Head, Dream Theater, Apocalyptica and Pendulum. The appeal of the album is staggering and has not diminished over the years but in fact, has grown in stature and influence. The aforementioned American progressive metal band Dream Theater went so far as to cover the entire album in concert. It is something said band has done with other artists' masterpieces, including Deep Purple's *Made In Japan* and Pink Floyd's *Dark Side Of The Moon*.

Matt Harvey of Exhumed, the American death metal band who released their debut album *Gore-Metal* in 1998, spoke about the influence *Master Of Puppets* had on him (Justin M, Norton interview, *Hellbound.ca,* 2001): "I got the twelve tapes for a penny deal in *Hit Parader* and one of the tapes was MASTER OF PUPPETS. I remember putting it on and I was like: 'Fuck, something just happened!' That night my whole life direction changed. I was like: 'OK, cool. This is what I'm into now'. From there things got heavier and heavier".

Lars Ulrich say some four years later (Bernard Doe interview, *Metal Forces*, 1990): "...looking back, personally, even though most people say that *Master Of Puppets* was the definitive Metallica album, I think I would probably take *Ride The Lightning* as my most favourite album. Not that I'm gonna criticise the other stuff. You know I hate all that shit when people say like 'Well, that band on the first album is not really for us'. Fuck you it was, it's got your band name right here. It cringes me when people talk like that. I mean, every interview that Joe Elliott [Def Leppard frontman] does, he always denies their first album..."

MASTER OF PUPPETS (SINGLE)

'Master Of Puppets' was only released as a single in France and the inly single issued from the album of the same band, Metallica's third studio opus.

MAY, BRIAN

Brian May is undoubtedly one of rock music's greatest and best-known guitarists. Regularly appearing in 'The World's Greatest Guitarists' polls and such lists, Brian May is a living legend and an icon to musicians of all ages. As a member of Queen, he is a household name and his innovative signature guitar riffs are world famous. Some of his most recognised songs for Queen include 'We Will Rock You', 'Tie Your Mother Down' and 'Fat Bottomed Girls'. His musical career outside of Queen was kick-started with the *Star Fleet Project* in 1983 before two solo albums (*Back To The Light* and *Another World*) with the Brian May Band in the 1990s as well as his soundtrack compositions and many musical collaborations as a guitarist, producer and songwriter throughout his career. He's also collaborated with the West End theatre actress Kerry Ellis. He is a passionate activist and animal welfare charity enthusiast, an avid and popular blogger as well as an author and holds a PhD in Astrophysics. He is especially fond of Metallica and an influence on the band.

MCGOVNEY, RON

Prior to what is considered to be the first line-up of Metallica (singer/guitarist James Hetfield, drummer Lars Ulrich, guitarist Dave Mustaine and bassist Ron McGovney) Metallica experimented with various guitar and vocals sounds; creating a combination which was essentially the same as Diamond Head's. The band all along wanted to have a frontman like their heroes Iron Maiden and Deep Purple.

With the newly hired bassist Ron McGovney of Hetfield's former band Leather Charm, Metallica played their initial live show at Radio City in Anaheim, California on March 14, 1982. James Hetfield said to *Kerrang! Legends: Metallica*: "There were a lot of people there, maybe 200, because we had all my school friends and all Lars' and Ron's and Dave's buddies. I was really nervous and a little uncomfortable without a guitar and then during the first song Dave broke a string. It seemed to take him eternity to change it and I was standing there really embarrassed. We were really disappointed afterwards. But there were never as many people at the following shows as there were at that first one".

The band's first ever live setlist looked like this: 'Hit The Lights', 'Blitzkrieg', 'Helpless', 'Jump In The Fire', 'Let It Loose', 'Sucking My Love', 'Am I Evil?', 'The Prince' and 'Killing Time'.

McGovney's impressions of Ulrich drumming skills were not exactly favourable but with the new line-up amendments they started jamming straight away. McGovney was a budding photographer at the time often seen taking his camera into gigs and photographing bands live.

Ron McGovney to Pat O'Connor of *Shockwaves* in 1997: "I knew James [Hetfield] in junior high but didn't really start hanging out with him till our freshman year in high school. I remember having James in my driver's ed class, James had drawn a big picture of Steven Tyler on his Pee-chee and I wrote 'Fag' across his face, just to piss James off, and he had a fit in class. But then they started getting me into hard rock, I had been into Foreigner and Boston... bands like that, but then they got me into bands like UFO. I started taking acoustic guitar lessons when I was a fourteen, a freshman in high school".

Lars Ulrich explained to *Metal Forces*' Bernard Doe in 1984: "I think James [Hetfield] and I always thought that the initial line-up of Ron [McGovney] on bass and Dave [Mustaine] on lead guitar wasn't people [*sic*] who we were going to take all the way. We always knew that when someone better came along Ron and Dave would have to leave. So when Cliff [Burton] came around, out went Ron and with Dave we never really thought he was as good a lead guitar player we wanted for the band and also he had a problem as when he had had a few to drink he would become extremely obnoxious and very hard to control and a few times he put us in some very embarrassing situations".

After about three shows in San Francisco in total, McGovney played one of his last gigs with Metallica in November, 1982 at Mabuhay Gardens and then his final appearance with Metallica was at The Old Waldorf on November 29 where they recorded the now famous *Live Metal Up Your Ass* demo. A month or so later McGovney sold all his equipment and quit the rock scene. "I would have been better off as a paid road manager rather than the bass player, I probably would have been more respected. But like I said, that's all history", he said in 1997 to *Shockwaves*' Pat O'Connor.

MCIVER, JOEL
Distinguished metal journalist and author Joel McIver has penned mammoth books on Black Sabbath, Slayer and Metallica as well as a

number of other admirable books, including Queens Of The Stone Age, Slipknot and a genre book on extreme metal. In 2009 he published three books: biographies of Tool and the deceased Metallica bassist Cliff Burton and one called *100 Greatest Metal Guitarists*. He has also appeared in radio show, documentaries and DVDs. His website is *www.joelmciver.co.uk*. Here is an interview the author did with McIver in 2008/09.

Why did you decide to write a book on Slayer?

There was an obvious gap in the market for a book on the band. I've always been mystified by that fact and wanted to supply an obvious demand. Also, I love their music to an almost unhealthy degree!

Did you approach the band's management? What was their response?

I did, yes, with a view to making it the official Slayer book. I had a couple of long conversations with their manager Rick Sales and sent them all copies of my Metallica book, so they could see that I was a serious author and that I had some experience of writing about heavy metal in general and thrash metal in particular. The band were tentatively interested but obviously too busy to give it much thought, and in the end they hadn't made a decision one way or the other by the time my deadline arrived. So I thanked them for their time and wrote the book without their involvement. I'm sure they'll do an official book one day.

In terms of research material, how do approach the writing of a book? With Slayer, for example, there is a lot of information to work with so it must be a daunting task?

For me, value for the reader is always top of the agenda. Any writer can cobble together a book made up of old text stolen from the Internet. I always aim to provide information that isn't available anywhere else, thus giving the book value and the reader a reason to purchase. This involves interviewing the subjects, their associates, eyewitnesses, and other people with first-hand information. Once I've done a gazillion interviews, I use them to add colour to the basic chronology. Of course, you may not be writing from a chronological perspective – I've written books about specific albums and films which require a lot of critical analysis, for example – but a band biog usually reads better if it's organised along a timeline.

If you find this daunting, treat it as a challenge and step up! The worst case scenario is that you do your best but the book flops. No big deal, you dust yourself off and resolve to do better next time.

Given the similarities does your Slayer biography make a suitable companion to your book on Metallica?

Yes, absolutely. Anyone interested in 1980s thrash metal will enjoy both books, and there's a lot of common ground in later years too.

Has Lars Ulrich or any of the band read your Metallica bio Justice For All?

I don't know, but I doubt it. Their legal team will have checked it for libelous material, for sure.

Can you tell me about your background in music writing?

I started as an occasional contributor to various magazines in 1996: I was a teacher at the time. I moved into full-time journalism in 1999 when *Record Collector* needed a Production Editor. This was a great training ground for me as a writer: within a short time I was learning to edit text, write reviews, commission writers, manage a production schedule and so on. It was chaos at times (the publisher back then was a sociopath and the editorial team were divided by differing loyalties) but that was just part of the challenge. I wrote my first book the same year and have continued to write a book or two every year since then. My Metallica biog sold well enough to allow me to quit *Record Collector* in 2005 and work from home, which I love as I don't have to deal with company politics, commute into London or work for idiots. I've built up my freelance journalism over the years too: I contribute every month to *Metal Hammer*, *DVD Review*, *Rhythm*, *Total Guitar*, and *Bass Guitar* and (still) *Record Collector*; I occasionally write for *Classic Rock*, *Future Music*, *Acoustic* and *Modern Drummer*; and mags, I've written for in the past include *Kerrang!*, *Terrorizer*, *Total Film*, *Music Mart* and *Rock Tribune*. I do a fair few liner notes for major and indie record companies as well as the odd bit of radio, TV and DVD.

Who are you music and non-music influences?
The music I love most is extreme metal, funk, classical and some jazz and hip-hop as well as the usual sixties to nineties biggies. My 'non-music influences', you might say, are my wife and kids and my love of films and sleep.

What do you think about contemporary rock writing compared to the eighties when Metal Hammer *and* Kerrang! *first started out?*
I was given a couple of *Kerrang!* yearbooks by David from Akercocke

recently and I was amazed by how naive the writing was back then. I'm sure Mick Wall and Malcolm Dome, who are great writers, would agree that the "kranium-krushin" style they used back then seems pretty obsolete now. Then again, I loved the way that in any given issue of *Hammer* or *Kerrang!* the Editor would happily include features on Rush, Styx, Lita Ford, Bon Jovi, Deep Purple, Anthrax, Morbid Angel, Warrant, Poison, Venom, FM and Cheap Trick and not give a toss that they had very little in common.

Which of your books has been the hardest to write?
The Black Sabbath book I did in 2006, partly because it was so big – one hundred and seventy five words – but also because I wanted it to be the best in its field. No easy feat when there are already several books on the subject by very respected writers. It turned out OK though.

What challenges did writing and researching 100 Greatest Metal Guitarists present?
Writing any kind of list of best guitarists, opera singers, chicken farmers etc., is bound to attract controversy, and in the heavy metal zone (which is populated largely by young, sensitive people) even

more so. I knew that releasing a list like this on a big, well-distributed publisher would cause feathers to fly and so it has. My challenge was to prove that a list book can be meaningful and arguable without merely being controversial, so I took special care to place each of the hundred guys at a place on the list which could be backed up with solid technical reasoning. I think I pulled it off, but I've still been called every name under the sun (to my amusement, I should add).

What did you learn about Cliff Burton when writing your biography of him?

I'd always suspected that Cliff must have been an unusually mature bloke despite his tender age, and wise beyond his years, and this was confirmed to me by the many interviews I did with those closest to him. I wanted at all costs to avoid painting a picture of him as a saint, which would have been very easy to do: I just wanted to tell the truth about who he was and what he achieved. Even so, he still came across as a unique individual, the Mozart of the heavy metal bass – and I don't say that lightly.

Do you think Burton would still be in Metallica if he was alive today?

Who knows. I think Metallica would have taken a different path after *The Black Album* [aka *Metallica*] with him in the band, perhaps in a more southern-influenced and/or progressive direction. He said not long before his death that he could see Metallica playing softer music in years to come.

You've written the first biography of Tool. What do you like about their music?

Its complexity and its depth. That band are true pioneers, even though they only emerge into the spotlight every few years. A band like Tool take years to understand.

What can you tell me about your book project with the legendary Glenn Hughes?

Glenn's autobiography, which I suggested to him back in 2005, is going to be a milestone in rock writing. Not because I'm so awesome or anything like that (I hasten to add), but because he has done things in his life that would have killed most of us several times over and still survived to tell the tale –literally. On the one hand, the format will be recognisable to most readers of rock biogs (the stadium years; the drugs; the recovery; the solo career), but on the other, the angle that

Glenn's memories have taken don't just focus on the debauchery, although there's plenty of that – in gobsmacking detail. He's also taken an honest, no-bullshit stance towards the nature of rock 'n' roll stardom and addiction that is entirely new. There are rock-star autobiogs which drone on for ages about drugs and sex until it becomes tedious: this book won't ever become that way, I promise you. We're looking to publish in time for Christmas '09.

MEGADETH

Megadeth was of course formed by Dave Mustaine after he was ousted from Metallica in 1983. Mustaine was joined by bassist Dave Ellefson and Greg Handevidt. They would become one of the genre's most successful bands and would join Metallica and Anthrax as part of the Big Four. After the release of their debut album *Killing Is My Business... And Business Is Good* Lars Ulrich told *Metal Forces'* Bernard Doe: "I was expecting the first album to be a lot like Metallica, but I think it's great Dave's [Mustaine] taken a completely different approach and tried to be totally different to anything we had done with him".

Anthrax's Scott Ian said to Jon Wiederhorn of *Noisecreep* about Megadeth's debut album: "I remember Dave playing me the demos to that record. We were on tour with Raven and we were playing the

Country Club in LA. We were sitting in someone's car and he was playing me the demos to 'Skull Beneath The Skin' and we were just like, 'Holy shit', banging out heads and listening to this stuff. That record still absolutely holds up. There are some amazing riffs. And to be able to get kicked out of Metallica after having written a lot of *Kill 'Em All*, and then come back with *Killing Is My Business* and be able to churn out all those great riffs and great songs is no small accomplishment".

What Mustaine had done was form a band and turned it into a living breathing animal that was totally separate from Metallica. Megadeth have their own sound and identity that is different from Mustaine's former band. There have been many line-up changes in Megadeth's long history and in 2002, the band was briefly disbanded after Mustaine had nerve damage on his left arm. With thirty million albums sold worldwide and ten Top 40 albums in the United States their legacy is assured despite the erratic nature of the band. They released their thirteenth album *TH1RT3EN* in 2011 followed by *Super Collider* in 2013. The band announced that *Dystopia* would be released in 2016.

Their most successful albums are *Killing Is My Business... And Business Is Good* (1985), *Peace Sells... But Who's Buying?* (1986), *So Far,*

So Good... So What! (1988) and *Rust In Peace* (1990).

CURRENT MEMBERS:

Chris Adler (Drums, 2015-)

David Ellefson (bass/backing vocals, 1983-2002, 2010-)

Kiko Loureiro (guitar/backing vocals, 2015-)

Dave Mustaine (vocals/lead guitar, 1983-2002, 2004-)

FORMER MEMBERS:

Mike Albert (Guitar, 1985)

Chuck Behler (Drums, 1987-1989)

Chris Broderick (Guitar, 2008-2014)

Dijon Carruthers (Drums, 1983)

Jimmy DeGrasso (Drums, 1998-2002)

Glen Drover (Guitar, 2004-2008)

Shawn Drover (Drums, 2004-2014)

Marty Friedman (Guitar, 1990-2000)

Greg Handevidt (Guitar, 1983)

Kerry King (Guitar, 1984)

James LoMenzo (Bass, 2006-2010)

James MacDonough (Bass, 2004-2006)

Nick Menza (Drums, 1989-1998, 2004)

Al Pitrelli (Guitar, 2000-2002)

Chris Poland (Guitar, 1984–85, 1985–87, 2004)

Gar Samuelson (Drums, 1984-1987)

Jeff Young (Guitar, 1987-1989)

SESSION MUSICIANS:

Chris Adler (Drums, 2015-)

Vinnie Colaiuta (Drums, 2004)

Jimmy Sloas (Bass, 2004)

MECURY, FREDDIE

Regularly voted the greatest frontman of all time, Freddie Mercury fronted Queen from 1970 until his death in 1991. Of the 17 songs featured on Queen's *Greatest Hits* album, he wrote ten: 'Bohemian Rhapsody', 'Seven Seas Of Rhye', 'Killer Queen', 'Somebody To Love', 'Good Old-Fashioned Lover Boy', 'We Are The Champions', 'Bicycle Race', 'Don't Stop Me Now', 'Crazy Little Thing Called Love' and 'Play The Game'. He has posthumously been inducted into the Rock And Roll Hall Of Fame, the Songwriters Hall Of Fame, the UK Music Hall Of Fame and the Hollywood Walk Of Fame. A film based on his life is said to be in development. The legend lives on. Metallica performed at the Freddie Mercury Tribute Concert in 1992.

MEGAFORCE DEMO

The last Metallica demo to feature Mustaine. It was recorded on March 16, 1983. The demo was recorded to introduce Cluff Burton to potential record label bosses. The band won a contract with Megaforce Records.

MEGAFORCE RECORDS

An indie record label that was founded in 1982 by Jon and Marsha Zazula. Their firs signing was Metallica and other metal artists include Anthrax, Overkill and Testment.

MEMORY REMAINS, THE

The first single from Metallica's 1997 album *ReLoad*. The band first performed it live on July 2, 1996. Marianna Faithful, the '60s British singer performs backing vocals on it.

MERCYFUL FATE

Mercyful Fate was also a major influence on the young Dane, Lars Ulrich. The metal band had formed in Copenhagen in 1981 featuring former members of Black Rose and Brats. They released *The Mercyful Fate EP* in 1982 and followed it up with their debut album Melissa in 1983. It has become one of the most enduring albums in metal and Mercyful Fate led the way for lots of the bands in the various extreme ends of metal, including, death, thrash, speed, progressive, power and black. Their second album *Don't Break The Oath* (1984) is also a stone cold heavy metal classic. Fronted by King Diamond, they were also an incredibly powerful live band and coming from Denmark, Ulrich was especially fond of the band. Some of their music was very intricate and progressive but it would be some time before critics would truly appreciate the sheer power and exhilaration of the band's music. They had an enormous impact on the American thrash metal scene and their influence lasts to this day.

METAL

Metal had started with Black Sabbath following on from the hard blues-tinged rock bands like The Who, The Kinks, Led Zeppelin and Cream and then it progressed to heavier heights with the second metal band (also from the Midlands), Judas Priest. Hard rock bands Deep

Purple and UFO were (are) not metal but they appealed to the same fanbase. Of course there were other subgenres such as glam rock with bands like T-Rex and Queen and Slade, The Sweet et al and prog rock with ELP and in some ways they all had a major part to play in the development of metal and paved the way for the rise of American metal in the 1980s. There are many sub-genres of metal from speed and thrash to prog, death, black and power metal.

METAL BLADE RECORDS

Founded by Brian Slagel. He label's first release was *The New Heavy Metal Revue Presents Metal Massacre*, and included Metallica, Ratt, and Black 'N Blue.

METAL UP YOUR ASS

Just had Saxon had trouble with their original name of Son Of A Bitch, Metallica had disagreements with their label and distributors over the album title of their debut album, initially dubbed *Metal Up Your Ass*. They got a call from the label telling them they had to change the name. Consequently, because of the fuss surrounding the word 'ass' in the title Metallica changed the album's name to *Kill 'Em All*. As with rap and hip-hop music in the noughties, heavy metal was the cause of attacks and rebuttals from conservative voters and right wing fundamentalists and religious fanatics throughout the 1980s so record companies were often cautious about censorship fearing it would damage sales and give bad publicity. The name of Metallica's debut came from something Cliff Burton said after hearing that the label and management objected to *Metal Up Your Ass*. Kirk Hammett recalled to Jaan Uhelszki of *Music Radar* in 2008: "Cliff said, 'You know what? Fuck those fuckers, man, those fucking record outlet people. We should just kill 'em all... Someone, I can't remember who, said, 'That's it! That's what we should call the album'".

The band later released official T-shirts with the original album cover and title *Metal Up Your Ass*. A live bootleg from 1982 is also in existence with the original title and album artwork.

METAL UP YOUR ASS LIVE

Metal Up Your Ass Live was recorded thereafter at the Old Waldorf in San Francisco on November 29 1982.

The early Metallica demos became sought-after items amongst metal tape trading collectors. Even though some fans complained that Metallica were too fast to be a metal band or even too punk, they offered something new and vibrant. Bernard Doe who went on to co-found and edited the (no defunct) UK magazine *Metal Forces* said to the author in 2011: "Metallica were already having a big influence on the underground metal scene. Now, absolutely no one, if they're being honest, could have predicted just how popular Metallica would become at that point, but it was clear even then that they were extending the boundaries of heavy metal and spearheading something very special".

METALLICA

"Well, Cliff Burnstein who signed us to our new management deal in the States has this big belief that what we are doing will be the next big thing in heavy metal, especially in the States which is something like 80% of the market, and this whole Ratt, Mötley Crüe, Quiet Riot, Black 'N Blue thing will get kinda old and die out and that Metallica will lead the way in a sort of new true metal trend", said Lars Ulrich to *Metal Forces'* Bernard Doe in 1984. "One step further than say Iron Maiden who are at the moment the most extreme metal band with major success". Those words would prove rather prophetic...

Metallica literally changed the face of metal. They didn't do it with one album, of course; they did over a period of time. They built up a fanbase and conquered the metal world all almost single-handedly.

They had a passion for metal; it wasn't about the scene, or the money or even the booze and women – it was all about the music. It was about metal. Signing to Q-Prime management company made them megastars but their foundations were based on a DIY approach inspired by the New Wave Of British Heavy Metal bands, in particular Diamond Head; a gruff working class band from Stourbridge in the English Midlands.

Upon meeting each other in the fall of 1981 in Downey, California, Ulrich and Hetfield became fast friends through a shared love of rock and metal. "Certainly the first time Lars and I got together for a jam [forming a band] didn't happen, there was no vibe", Hetfield said to *Kerrang! Legends: Metallica*. And when he came to me with an opportunity to be on a record that was pretty interesting. At that time in my life I wanted to play music, I didn't want to work".

Ulrich opened up a whole new world of metal for Hetfield and not only introduced him to some of the obscure NWOBHM bands but also other European metal outfits too. "I had heard of Iron Maiden and Def Leppard, but not too many of the other, more obscure, English metal bands", confessed Hetfield to *Guitar World* in 1998. "So when I first met up with Lars, I would spend days just going through his record collection, taping over my REO Speedwagon cassettes with bands like Angel Witch and Diamond Head and Motörhead. I was in heaven at his house".

Even though a band had not yet been officially formed, Ulrich got in touch with Metal Blade Records founder Brian Slagel about the possibility of recording a track for the upcoming metal compilation, *Metal Massacre*. The answer from Slagel was an affirmative nod of the head.

In October, 1981, Ulrich formed a band with Hetfield and through Ulrich's close metal lovin' buddy Ron Quintana, Metallica was born.

Ron Quintana told the author of this book in 2011: "Lars and I met on top of Strawberry Hill on the island in the middle of Stow Lake in deepest Golden Gate Park at midnight or so one Friday Night (or Saturday) in January, 1981. Our friends went there every weekend with Ghetto Blasters and tons of Budgie/Priest/Scorps/Maiden/Motörhead, etc.; tapes to blast as loud as we wanted and not attract the cops (although they did trudge up there a time or two trying to catch us underage kids drinking and screamin' til 3a.m.). Lotsa cases of beer or other bottles and rarely a keg as it took so long to lug up there. Our East Bay buddy Rich Burch...actually met him first that day on Telegraph in Berkeley and attacked Lars when he saw all the rare patches and buttons on his denim jacket! He invited Lars to our Banger Party and all of us quizzed him on all the NWOBHM bands he'd seen that we'd only heard about! His and my favourite band was Diamond Head at that moment so we hung out the most. Later, he drove me [and] then Rich home, but we talked metal in his huge brown AMC Pacer car that is something of a joke to car enthusiasts for hours! We hung out every time he visited north from Newport Beach through summer".

Quintana remembers the almost obsessive enthusiasm Ulrich had for heavy metal: "Lars was totally a metal fan and hardly ever mentioned tennis, or his famous father 'til much later. We'd all collected any info in the Bay Area on the NWOBHM in 1979 and 1980 from *Sounds*, *NME* or *Melody Maker*. I immediately loved 'Am I Evil?' from a BBC recording as well as a London live recording from 1980 that featured my other favourite, 'Dead Reckoning'. Lars actually loved that tape (before I made him a copy) that he jammed my Fisher tape deck listening to the lyrics over and over one day he came to visit! I still have that broken wreck in the basement somewhere!"

1981 to 1989 was the period in which Metallica were outlaw metal musicians with a don't-give-a-fuck attitude that literally promised them not only cult status but crowned them kings of the underground American metal scene but of course, they became bigger than that. Much bigger. Subsequent decades saw them attacked and criticised by their fanbase for betraying their metal roots but in the beginning, they were adored; they were unique and innovative. Metallica knew what metal fans wanted; what they craved. It was all about full-throttle riffs, aggressive vocals, pounding drums and a kick-arse bass. It was thrash fuckin' metal, American style.

Metallica created their best work in this era: is it any wonder that *Ride The Lightning* and *Master Of Puppets* constantly come up in various polls of classic albums or great riffs both within and out of the metal genre. Those albums along with their debut *Kill 'Em All* and their fourth opus *...And Justice For All* have stood the test of time and hold up alarmingly well in the 21st Century when metal has become in many respects a lot more technical. There is a naivety about those first four Metallica albums but also an honesty, a rawness and large doses of aggression which is now lost in time. Metallica is a different type of band these days and they could never replicate what they created during that era; if they wanted to they would have probably done it by now, anyway. Those albums were as much about youth as anything else.

Those first four albums by Metallica remain cornerstones in

heavy metal. While ...*An Justice For All* still causes contention within the Metallica fanbase, there's no doubt that the early years of Metallica from 1981 to 1989 laid down the foundations for the birth of American metal. Metallica were literally the bridge between the British heavy metal bands of the late 1970s and the American bands of the 1980s. Metallica also spearheaded the famed Bay Area thrash scene and led the Big Four of the thrash bands with the remaining three being Megadeth, Slayer and Anthrax. The holiest of the unholy of American thrash.

Metallica have yet to make anything as groundbreaking as those first four (or in a lot of fans minds, three) albums. They represented a period in their career when they were young, hungry and just different. They were angry too. Very angry. Since then, they have never been afraid to move on and change and adapt their sound and musical identity. Perhaps it's the case that they'll never make anything as bold or technically accomplished as *Master Of Puppets* and whether that's because Cliff Burton was in the band will never been known, only speculated. *Kill 'Em All*, *Ride The Lightning* and *Master Of Puppets* proved that Burton was perhaps the most fundamental figure in Metallica; it can be argued that he was certainly the most technical. *...And Justice For All* was certainly a strong album despite the obvious change in musical direction from its three predecessors but it marked the end of an era for sure and those that came after were nowhere near as profound.

The band was formed in 1981 and have released nine studio albums and sold over 100 million albums worldwide. Former members of the band include the late bassist Cliff Burton, Ron McGovney and James Newsted and guitarist Dave Mustaine. Robert Trujillo now plays bass. Their latest album at the time of writing was 2009's *Death Magnetic*.

Will Metallica ever end? Will they call it a day?

"Well, death doesn't stop it, pyrotechnics don't stop it, people leaving don't stop it", Hetfield said to writer Greg Prato of *Brave Words* in 2008. "Yeah, what does stop it? Bus accidents, all that, I don't know. I think when Lars and I decide to not do it or we don't feel it or something happens to one of us then it probably stops. But that doesn't mean the spirit of Metallica or the love for it stops. Writing music will always be a part of me and my expression".

CURRENT MEMBERS:

Kirk Hammett (Lead guitar/backing vocals, 1983-)

James Hetfield (Lead vocals/guitar, 1981-)

Robert Trujillo (Bass/backing vocals, 2003-)

Lars Ulrich (Drums,1981-)

FORMER MEMBERS:

Cliff Burton (Bass/backing vocals, 1982–86)

Ron McGovney (Bass/backing vocals, 1982)

Dave Mustaine (Lead guitar/backing vocals, 1982–1983)

Jason Newsted (Bass/backing vocals, 1986–2001)

SESSION MUSICIANS:

Bob Rock (Bass, 2002–03)

METALLICA (THE BLACK ALBUM)

In October, 1990, Metallica recorded their fifth album at One On One Studio in Hollywood with the revered and appropriately named Bob Rock; known for his work with Aerosmith, Bon Jovi, The Cult and famously Mötley Crüe on their hair metal classic *Dr. Feelgood*. They had a batch of songs which had been written over a two month period during the summer and had recorded demos in mid-September. Metallica and Rock spent about a week recording at Little Mountain Sound Studios in Vancouver; the home of the influential and highly respected producer Bruce Fairbairn (RIP) and Bob Rock. It wasn't an easy album to make by any band's standards and the costs of the album were huge after they remixed it three times at a cost of one million dollars. The album also brought some personal upheavals. There were clashes of personalities and creative differences between the band and Rock, which have been publically acknowledged by Metallica. Rock had changed the way the band had previously recorded: for example, he would have them record their parts together rather than separately. Perhaps some Metallica fans would like the original tapes to be given to producer Rick Rubin? While the production on *Metallica* is polished; the best produced thrash metal album is Slayer's classic, *Reign In Blood*. After the release of the album hardcore Metallica zealots even went so far as to create a petition to stop Rock from producing any more Metallica albums.

When *Metallica* (dubbed *The Black Album* by fans due to its black cover sleeve) was released in August, 1991, it hit Number 1 in ten countries, including their native United States. It gave the band their first dose of major global mainstream attention. It spawned six singles: 'Enter Sandman', 'Don't Tread On Me', 'The Unforgiven', 'Nothing Else Matters', 'Wherever I May Roam' and 'Sad But True'. Since its release it has sold 22 million copies worldwide making it one of the most successful albums in history, regardless of genre boundaries. The album has since been featured in many polls, including *Rolling Stone*'s 'Essential Recordings Of The '90s', *Spin* magazine's '90 Greatest Albums Of The 90s' and *Q* magazine's 'Best Metal Albums Of All Time'.

METALLICA BY REQUEST

A Metallica tour from March to August 2014. Fans got to vote for the song played before 'Seek & Destroy'.

METALLICA COLLECTION, THE

Metallica's digital box set that was release don iTunes Store in April 2009. It features all of their studio albums plus bonus material.

METALLICA – THE VIDEOS 1989-2004

A video album by Metallica released in 2006. It contains all the band's videos from 1989 to 2004.

METALLICA THROUGH THE NEVER

A concert film with a title derived from the Metallica song 'Through The Never'. The film follows a roadie called Trip (Dane DeHaan) with live footage from Metallica recorded in Vancouver and Edmonton in August 2012. A live soundtrack was also released.

MONSTERS OF ROCK TOUR

On August 20, Metallica played a warm-up gig at the famed London venue 100 Club and then from August 22 to August 30 Metallica toured Europe as part of the Monsters Of Rock Festival Tour although the 'tour' only included three shows: they returned to England on August 22 to perform for the second time at the famed rock stronghold, Castle Donington and thereafter they played two shows in West Germany. The Donington Festival was again headlined by Bon Jovi with Metallica third on third bill under Dio. The other acts included Anthrax, W.A.S.P. and Cinderella. During the tour, their regular setlist looked like this: 'Creeping Death', 'For Whom The Bell Tolls', 'Fade To Black', 'Leper Messiah', 'Welcome Home (Sanitarium)', 'Seek & Destroy', 'Master Of Puppets', 'Whiplash', 'Am I Evil?' and 'Battery'. Metallica were not too impressed with their Donington performance as it was the first time (discounting the 100 Club gig in London) they'd played live in several months.

Broadcasters and presenters, The Baileys Brothers (Mick and Dez) were there to introduce the bands. Dez Bailey recalled in 2011:

"The 1987 MOR saw a divide between rock fans as they were those who wanted their music fast hard and heavy as in Metallica and those who wanted it glam and commercial (Cinderella and Bon Jovi). I think if the Bailey Brothers hadn't had walked out on stage and pulled the audience together they would have been trouble for sure. As for hanging with Metallica, well we had all-ready seen what the guys were capable of in Germany when we were on the bill with them at the Lorely Festival and interviewed many of the acts for Sky [TV] but by the time the MOR came around they were huge. Our memory of them playing there was awesome and we probably witnessed one of the best metal acts since Judas Priest, the intense power and musicianship put them in another zone. Metallica were a movement an arrow head that said fuck your glam and pop rock move over or we will kick your ass. We were more concerned in making sure the fans had some cool music throughout the day than hanging with the bands we could do that at the after show party, yeah the usual norm was to stick a tape on and piss off to the bar and leave the fans to it but we changed that mind set and at least gave the fans some respect".

Metallica returned to the same tour in 1988 on a USA road jaunt. They also played on the European tour in 1991.

MOTÖRHEAD

Motörhead are unquestionably the underdogs of the British hard rock/heavy metal scene and have been since the band was formed in 1975 by the late Ian "Lemmy" Kilmister who had been famously fired from Hawkwind. The band began as a sort of power-trio during the zenith of punk and prior to the New Wave Of British Heavy Metal. Their three now iconic albums Overkill from 1979, *Bomber*, also from 1979 and 1980's *Ace Of Spades* as well as 1981's *No Sleep 'Till Hammersmith* were of great influence and inspiration to the North American thrash and speed metal bands of the 1980s. Lemmy and Metallica are good friends.

Joel McIver – author of the Motörhead *Over The Top* – said to the author in 2011 that Metallica were chiefly inspired by the English band because of "the aggression and speed of the music, as well as Lemmy's image and refusal to dilute his message".

The band's fusion of punk rock and heavy metal meant that they were one of few bands that appealed to both rock and punk fans alike. Motörhead have rarely slowed down with a constant stream of albums and a seemingly never-ending touring regime.

Lemmy has also become embedded in popular culture because of his image (cowboy hat, boots and warts) and his witty, sardonic personality. He died during the writing of this book.

There is an honesty and relentless energy about Motörhead that still makes them relevant to a modern rock audience. Go to a Motörhead gig and there will be fans of all edges bridging the generation gaps. The line-up of Motörhead has altered over the years. Fans prefer the classic line-up of Lemmy on bass/vocals, drummer Phil "Philthy Animal" Taylor and guitarist "Fast" Eddie Clarke. For many years the band has been settled with drummer Mikkey Dee and guitarist Phil Campbell. Both bands have rarely made missteps though such opinions are entirely subjective and they are perhaps more popular now since their relative heydays.

They have sold thirty million albums worldwide, approximately fifteen million of which has been sold just in the USA. What is so great about both bands is that they have their own style, image and fanbase and care little – if at all – about passing musical trends. Motörhead's album covers are known for their striking imagery which features the band's stunning logo which was designed by artists Joe Petagno in 1977. The logo is generally known as the 'Snaggletooth' but has also been called the 'War-Pig'. It has certainly helped sell the band a significant about of t-shirts.

Metallica have covered 'Damage Inc' which has been performed with Lemmy onstage. They also covered 'Overkill' which features on *Garage Inc.* Ironically Motörhead covered 'Whiplash' for the Metallica tribute album *Metallic Attack* and won their first and only Grammy for it in 2005 for 'Best Metal Performance'. With Lemmy's death in 2015 the band was quite clearly over.

MUDVAYNE

Formed in Illinois in 1996, Mudvayne signed a record contract with Epic in 1998 and released their debut CD *L.D.50* in 2000. It got some good reviews and it obviously helped take the band in the right direction. Their style of metal was more alternative and intelligent (they're influenced by progressive rock/metal) than many of their nu-metal peers. By the time their second album (*The End Of All Things To Come*) was released in 2002 they changed their stage names and wore make-up on stage. The band hit the road in 2003 for the Summer Sanitarium tour with Linkin Park, Limp Bizkit and headliners Metallica. Previously, Mudvayne and Linkin Park had toured on the 2001 Ozzfest jaunt. They've never been a massively successful band but the success they've had has been constant, which is obviously aided by a very loyal fan base. Studio albums were released in 2005

(*Lost And Found*), 2008 (*The New Game*) and 2009 (*Mudvayne*).

MUSTAINE, DAVE

Dave Mustaine was born on September 13, 1961, in La Mesa, California to Emily – who was Jewish – and John Mustaine. Raised as a Jehovah's Witness, Mustaine's parents divorced and he was raised mostly by his mother and sisters. Relationships between Mustaine and his father were somewhat estranged. Mustaine moved out of the family home aged fifteen and rented an apartment and survived by dealing drugs; one of his clients was a record store clerk who in exchange for drugs gave Mustaine records by artists like Iron Maiden and Judas Priest et al.

"Well, the stuff that I liked growing up was AC/DC, Led Zeppelin, but I also liked The Beatles and guys like Cat Stevens and Elton John", he explained to PD Freeman of *MSN Music* in 2011. "The music I liked was very eclectic. A lot of it was from the British Invasion. The guitar influence that affected my songwriting came from the New Wave Of British Heavy Metal. So I would have to say my whole style is supported around the whole blues thing, and going into making a thrash style… I guess because I had such a horrible life growing up, going from place to place not knowing what I was gonna do and ending up being homeless, there was a lot of pain and a lot of anger that was coming out through my guitar playing. I listen to other people play guitar, and when they play it, they can make it sound beautiful and write real pretty songs and stuff like that. I'm just incapable of doing that. I have this built-in governor that when the song gets a little too happy, something in the back of my head just goes, 'Crap', and just stops it. I can't proceed with it. I don't know why".

Mustaine was in awe of those bands so much so he picked up an electric guitar (a B.C. Rich) and began playing in the 1970s.

Mustaine explained to Robert Pally of *Ear Candy* in 2002 his reasons for getting into music: "I liked playing music and I liked the lifestyle that went along with it if you were in a band. Because it was a kind of like you are in a gang. Every time you went into the other gang had to give up their girls. It was fun for me... It was really cool to experience traveling and meeting people, and playing in front of people around the world".

Prior to joining Metallica, Mustaine was in a band called Panic which he left to join Ulrich and Hetfield's metal venture. Things would never be quite the same again for any of them from this point onwards.

Metal fan Bob Nalbandian who wrote for the metal rag *The Headbanger* told the author in 2011, "I really dug Dave Mustaine in

Metallica. When he first joined he was really the only truly accomplished musician; Lars was just starting out on drums and James was only singing at the time; he didn't really find his vocal identity until much later (around *Ride The Lightning*). But I thought Dave really added the driving fuel and brash attitude that really carried the band over the top".

Members of Metallica were becoming increasingly frustrated with Dave Mustaine's volatile temper around 1982/83 due to his well-known drug and drink problems which has spoken about at length in interviews. "Dave Mustaine was really the face of the band", Ulrich said in *Kerrang! Legends: Metallica*. James was the lead singer but Mustaine did all the connecting with the fans from the stage, because James was still incredibly shy. Mustaine was certainly a character, but it just became too much for the rest of us, particularly with his mood swings. James and Cliff and I were happy, silly drunks, but Mustaine could get really aggressive and it just stopped becoming fun. That outweighed any fear we had of replacing him".

Relationships between Hetfield and Mustaine during 1982 to 1983 were especially fragile. Mustaine was said to have had an aggressive and volatile temper which was the cause of many arguments within the band.

On April 11 1983, Mustaine was out of the band as they were just beginning session work for their upcoming album. Mustaine's last gig with Metallica was on the Saturday at The Rods and then on the following Monday the band packed up and loaded Mustaine's gear into a car and drove him to Port Authority Bus Terminal. Mustaine was sent home on a four day bus journey from the East Coast to the West Coast. On the journey back to LA Mustaine wrote down some lyrics on a muffin wrapper which became the song 'Set The World Afire'. 'Set The World Afire' appears on the Megadeth album *So Far, So Good...So What!* from 1988. There would be a lot of animosity and public feuds between Mustaine – who went on to find success on his own terms – and the guys in Metallica for quite some time. On their debut album *Killing Is My Business...And Business Is Good*, Megadeth would record the Metallica demo 'The Mechanix' as 'Mechanix' from the *No Life 'Til Leather* tape which Metallica recorded and renamed 'The Four Horsemen Of The Apocalypse' for *Kill 'Em All.*

Ron Quintana – a close buddy of Lars Ulrich and a metal anorak who founded the cult magazine, *Metal Mania* – told the author of this book in 2011: "Metallica shows were always insane! Dave [Mustaine] was always the drunkest one in the club! He usually got into fights he didn't start but often finished! James seemed mellow at first ('til he got drunk) then him and Dave would get into some trouble almost every night! Lars was the instigator, but Dave often just got in trouble on his own, and Dave did not look for fights, but his charisma (way more than James) often got girls following him then their jealous boyfriends would start shit and Dave would usually kick their ass! Dave always drank more and faster than everyone else and would often pass out early. You did not wake Dave then or else... When they kicked Dave out in April, I really thought it changed their dynamic and didn't expect them to ever be huge, until about *Master Of Puppets* Tour [Damage, Inc. Tour, 1986 to 1987] then I realised there was no stopping them!"

MY APOCALYPSE

This was the second single from Metallica's *Death Magnetic* album and their forty-first singe in total. It was released in late 2008.

N

NALBANDIAN, BOB

Nalbandian is a well-known name in rock and metal circles having covered the scene since the early 1980s. Nalbandian has been writing about rock since 1981 when he penned a review of Tygers Of Pan Tang for the now legendary metal fanzine *Metal Mania*. But he is best known for the excellent site *Hard Radio* at www.hardradio.com. With Carl Alvarez he is responsible for the documentary *Inside L.A. Metal*. Here is an interview the author did with Nalbandian in 2011.

When did you first come across Metallica?

I first came across both Lars and James months before Metallica had formed. I grew up in Huntington Beach, CA (less than an hour south of Los Angeles) and Lars lived in Newport Beach in the early '80s. My good friend Patrick Scott came across Lars from a recycler ad he put out when he was looking to form a band. Both Patrick and I were totally into the NWOBHM scene and Lars's ad read something like "Forming a metal band, influences Motörhead, Saxon, Diamond Head and Tygers Of Pan Tang'" or something like that, which caught Pat's attention. A couple days later Patrick invited me to Lars's house (he lived in a condo with his parents) and we were freaking out on his amazing record collection! I had met James around the same time outside the local rock/metal club The Woodstock in Anaheim.

How did they compare to other metal bands in California?
They were obviously much faster and much more European influenced as far as their music goes, which we loved. When they first started out playing the OC and LA clubs they were performing primarily covers of Diamond Head, Sweet Savage, Blitzkrieg, etc., but nobody (except for people like Pat and I) knew that they were covers since those bands were obscure here in the US. They performed well in Orange County but they definitely didn't fit in with the LA club scene, which was heavily glam at the time.

What do you remember about the time when you first interviewed them?
I don't think I actually interviewed the band for my fanzine *The Headbanger*. We hung out at the shows and stuff but I never actually did a full interview with them at the time. I only did a few reviews and articles of them in the early days and then I interviewed Dave Mustaine for *Headbanger* when he first left Metallica, this was in

January 1984.

What were your thoughts on Dave Mustaine?

I really dug Dave Mustaine in Metallica, when he first joined he was really the only truly accomplished musician, Lars was just starting out on drums and James was only singing at the time, he didn't really find his vocal identity until much later (around *Ride The Lightning*). But I thought Dave really added the driving fuel and brash attitude that really carried the band over the top.

What did you think of Ulrich when you first met him?

To be honest, he seemed like a spoiled, snotty kid when I first met him! I hadn't really met many people from Europe at that time so it was kind of a new experience for me, he had a bit of that European sarcastic attitude which kind of put me off at first but I got to know and appreciate later.

What do you remember about the early Metallica gigs?

They were definitely pretty amateurish. I saw their first show at Radio City (small club in Anaheim next door to The Woodstock) and I saw their second show opening for Saxon at the Whisky (which was quite a leap!). Like I said, they played 80% cover songs (I think only two originals). But they developed rather quickly. I think one of the last shows they played before moving up to San Francisco was opening for Y&T at the Woodstock and I really noticed the band improved immensely. James was playing rhythm guitar at that point and that's when I first really saw the true potential for Metallica to make it big.

Why are the first four albums so important in their back catalogue and in metal in general?
Because they are arguably their best efforts and totally groundbreaking metal albums! I think they were so young and hungry and full of testosterone at that time and they just captured every bit of that energy on those first four records. Not to mention the songs are amazing!

What are your thoughts on ...Justice?
Didn't like it as much. I thought *Master* was a much stronger album. I didn't really care for the production of *Justice*, way too dry sounding, and also thought the songs were too long and drawn out.

Many have criticised Justice. Do you think it showed just how

integral Cliff Burton was on the first three releases?

In a way yes, but obviously Jason had very little involvement on *Justice* and since Lars and James were the main songwriters I don't think Justice would have differed a whole lot if Cliff were alive and still in the band at that point. I think the latter albums would likely have been a lot different if Cliff was still around for those recordings.

Do you think the band compromised their thrash roots too much with **The Black Album** *and the albums thereafter?*

I actually really loved *The Black Album*, and still do. I think they pretty much did all they could as far as making a thrash album after *Justice* and rather than repeating themselves they recorded a totally different, but equally classic recording with *The Black Album*. I think with *Load*, *Reload* and *St. Anger* they may have lost their focus too much!

Did you think they would become so big??

Never in a million years. I thought they had the potential to be big on an underground level like a Motörhead or something, but never did I think they would become the biggest metal band in the world!

NEW WAVE OF BRITISH HEAVY METAL (NWOBHM)

Between 1979 and 1981 aspiring rockers formed bands literally all over the UK. Not confined simply to the popular cities such as London and Birmingham, these bands also came from as far afield as Sheffield, Newcastle and Manchester. They took a basic DIY approach to their music; much of it was self-released though some bands did attract the notice of London record labels. The big league NWOBHM players included Iron Maiden, Def Leppard, Saxon, Diamond Head, Tygers Of Pan Tang, Girlschool and Venom while lesser known names such as Blitzkrieg, Samson, Sweet Savage and Demon also spring to mind though there were many, many more bands from that era. Most of them, however, have faded into the annals of metal history.

The interesting thing about the NWOBHM bands is that there was more to their music than just good old electric riffs; some bands like Paul Di'Anno era Iron Maiden were inspired by punk music as much as they were heavy metal and hard rock. The sounds of Birmingham metal band Black Sabbath – the pioneers of the genre – and London hard rockers UFO can be heard in their music for sure. Maiden were progressive too. There was certainly a punk aspect to the New Wave Of British Heavy Metal bands and it was the two sides of the coin as it were that inspired the young Lars Ulrich.

Metal had started with Black Sabbath following on from the

hard blues-tinged rock bands like The Who, The Kinks, Led Zeppelin and Cream and then it progressed to heavier heights with the second metal band (also from the Midlands), Judas Priest. Hard rock bands Deep Purple and UFO were (are) not metal but they appealed to the same fanbase. Of course there were other subgenres such as glam rock with bands like T-Rex and Queen and Slade, The Sweet et al and prog rock with ELP and in some ways they all had a major part to play in the development of metal and paved the way for the rise of American metal in the 1980s.

Punk came along in the mid-1970s and was localised to London and New York. The only American punk band to have any real effect on the British scene was the RAMONES.

The London scene spawned the likes of The Clash and the Sex Pistols, arguably the most famous punk bands of all time. Punk was more than just a style and type of music; it was a sub-culture; a fashion; a movement that impacted on Britain's disenfranchised and angst-ridden youth. The style of music has endured and manifested itself in various subgenres and fashions over the years. The anti-authoritarian punk attitude and DIY approach to releasing music had a fundamental impact on the NWOBHM bands, which in turn affected a certain young Danish born drummer. Ulrich was well-versed in music and it was primarily European rock and metal that he adored.

For the author's book on the early years of Metallica (IMP Books, 2012) NWOBHM author and journalist John Tucker wrote a foreword which is worth publishing here:

Metallica, the NWOBHM and Diamond Head...

It's the stuff of dreams, really. Inspired by the New Wave Of British Heavy Metal and almost obsessed by a track called 'It's Electric' a young man hops on a plane and flies halfway round the world to see his favourite band. He even gets to meet them after the show. In the ensuing conversation he reveals that he hasn't put any thought into what happens next: he's come straight from the airport to the gig and has no idea where he's going to stay. The guitarist, mightily impressed with the guy's determination, suggests he comes and stays with the band, and he does, spending the first few nights at the guitarist's house and then later staying with the singer – and their respective parents! All the while he not only snaps up all the NWOBHM releases he can get his hands on, but also watches his favourite band as they write rehearse and perform songs, soaking everything up. When he returns to the States he places a 'musicians wanted' ad, and Metallica is born.

The enormity of the meeting between the young Lars Ulrich

and Diamond Head in July, 1981 cannot be understated, and can probably best be measured by the 'What if's'. What if Ulrich had missed the gig? What if the members of the band hadn't wanted to engage with their fans that night? What if the young soon-to-be drummer hadn't been given the opportunity to hang out with the band, had not learned how to craft a song or what it takes to keep a band on the road. Quite simply, there would not have been a Metallica; or had Ulrich eventually formed such a band anyway it would not have been as inspirational and pivotal to the development of metal as it is today.

The sound of the band's early albums, which went on to influence so many other bands, was highly derivative of the NWOBHM in general and Diamond Head in particular. In Metallica, Ulrich took the style of the NWOBHM (and the aggression of Motörhead) and infused it with both his and Hetfield's own enthusiasm and the burgeoning local sound to develop a hybrid which soon became the springboard for the speed/thrash metal boom of the mid-1980s.

Metallica's early sets featured a number of NWOBHM covers including the likes of Blitzkrieg's 'Blitzkrieg', Savage's 'Let It Loose' and Sweet Savage's 'Killing Time' as well as 'Helpless', 'Sucking My Love', 'Am I Evil?' and 'The Prince' – quite a healthy chunk of Diamond Head's first LP. And as they began to write their own material the nods to

Sean Harris's and Brian Tatler's songs and style were as obvious as the beers in the Americans' hands. From the speed of their tunes, to the numerous riffs and time-changes in lengthy sprawling compositions, the bulk of the material on *Kill 'Em All* drew heavily on Ulrich's fascination with Diamond Head. Let's not forget that not only were Diamond Head one of the fastest bands around at that time, but they'd also been awarded the accolade of having 'more great riffs in a single song than Sabbath had on their first four albums', and there's no way either fact escaped the young drummer. 'Hit The Lights' and 'The Prince' are more than just distant cousins – the pacing, the construction, the frenetic lead breaks; and the section just before Hammett's solo is pure Harris/Tatler. The time change midway through 'The Four Horsemen', the middle section of 'Whiplash' (ironically, in this case the slower part of the song), the opening and ending to 'No Remorse' (which also features some trademark Iron Maiden runs) – it's all there in the material that was being composed in a bedroom in Stourbridge several years earlier. In fact, pretty much the only part of the album that doesn't have some kind of relationship with Diamond Head is Cliff Burton's bass solo.

By *Ride The Lightning* Metallica were beginning to develop their own style, although the comparisons are still apparent in some of the riffs, the length of the songs and the fact that neither band was really comfortable with trying to write commercial songs to order: 'Escape', Metallica's one real attempt at writing a 'single' – not that it was ever released as such – sounds as unconvincing and unhappy as Diamond Head's 'Call Me'.

"Diamond Head were 50% of what ended up being Metallica", Ulrich once famously admitted and to Metallica's credit they've never attempted to disguise the fact; in fact, they have gone out of the way to help all the bands that influenced them by recording covers of their songs and thus earning royalties for them. Metallica's biggest debt though is definitely owed to Diamond Head, and this was finally repaid in July, 2011 when the massed ranks of the Big Four of thrash metal flanked Tatler at Sonisphere for a massive rendition of 'Am I Evil?'. The smile on the English guitarist's face said it all.

NEWSTED, JAMES

James Newsted was born in Michigan in 1973. He grew up on a diet of hard rock and metal listening to the records owned by his older brothers.

Metallica held auditions in California for a new bassist. Over fifty musicians tried out, including Les Claypool of Primus and Troy

Gregory of Prong. After Armored Saint's *Raising Fear* recording sessions, the band contacted bassist Joey Vera about replacing the late Cliff Burton but needless to say nothing came of it but it would have been an interesting collaboration considering the heaviness of Armored Saint.

Also, amongst the auditionees was a dude named James Newsted, Flotsam And Jetsam bassist. He recalled to *Metal Rules* in 2033: "My friend woke me up at six in the morning and said, 'Cliff's gone'. I said, 'No fucking way. Why are you doing this to me this early in the morning?' And he said, 'No, it's real. Go look in the paper'. So, I looked in the paper and I had this epiphany watching and just thinking and I was like, 'I'm going to be the dude. I'm going to do it. If they're going to go on then I'm the man. I'm going to do it'. And from that minute on I wasn't going to let anybody else get it".

During the audition period, Newsted went so far as to learn the entire Metallica setlist and so impressed was the band with Newsted that they invited him to Tommy's Joint in San Francisco after the auditions. "I was one of the biggest fan of the band before I went in", Newsted told *Rolling Stone* in 2009.

Metallica played their first live performance with new bassist James Newsted at the County Club in Reseda, California. Such was the humour and mischief between the members; they tricked Newsted into eating some Wasabi (Japanese horseradish) as a kind of initiation test.

James Newsted said in 1989: "Well naturally somebody had to be able to be strong enough to take on what was about to happen. Not just somebody that could play but somebody that also was able to take it mentally as far as taking Cliff's place, living up to all the people in the family and all the crew people and all. There was forty or 45 people tried out and they wanted to find someone that could take it in all aspects, ya know. They had a million people that could go veroumarrarr and all that shit, but that's only part of it, actually".

He left Metallica on January 17, 2001. He was later replaced by Robert Trujillo, formerly of Suicidal Tendencies and Ozzy Osbourne's band.

NINE INCH NAILS

The brainchild of Trent Reznor, Nine Inch Nails is perhaps the most influential industrial metal band of all time (although NIN, as they are commonly known, is a one-man band with Reznor only hiring musicians for the road). NIN's breakthrough album was 1994's *The Downward Spiral*, which was recorded in a specially built studio in the house in Beverly Hills where the Shannon Tate murders were committed by Charles Manson's hideous cronies. Reznor has also worked with Marilyn Manson and Rob Halford; he scored the soundtrack to the David Lynch film *Lost Highway* and has remixed songs by Megadeth, David Bowie, U2, Peter Gabriel and allegedly Queen. They are known for electronic beats, digital programming, heavy guitars, experimental sounds and distinctive remixes. They have released eight studio albums with 2013's *Hesitation Marks* being the latest.

NO LEAF CLOVER

This live single from S&M was released as a single by Metallica and the San Francisco Orchestra. It was the band's fourth Number 1 single on the *Billboard* Hot Mainstream Rock Tracks.

NO LIFE 'TIL LEATHER

No Life 'Til Leather was released in July 1982. It was the band's first officially released demo and their most widely-circulated one too. It would have a major impact on the band's subsequent debut album. It features 'Hit The Lights', 'The Mechanix', 'Motorbreath', 'Seek & Destroy', 'Metal Militia', 'Jump Into The Fire' and 'Phantom Lord'.

Brian Ross of Blitzkrieg told the author in 2011: "My first brush with Metallica was way back when I was doing a bit of A&R work at Neat Records in Newcastle [England.] Lars had sent a copy of the *No Life 'Till Leather* demo to Neat. They were after a deal with the label that had all their favourite NWOBHM bands on it, Dave Wood, the M.D. at Neat, gave me a pile of demos to listen to, among them the Metallica one. What immediately struck me was that here was an American band that sounded like a NWOBHM band. I was quite impressed by them and so I recommended to Dave that he sign them to Neat Records. The other A&R rep at Neat was a guy called Russ Conway; he did not agree and said that signing them would be a mistake and that in his opinion they would never amount to anything. Russ was, as I recall a U2 fan so whether that has any bearing on his judgment, I don't know. I also don't know why Dave Wood sided with Russ on this one but I guess he has grown to regret that decision".

In the end, *No Life 'Till Leather*, their latest demo, was funded by Kenny Kane for an imprint of Rocshire Records called High Velocity in Orange County. It was recorded at an eight track studio called Chateau East in Tustin. However, the label was punk oriented and Kane did not think the band were punk enough when he heard the demo so the band self-released it.

NOTHING ELSE MATTERS

'Nothing Else Matters' was the third single from *The Black Album* and issued in 1992. It is one of the band's most popular tracks especially onstage.

NOTHING ELSE MATTERS '99

This live version recorded for *S&M* features orchestra from Michael Kamen and was released in 1999 as a single.

NOWHERE ELSE TO ROAM TOUR

A Metallica world tour from January to July 1993.

O

ONE

'One' was the third and final single released from ...*And Justice For All*. It is an anti-war song. It was Metallica's first Top 40 hit in the US.

ORGULLO, PASION, Y GLORIA: TRES NOCHES EN LA CIUDAD DE MEXICO

A Portuguese version the Metallica live set *Pride, Passion And Glory: Three Nights In Mexico City*, which was recorded at Foro Sol, Mexico City, Mexico on June 4, 6 and 7, 2009 during the World Magnetic Tour.

OVERKILL

A groundbreaking album by the British band Motörhead. It was released in 1979 via Bronze Records, their first release for the label. It had a major impact on the Bay Area and American metal scene of the 1980s. It is general regarded as one of the greatest metal albums ever. Lars Ulrich hailed it as a pivotal influence on him.

P

PANTERA

Metallica and Slayer were a major influence on the Texan metal band Pantera but primarily an influence on the band's singer Phil Anselmo. Pantera's influences were wide ranging from KISS to Van Halen to Black Sabbath. They began as a high school glam metal band with after three albums (released between 1983 and 1985) they recruited Phil Anselmo from Louisiana in 1987. The band then released their heaviest album to date, *Power Metal*, in 1988 before completely changing their look and sound for their major label debut *Cowboys From Hell*, which came out via Atco in 1990. Four studio albums followed until the band dissolved in the 2000s. Dimebag Darrell, who was originally known as Diamond Darrell after the KISS song 'Black Diamond', was a huge blues fan and was well schooled in blues rock. He would listen not only to American hard rock but also country and blues and was a self-taught guitarist. Pantera was perhaps one of few metal bands of their generation that still retain touches of the blues in their sound which was heavy, often fast and "sludgy" but always melodic. Anselmo brought with him much heavier influences from the tape-trading scene that promoted the underground metal bands of the era. Pantera have sold over twenty million albums worldwide and are hailed as one of the most influential bands in American metal history. They had a particularly unique sound that was groove and thrash metal rolled into one melting pot of ideas.

With Anselmo's distinctive Rob Halford style voice and Dimebag Darrell's utterly brilliant guitar wizardry, Pantera were a saving grace for metal fans in the 1990s, a time when metal had been shunned and ignored by the mainstream. Pantera was rife with internal troubles throughout the 1990s leading to their eventual split in the early 2000s. As well as releasing some masterful albums and becoming one of the most talked about live bands of the 1990s they got to tour with their heroes KISS and Black Sabbath but sadly not Van Halen. The late Dimebag Darrell who was killed onstage by a fan in Columbus, Ohio in December 8, 2004 is hailed as one of the most important metal guitarists of all time, and rightfully so.

PAPA ROACH

Formed at Vacaville High School in California in the mid-nineties, Papa Roach signed a record deal with Dreamworks in 1999 and released their breakthrough album *Infest* the following year. (Previously, they had released *Old Friends From Young Years* on an independent label). *Infest* was a significant hit top 10 in both the US and UK) and went Platinum three times. The band quickly became one of the major players on the alternative metal/nu-metal scene. They played on the Main Stage on the 2001 Ozzfest and also hit the stages of other major metal festivals around the globe. Drummer and co-founder Dave Buckner left in 2007; Tony Palermo replaced him on the drum stool thus making him a fully-fledged member with singer Jacoby Shaddix, guitarist Jerry Horton and bassist Tobin Esperance. As the nu-metal scene faded around 2002/03 the band's sound changed somewhat and their record sales dipped: they released albums in 2002 (*Loveheattragedy*), 2004 (*Getting Away With Murder*) and 2006 (*The Paramour Murders*). Nu-metal may be dead but of the bands that remain Papa Roach are surely one of the hardest working outfits around. They released *Time For Annihilation* in 2010, *The Connection* in 2012 and 2015's *F.E.A.R.*

PEACE SELLS...BUT WHO'S BUYING?

Megadeth's 1986 album. It was their second release and again, a stone cold thrash metal classic. It was the last album to feature drummer Gar Samuelson and guitarist Chris Poland. The album regular appears in various 'best' and 'greatest' metal album polls. It was remixed and remastered in 2004. It is included in Martin Popoff's *Top 500 Heavy Metal Albums Of All Time*.

P.O.D.

P.O.D. stands for Payable On Death. The band formed in 1992 in San Diego, California and their breakthrough album came with 1999's *The Fundamental Elements Of Southdown*. The band, who are Christians and their faith often has a role in their music, released their fourth album *Satellite* on 11th September, 2001. The album was another commercial success and gave the band a Grammy nomination ('Best Metal Performance') for the song 'Portrait'. P.O.D. became one of the more popular nu-metal bands. 2003's *Payable On Death* caused controversy with fellow Christians because of its occult themed cover and although it made the Top 10 in the *Billboard* 200 sales were not as high as expected, which was typical at the time for nu-metal bands as the genre was rapidly slipping in popularity. P.O.D. toured hard on the festival circuit and they (along with Hoobastank and Story Of The Year) supported Linkin Park on the 2004 North American leg of their *Meteora* world tour. (Previously, Linkin Park had supported P.O.D. prior to the release of *Hybrid Theory*). 2006's *Testify* marked a change in sound for the band and it was also the last album to feature guitarist Jason Truby. Similarly to many bands of their ilk they left a major label (in their case Atlantic) and joined a much smaller one (Rhino) and a *Best Of* album was released thereafter. In 2008, they released *When Angels & Serpents Dance*, and although sales were not as high as what they'd achieved during their peak, the album still made it into the top 10 in the *Billboard* 200. They released *Murdered Love* in 2012 and *The Awakening* in 2015.

POLAND, CHRIS

As lead guitarist Poland played on various Megadeth albums from 1985 to 2004 including 1985's *Killing Is My Business...And Business Is Good!* and its follow-up 1986's *Peace Sells...But Who's Buying?*. He is now a member of OHM, a jazz rock fusion band.

POOR TOURING ME

Metallica supported *Load* around North America and Europe from September 1996 to May 1997.

POOR RE-TOURING ME TOUR

Metallica were on the road from March 1998 to April 1999 in support of *ReLoad*.

POWER METAL

The first proper Metallica demo (though never officially released), the band recorded was called *Power Metal*, which initially had Hetfield singing like Sean Harris formally of Diamond Head but Hetfield amended his vocals to make himself sound rougher. An obscure demo called *Ron McGovney's 82 Garage Demo* was never released though it does contain 'Hit The Lights' and 'Jump In The Fire' while the rest of the eight track demo was made up of cover songs from Sweet Savage, Diamond Head and Savage. It was recorded on March 14, 1982 in McGovney's garage and preceded the *Power Metal* demo by a few weeks. It was recorded in April, 1982, in McGovney's garage. It contained four original songs: 'Hit The Lights', 'Jump In The Fire', 'The Mechanix' and 'Motorbreath'. Ulrich and his buddy Pat Scott personally mailed copies of their demos to as many record companies around the world as they could afford.

Rob McGovney said to Pat O'Connor of *Shockwaves* in 1997: "It's funny how that demo was labelled the *Power Metal* demo. The story is, I went to make Metallica business cards to send to the club promoters along with our demo. The card was supposed to just have the 'Metallica' logo and a contact number. But I thought it looked too plain and decided it should say something under the logo. I didn't want to put 'hard rock' or 'heavy metal', so I coined the term 'Power Metal', I thought it had a nice ring to it. No band had used that term before as far as I knew. I remember bringing the business cards to the band and Lars got so pissed off at me. He said, 'What did you do! What the hell is 'Power Metal?!' I can't believe you did such a stupid thing! We can't use these cards with the words 'Power Metal' on it!'. So, that's how that tape became known as the *Power Metal* demo".

PUBLIC ENEMY

In the eighties when hip-hop and rap had social meaning and it wasn't all about bling and how many millions are being made, Public Enemy were at the forefront of the scene. Back then, rap groups were conscious of politics, religion and race. The group was formed in 1982 in Long Island, New York and was eventually signed to Def Jam Recordings, a label co-founded by legendary producer Rick Rubin. *Yo! Bush Rush The Show,* their debut album, was released in 1987, but it was the released of their sophomore opus *It Takes A Nation Of Millions To Hold Us Back* that recognised the group as serious artists tackling issues of race and politics. The album contains the song 'Bring The

Noise' which was later re-recorded (in 1991) with the thrash metal band Anthrax. The collaboration between rap and metal led to nu-metal later in the decade. Without question the song influenced nu-metal and rap rock as did the Aerosmith/Run-DMC collaboration on 'Walk This Way' which preceded 'Bring The Noise'.

PUDDLE OF MUDD

Despite releasing two albums in the nineties (*Stuck* and *Abrasive*) it was not until a deal was signed with Geffen (and their subdivision label Flawless Records, owned by Limp Bizkit's Fred Durst) and *Come Clean* was released in 2001 that they achieved mainstream recognition and success. Sales of the album and consequently the band's profile was aided by the hit singles 'Control', 'Blurry', 'Drift And Die' and 'She Hates Me'. As nu-metal was on the slide the band's next big Geffen release was *Life On Display* in 2003 which didn't shift nearly as many copies as its predecessor. The band released *Famous* in 2007 and seemed to have slipped off the radar since. In 2011 they released a covers album called *Re:(disc)overed*.

PUNK

Punk came along in the mid-1970s and was localised to London and

New York. The only American punk band to have any real effect on the British scene was the RAMONES. The London scene spawned the likes of The Clash and the Sex Pistols, arguably the most famous punk bands of all time. Punk was more than just a style and type of music; it was a sub-culture; a fashion; a movement that impacted on Britain's disenfranchised and angst-ridden youth. The style of music has endured and manifested itself in various subgenres and fashions over the years. The anti-authoritarian punk attitude and DIY approach to releasing music had a fundamental impact on the NWOBHM bands. These days punk is more limited to pop punk with bands such as Blink-182 and Wheatus.

Q

Q-PRIME MANAGEMENT

After the release of *Ride The Lightning* Metallica were offered a deal by the UK label Bronze Records but after a few weeks of careful consideration they declined. The biggest and most important event of 1984 was the band's meeting with Michael Alago, Elektra Records A&R representative and Cliff Burnstein, co-founder of Q-Prime Management both of them attended a Metallica gig in September and so impressed were they with Metallica's performance that the signed the band to both Elektra Records and Q-Prime Management. However, the band themselves were not that impressed with their performance. "It was really funny, because as soon as we got off stage we all agreed it was probably one of the worst gigs we've ever done", Ulrich said to Bernard Doe of *Metal Forces* in 1984.

Metallica were pleased with Burnstein who was known for his work with AC/DC, Def Leppard and Dokken and would in time turn Metallica into a global force. It would be one of the best things that happened to Metallica. Also, Elektra Records would give a lot of time, effort and money into promoting their new band and it wasn't one of those huge record companies where bands would get lost in an extensive catalogue of artists thus every artist was treated with the same degree of energy and enthusiasm and given ample time.

QUEBEC MAGNETIC

A live concert from Metallica released on DVD in December 2012. It was filmed in Colisee Pepsi in Quebec City on October 31 and November 1 2009.

QUEEN

Queen are one of the most successful British rock bands of all time with sales of estimated somewhere between 150 and 300 million. They have won just about every major award possible in the music and entertainment industry. They're origins were in glam rock with touches of prog and heavy metal before they became a fully-fledged stadium rock band in the 1980s. They have influenced amongst others, Guns N' Roses, Van Halen, Foo Fighters, The Smashing Pumpkins, Nirvana, Iron Maiden, Anthrax and Dream Theater. Some of their most famous albums include *A Night At The Opera* (1975), *News Of The World* (1977), *The Game* (1980) and *A Kind Of Magic* (1986). The band was comprised of singer Freddie Mercury, guitarist Brian May, drummer Roger Taylor and bassist John Deacon. Between 2004 and

2009 Taylor and May reformed Queen with Bad Company singer Paul Rodgers. They played two world tours and recorded one album, *The Cosmos Rocks*. The band is now fronted by American singer Adam Lambert, however long that partnership/collaboration may last. Metallica covered 'Stone Cold Crazy' which they have also performed live.

QUINTANA, RON

Quintana is the founder of the much missed *Metal Mania* magazine. Here is an interview the author did with Quintana in 2011. Some quotes have been used elsewhere in the book, but here is the full interview:

When did you become friends with Lars Ulrich?
Lars and I met on top of Strawberry Hill on the island in the middle of Stow Lake in deepest Golden Gate Park at midnight or so one Friday Night (or Saturday) in January, 1981. Our friends went there every weekend with Ghetto Blasters and tons of Budgie/Priest/Scorps/Maiden/Motörhead, etc. tapes to blast as loud as we wanted and not attract the cops (although they did trudge up there a time or two trying to catch us underage kids drinking and

screamin' til 3a.m).. Lotsa cases of beer or other bottles and rarely a keg as it took so long to lug up there. Our East Bay buddy Rich Burch ('Bang that head that doesn't Bang') actually met him first that day on Telegraph in Berkeley and attacked Lars when he saw all the rare patches and buttons on his denim jacket! He invited Lars to our Banger Party and all of us quizzed him on all the NWOBHM bands he'd seen that we'd only heard about! His and my favourite band was Diamond Head at that moment so we hung out the most. Later, he drove me [and] then Rich home, but we talked metal in his huge brown AMC Pacer car that is something of a joke to car enthusiasts for hours! We hung out every time he visited North from Newport Beach through summer.

Was Ulrich a metal fan before you meet him?

Lars was totally a metal fan and hardly ever mentioned tennis, or his famous father 'til much later. We'd all collected any info in the Bay Area on the NWOBHM in 1979 and 1980 from *Sounds*, *NME* or *Melody Maker*. I immediately loved 'Am I Evil?' from a BBC recording as well as a London live recording from 1980 that featured my other favourite 'Dead Reckoning'. Lars actually loved that tape (before I made him a copy) that he jammed my Fisher tape deck listening to the lyrics over and over one day he came to visit! I still have that broken wreck in the basement somewhere!

Can you tell me the story behind the name "Metallica"?

Lars and I joked about starting a record store/band/metal magazine together sometime; we each showed each other lists of names, I thought he liked 'Skull Orchard' best. I wasn't impressed with Red Vette, TurboCharger, Lightning Vette or some of his list. Eight months later he called to tell me he'd liked Metallica for a name best and was jamming with some friends using that name, I'd already started *Metal Mania* in August, 1981 so I didn't mind. I always felt bad about hoisting such a goofy name on such naive LA kids!

What do you remember about those early Metallica live shows?

Metallica shows were always insane! Dave was always the drunkest one in the club! He usually got into fights he didn't start but often finished! James seemed mellow at first ('til he got drunk) then him and Dave would get into some trouble almost every night! Lars was the instigator, but Dave often just got in trouble on his own, and Dave did not look for fights, but his charisma (way more than James) often got girls following him then their jealous boyfriends would start shit and

Dave would usually kick their ass! Dave always drank more and faster than everyone else and would often pass out early. You did not wake Dave then or else... When they kicked Dave out in April I really thought it changed their dynamic and didn't expect them to ever be huge, until about *Master Of Puppets* tour then I realised there was no stopping them!

R

RAGE AGAINST THE MACHINE

Hailed as one of the great bands of alternative metal, RATM are a politically-minded band, known for their powerful lyrics and very angry music. The cover to their self-titled debut album is the famous photograph of a Buddhist monk burning himself to death in Saigon in 1963 in protest to his government's regime. The 1992 album is often called one of the greatest albums of all-time. In a sense they certainly led the way for nu-metal and bands like Linkin Park owe a debt to RATM: they merged rap, funk, heavy metal and punk into their distinctive melting pot. Their third album *The Battle Of Los Angeles* was released in 1999 and like the first album it won huge critical praise and strong sales. RATM are also known as a powerful live band and after splitting up they reformed in 2007 to play festivals around the world. During the break drummer Brad Wilk, bassist Tom Commerford and guitarist Tom Morello formed the now defunct alt-rock band Soundgarden with Chris Cornell. Members of RATM have taken part in political activities and rallies.

REIGN IN BLOOD

Undoubtedly one of the greatest metal albums of all time Slayer's *Reign In Blood* is a pivotal release. It was unleashed in 1986 via Def Jam Recordings and was the band's first collaboration with famed producer Rick Rubin. It is regularly polled in 'greatest metal albums' lists. It defined the thrash sound alongside Anthrax's *Among The Living*, Metallica's *Master Of Puppets* and Megadeth's *Peace Sells...But Who's Buying?*.

RELOAD

ReLoad was a sort of sequel or companion to 1996's *Load*. The initially idea was to release a double album but that proved too difficult in terms of recording so many songs at once so the band later recorded some more tracks between June, 1997 and October at The Plant Studio in Sausalito. Due to the lack of enthusiasm surrounding *Load*, *ReLoad* sold less than half-a-million copies in the United States during its first week of release and has sold about a million less worldwide than *Load*.

James Newsted explained to *Metal Edge* in 1997: "Rock 'n' roll will never die. And it really is that old cliche, how everything comes back again, but when it goes down to hide it comes back morphed into a stronger thing like a roach that goes and adapts against Liquid Plumber. It eats it and gets bigger. So when it comes back on a

Metallica album it's certainly a different beast. An enhanced beast".

Reviews of the studio opus were mixed. The now defunct *Musician* magazine said: "...greasy, driving, full of fat grooves, lyric and rhythmic hooks, and sonic curveballs...captures one of rock's greatest bands at its peak".

The album peaked at Number 1 in the United States and Number 4 in the UK. Four singles were released from the album: 'The Memory Remains', 'The Unforgiven II', 'Fuel' and 'Better Than You'. The latter single won the band a Grammy Award for 'Best Metal Performance'.

RE-LOAD PROMO TOUR 1997

Metallica played shows in the USA and Europe in November 1997 in support of *ReLoad*.

RIDE THE LIGHTNING

In October 1983, Metallica announced the demo tapes for *Ride The Lightning* which would wet the lips of metal fans who were eagerly awaiting their second studio album. They also spent time on tour from October to December. However, just before they commenced recording of the aforementioned demos for their second studio opus, they hit problems after a reported £40,000 worth of equipment was stolen from the band at a hotel in Boston just a week before a tour with Anthrax commenced. Metallica's guitar tech John Marshall kept them stored in the hotel room because of the extremely cold temperatures outside. After the theft, a cautious Lars Ulrich then flew to London earlier than scheduled to arrange the hiring of new gear. Hetfield's one million dollar Marshall Head was taken and it took some time for him to find a replacement that had the right Metallica sound. For the remaining three shows on the tour Anthrax loaned Metallica their stage gear. This prompted Metallica to write a song called 'Fade To Black'.

Metallica had now begun work on their second unholy opus. They wrote the album at a house over in El Cerrito. "Me and James each had a bedroom", Ulrich said in 1995. "Dave Mustaine...slept on the couch. Dogs running around. We had the old garage converted into a rehearsal room with egg cartons. It was the refuge, the sanctuary for everybody in the neighbourhood. People would come over and live there, hang there. It was a lot of fun – when you're nineteen".

Ride The Lightning was recorded between February 20 and March 14 at Sweet Silence Studios in Copenhagen, Denmark where the British hard rock band Rainbow and the Danish metal band Mercyful

Fate had recorded, which was a major source of appeal to Metallica. Kirk Hammett was a huge Mercyful Fate fan. He enthused to *Guitar World* in 1998: "Their stuff was so incredibly heavy and progressive for its time. Their guitarists, Hank Shermann and Michael Denner, wrote some of the best riffs of all time. Musically, they came from the same place that we did: old UFO, Iron Maiden, Diamond Head, Motörhead, Judas Priest, Tygers Of Pan Tang. Fate had an incredibly huge influence on us in the early days".

Metallica hooked up with producers Flemming Rasmussen and Mark Whitaker though the band largely produced the albums themselves.

Ride The Lightning was released in August, 1984. It peaked at Number 100 in the *Billboard 200* album charts and Number 87 in the UK Top 100 album chart. In France, the album was wrongly printed with a green rather than blue cover. The 400 green covers released by Bernett Records have become collector's items, highly sought after by fans. It may have been only minor dent in the charts for some, but for Metallica it was the beginning of their eventual global chart domination. Interestingly, the album was erroneously printed with green covers in French; of course, this now makes them collector's items amongst diehard fans. Despite Dave Mustaine's departure from the band he did received songwriting credits on 'Ride The Lightning' and 'The Call Of Ktulu'. The album gave birth to the following singles: 'Fade To Black', 'Creeping Death' and 'For Whom The Bells Toll'.

Critical opinion was more positive than the band's debut and reviews were far more widespread. However, some Metallica zealots had attacked the band for including a ballad ('Fade To Black') and accused them of selling out.

Metal Forces' Bernard Doe reflected to the author in 2011: "*Ride The Lightning* is over 27 years old and songs like 'Creeping Death', 'For Whom The Bell Tolls' and 'Fade To Black' still rank among Metallica's finest work. Actually, I remember the inclusion of the later prompted the first cries of 'sell-out' and 'wimps' from the underground hordes. So, even early on in 1984 Metallica were upsetting the so-called 'true' metal fans. But the truth was that they were already publically distancing themselves from the 'thrash' tag and had learnt that you didn't have to depend on speed to remain aggressive and heavy".

On future reissues, critics and reviewers would rave over the eight track opus. Whatever criticism that were aimed at the album – such as the sound quality – were almost irrelevant as the band had obviously crafted a strong selection of songs and were more technically adept than they were at the time of the recording of *Kill 'Em All*.

"I think generally most people have received it favourably and certainly a lot better than I think anyone in the band thought it would", Lars Ulrich said at the time to Bernard Doe.

Here's what the rock and metal scribes said in the noughties:

Sputnikmusic declared: "Metallica's sophomore release, *Ride The Lightning*, is a classic thrash album, a classic metal album, and just a regular old classic album in general… The guitar on the album is superb, with some of these riffs being some of Kirk's most memorable. The bass, particularly in 'For Whom The Bell Tolls', is remarkable, and just another reason why Cliff is worshipped by a large portion of Metallica fans. You need to buy this album if you have not yet heard it".

Steve Huey of *MSN Music* stated: "Incredibly ambitious for a one-year-later sophomore effort, *Ride The Lightning* finds Metallica aggressively expanding their compositional technique and range of expression. Every track tries something new, and every musical experiment succeeds mightily. The lyrics push into new territory as well – more personal, more socially conscious, less metal posturing".

The Metal Observer enthused: "Everything fits, sound, songs and atmosphere. And all of this just can mean one thing, just like hundreds of other metal journalists have done before: give this album the full rating. Let's just hope that Metallica sometimes might be able to release another hammer like this one, even though I have my doubts..."

However, *Punk News* had some criticisms: "*Ride* really only has two weaknesses: The Judas Priest tribute of 'Escape' sounds dated (even if it is enjoyable), and ending the record with the instrumental 'The Call Of Ktulu' seems to somehow slow the album's momentum even though it's the last song".

Martin Popoff, the revered Canadian metal historian and prolific author of books on the NWOBHM, Rush and Deep Purple said to the author in 2011: "Huge effect on me, this album had. I'll never forget dropping the needle on 'Fight Fire With Fire', along with the fact that the same day I brought the import of this record home, I had brought home Savatage (*Sirens*) and Savage (*Loose 'N Lethal*) forever a weird blue-and-white trio imprinted on my brain. The latter two had their charms, well, more than that, they are a couple of the greatest heavy metal albums of all time. But *Ride The Lightning*... there was a recognition that it was instant masterpiece, that the rules had changed, or there was a new frontier to be explored for those who were brave enough. Super-fast, progressive, lots of changes, changes in speed, and that was just the first two tracks, which I guess are probably the most masterpiece-like on the album, from a purely showing-off point of view. But yeah, it barely sounded like the same band as the one that made the drinking songs of *Kill 'Em All*, which, yeah, was sort of just like a more groovy and tuneful than average German thrash album. This was a pageant of searing mensa-like metal beyond what anybody had done. Beyond the first two tracks, it then fell to superlative songwriting, and the whole album was enveloped in a remarkable production job, remarkable in that it is both full-spectrum, no faults, and also, in that Zeppelin-like manner, obscure and eccentric at the same time, not that Zeppelin ever had that first 'no fault' bit to their otherwise goodly name. But yeah, with *Ride The Lightning*, any idiot metalhead could tell that these guys were far and above the best of the new breed, although most studious metalheads were also likely of the opinion that Metallica really were never going to be huge stars doing this kind of music, because it was just too challenging as well as sounding like two large millstones grinding together. Still, the album is full of catchiness, so who knows? But yeah, the point here was that we were witnessing truckloads of talent from a band who one would think was too young to be this good. This happened exactly twice before, with Mercyful Fate circa *Melissa* and with Judas Priest circa *Sad Wings*

Of Destiny. That was my belief anyway, at 21, an instant connection with those records, music by Satan, namely too smart for mortals".

The general consensus amongst metal fans is that *Ride The Lightning* is a stone cold classic; one of the greatest heavy metal albums in history. Its legacy is most definitely assured. In November, 1987, it was certified Gold while in 2003 it was certified Platinum a staggering five times. *Ride The Lightning* was listed positioned at Number 3 in *Metal-Rules* 'Top 100 Metal Albums Of All Time'. Also, *IGN Music* ranked it at Number 5 in their poll of 'Top 25 Metal Albums'. Even the once trendy British music mag *NME* rated it in their poll of 'The 20 Best 80s Metal Albums Ever'. In *Kerrang!*'s '100 Greatest Heavy Metal Albums Of All Time' (published in 1989), *Ride The Lightning* was situated at Number 7 although bizarrely Def Leppard's *Pyromania* was a position ahead! Also, in 1998 *Kerrang!* published '100 Albums You Must Hear Before You Die' had three Metallica albums except *Ride The Lightning*.

Looking back, James Hetfield enthused year's later (Douglas J Noble, *Guitar Magazine*, 'Load Era 1', 1996): "But, overall, I'd have to say *Ride The Lightening* is my favourite. *Kill 'Em All*, our first album, was already written when we went into the studio but *Ride...* was the first next step, when we started to discover the studio and what we could do in it. That was kinda the fun bit, and it still is".

RIDE THE LIGHTNING TOUR

Metallica kicked off the *Ride The Lightning* Tour on January 9, 1985, with co-headliners W.A.S.P. in the United States and support came from Armored Saint and Tank on selected dates. W.A.S.P. dropped out of the tour to support KISS on a major arena tour of the States. Jeff Waters of Annihilator, a Metallica fan, remembered to the author in 2006: "...a Metallica tour I remember seeing, which was fantastic, [was] with Armored Saint and W.A.S.P. ..."

Lars Ulrich explained why Metallica preferred to concentrate much of their time and energy on their European fans for much of 1984 in an interview with *Metal* Force in 1984: "We've only done about one and a half gigs in the US during [19]84 but there's been such a lot of shit with legal hassles in the US with the change of management, record companies, etc., so really under those circumstances for much of that time the only place we could work was in Europe".

During the 57 date tour, Metallica regularly played the following setlist: 'Fight Fire With Fire', 'Ride The Lightning', 'Phantom Lord', 'The Four Horsemen', '(Anesthesia) Pulling Teeth', 'For Whom

The Bell Tolls', 'No Remorse', 'Fade To Black', 'Seek & Destroy', 'Whiplash', 'Creeping Death', 'Am I Evil?' and 'Motorbreath'.

The tour included a performance in front of 70,000 metal maniacs at the Monsters Of Rock Festival at Castle Donington in England on August 17 where they came second from bottom of the bill after the Midlands pomp rock band Magnum. The other acts of the bill were Bon Jovi, Ratt, Marillion and headliners Bon Jovi. "British audiences though are strange", said Ulrich to *Metal Forces* in 1986. "But once you've convinced yourselves that just because you're being bombarded with two litre bottles of full piss, mud and ham sandwiches doesn't meant that they don't like you…"

Metallica also performed in front of 60,000 fans at California's Day At The Green Festival on August 31 with the Scorpions, Ratt, Y&T and Rising Force also on the bill. They felt more comfortable playing back in the States were people were more familiar with their music. They would wind up those recording sessions on December 27 with the final date of the *Ride The Lightning* Tour arriving on December 31, 1985.

ROCK, BOB

A distinguished producer, engineer/mixer, Bob Rock has worked on some of the biggest selling albums in rock history. Some of his credits include Metallica, Mötley Crüe, David Lee Roth, Skid Row and Aerosmith.

Amongst many others, he has produced the following albums:

Bryan Adams – *On A Day Like Today* (1998)

The Cult – *Sonic Temple* (1989)

Lostprophets – *Liberation Transmission* (2006)

Metallica – *Metallica* (1991)

Mötley Crüe - *Dr. Feelgood* (1989)

Skid Row – *Subhuman Race* (1995)

As a sound engineers/mixer he worked on albums by Aerosmith, Black N' Blue, Kingdom Come, Krokus, Loverboy and Survivor. As a musician he played bass on Metallica's critically mauled album *St. Anger* (2003) as well as albums by Mötley Crüe and Strange Advance.

A protégé of Bruce Fairbairn, Bob Rock was the sound engineer on the massive selling albums *Slippery When Wet* and *New Jersey*. He also produced the 1992 album *Keep The Faith*, which marked a turn in musical direction for the New Jersey lads.

In sum he played bass and produced *St. Anger* as well as his debut as producer for the band, *The Black Album*, *Load* and *ReLoad*, *Garage Inc.* (disc 1) and *S&M*. Many fans were not happy with the Metallica-Rock collaborations.

RON MCGOVNEY'S '82 GARAGE TAPE

Metallica recorded this demo tape in McGovney's garage in March 1982. Bootleg recordings of this tape exist. It features 'Hit The Lights', 'Jump In The Fire', 'Sucking My Love', 'The Prince' Am I Evil?' and 'Helpless'.

RUSH

Rush is a Canadian band that was formed in 1968 in Toronto. They went through various line-ups before settling on the long-lasting trio of singer/bassist/keyboardist Geddy Lee, guitarist Alex Lifeson and drummer Neil Peart. They have recorded twelve studio albums since their 1974 self-titled debut.

Metallica, particularly bassist Cliff Burton, was interested in the heavier end of prog rock and Rush was one of those bands. Formed in 1968 in Toronto, Rush began as a blues-tinted heavy metal band inspired by British Invasion bands like The Who, The Kinks and Led

Zeppelin et al before they fully embraced progressive rock and began incorporating synthesizers in their music. 1976's masterful opus *2112* was the band's breakthrough album after three previous releases. What Metallica loved about Rush was their sense of musicality, their originality and the melting pot of ideas and styles that was totally unique.

Jon Collins, author of the biography *Rush: Chemistry*, said to the author in 2011: "In some way thrash metal was an evolution of the more hair metal oriented bands; in some ways, it was a reaction to them and a return to more of the energy levels of the 1970s. I would imagine that Metallica musicians would undoubtedly have been influenced by the virtuosity of Rush; I wouldn't be at all surprised if they didn't take influence from that earlier period – up to *2112*. However, [19]80s Rush were the kind of thing that Metallica were reacting to, with their short hair, jackets and shoelace ties!"

Meanwhile, the Canadian writer Martin Popoff – author of the official Rush book *Contents Under Pressure* – told the author, also in 2011: "I think Rush absolutely was a huge influence on anybody trying to craft metal in 1982, 1983. Even though I never amounted to anything as a drummer, I know for sure I lived that exact same experience as lots of guys, my huge drum kit with nine tom-toms, in the attic of a buddy's house, lonely pursuit, 'Subdivisions' guy, learning all of Neil's [Peart] licks, able to play them all, just not as smoothly. That guy alone was a huge inspiration on all drummers, because he was such a musical drummer, with his tom fills being drum riffs. In fact, the technicality stopped just short of the crazy jazz guys, or even Bill Bruford. And that's what gave kids that magic opportunity, that possibility that if they worked hard enough, they could work their way through these licks which always sounded heroic and epic in the context of the band's weirdly bubbly and joyous hard rock sound (see 'Limelight' or 'The Spirit Of Radio'). Same thing for bass players. Guitar, I really don't know if Rush was really one of these big guitar inspiration bands. Nobody really talks about it, and for good reason. It's almost like the bass and the drums were metal in combative spirit, but Alex wasn't particularly metal all that often. Anyway, Rush was absolutely the instruction book for many bands. Not to get carried away here, it's not like all of these metal bands only listened to Rush. But Rush was a big part of that woodshedding, learning your instrument thing. And looking specifically at Metallica, sure, large swaths of the band's second, third and fourth albums are progressive metal, and who invented progressive metal, almost single-handedly? Rush. You can even hear Rush in Cliff Burton's bass sound, that buzzy bass, which I guess also, when a bass player wants to be heard, there's inspiration from Geddy, from Lemmy, from Steve Harris. And as an extension, you can hear the influence of Geddy in the fact that there are recurring prominent roles for the bassist in Metallica".

Indeed, Burton in particular loved the way prog rock bands like Rush in Canada and Jethro Tull and ELP in England introduced classical influences in their music as well as blues and folk. Ever since he was a teenager in Denmark, Ulrich has always loved rock and metal and the many subgenres.

RUSSELL, XAVIER

Now a successful film editor, Xavier Russell began writing for *Sounds* before he joined *Kerrang!*, which he wrote for until the mid-nineties. Xavier is still a fan of the music of his youth and has written for *Classic Rock*. He covered Metallica during the 1980s. Here is an interview the author did with Russell in 2009.

***How did you end up writing for* Kerrang!**

I started out writing for *Sounds* and I have to thank Geoff Barton for that. I used to phone him all the time in the mid-seventies giving him tips about new American hard rock and heavy metal. After a while he just said, *"You seem to know so much about this type of music, why don't you write an American import column for me?"*, and that's how it started. I got into *Kerrang!* when Geoff started using Dave Roberts from Silverwing more than me. So I jumped ship, when Dante Bonutto gave me a Santana album to review. I wrote under another name for that review: Zed. F Gore. I then went to San Francisco to cover Mötley Crüe and ended up discovering Metallica for *Kerrang!*, by now I was writing under my normal name.

Who were your contemporaries?

Geoff Barton of course, he turned me onto the likes of KISS, Aerosmith and Ted Nugent. I also liked the American rock writer Lester Bangs who used to contribute for *Creem* Magazine.

What was it like working with the likes of Mick Wall, Geoff Barton, Malcolm Dome and ex-scribes like Steve Gett, Mark Day, Dave Dickinson and Paul Suter et al?

It was great in the early days, when we were in Covent Garden. It was like one big party. Every writer had their own unique style. There were obviously certain rivalries and certain journalists like to hog the limelight, but I'm not naming names. They know who they are. My approach was slightly different, because I was a metal fan I tried to write from a fans point of view. Dave Ling was similar in that respect.

Did you have any rock writing influences when you first started?
Like I said before, Geoff Barton and Lester Bangs.

Who was your first interview with?
Mötley Crüe and Metallica both on the same day in San Francisco, 1982. You couldn't get two more different bands. The Crüe were just rowdy noisy party animals who were more interested in getting laid than listening to me waffling on about the brilliance and rawness of their album *Too Fast For Love*, while Metallica were the total opposite. Here was a band that would talk for hours about Iron Maiden, Saxon Venom and the like. They really did take their music seriously, that doesn't mean to say they didn't like to get wasted – they did, and their tipple back then was Carlsberg Elephant and frozen Absolute Vodka!

Can you tell me more about Metallica?
I first came across Metallica quite by accident. The year was 1982, I was in Concorde, California doing a piece and live review of Mötley Crüe who were just breaking big. A metalhead by the name of Ron

Quintana who ran the underground fanzine *Metal Mania*, thrust the now legendry *No Life 'Til Leather* demo into my grubby mits. I ignored the demo for a few days, and then got continually hassled by Ron asking if I'd played it yet. I finally gave it a spin and was totally blown away. I'd never heard anything quite like it before. The rawness, the speed of the songs and the sheer energy all combined to make Metallica the next big thing.

As luck would have it they were due to play a 'Metal Monday' at the legendry Old Wardorf set in San Francisco's financial district! The power and brutal music Metallica played that hot sweaty night, very nearly started an earthquake, the nearby Pyramid Building was swaying to the thunderous chords of 'The Four Horsemen'. This was Metallica Mark II: Ron McGovney (bass), James Hetfield (guitar), Lars Ulrich (drums) and Dave Mustaine (guitar). What was so refreshing about the band back then was there sheer energy, enthusiasm and brutal speed. I'd never seen anything quite like it, the power and adrenalin was amazing, the sweat flew off the stage as Messrs. Hetfield and Mustaine went into battle. Both were very similar in look and style, but it did feel like they were trying to push each other out of the way and hog the lime light – needless to say Hetfield eventually won! I got talking to them after the show, and they more interested in talking about Saxon and Venom than me asking them about the current state of the LA metal scene!

I did end up interviewing the band for *Kerrang!*, and the piece was entitled *'M.U.Y.A' (Metal Up Your Ass!)* It was the first time Metallica had been properly covered by the European press, apart from an article in *Metal Forces*. Over the years I got to know the band quite well, and recently returned from Cleveland, Ohio where I was invited to see the band being inducted into legendry Rock And Roll Music Hall Of Fame – the first thrash band to be inducted! I covered the story for *Classic Rock*.

Did you have any bad interviewing experiences?

Yes, Blue Öyster Cult in 1983. They were always one of my favourite bands. I got to know Albert Bouchard quite well, but he sadly left the band. I interviewed Buck Dharma in a studio in San Francisco where he was mixing *Revolution By Night*. He played back some of the new album, and could tell I wasn't really impressed. So I started to try and talk about the old days and how they got their amazing name. He was having none of it, and just froze. When I played the interview back later I realised it was a total disaster and one of the shortest I'd ever done.

Did the magazine pay for you to travel abroad to interview bands?

No, the magazine never paid. It was always the record companies or the band's management.

Do you have any 'on the road' stories?

Too many to mention here. My favourite Metallica article was an 'on the road' feature I did for *Extra Kerrang!* in 1986/7. The band were playing on a double bill with Armored Saint. The Saint, possessed a very gifted bassist by the name of Joey Vera, who was later offered the Metallica gig when Cliff tragically died, but remained loyal to the Saint cause – a big mistake if you ask me. As it was a 'road feature', we needed a shot on the bus. Photographer Ross Halfin was being lazy so and so and refused to take pictures and went back to his bunk on the bus and crashed out. I was having none of it and asked the band what they thought: they all proceeded to pull their knobs out and aimed them in the direction of Halfin – you've never seen a man or a camera move so fast. He clicked one black and white group shot and went straight back to sleep. Needless to say the picture was used in the finished article. So I was proved right. I also broke a golden rule of playing back my Armored Saint interview on the Metallica tour bus, before I'd even had a chance to listen to it myself. Metallica and especially Lars spent the rest of the trip quoting various bits of text back to John Bush and Joey Vera of the Saint – they took it well, and thankfully saw the funny side. Looking back now perhaps I shouldn't have done that. Not very professional.

Did you get to meet any of your rock idols?

Yes, Eddie Van Halen, Ronnie Montrose, Ted Nugent, all of Blue Öyster Cult, Lynyrd Skynyrd, Molly Hatchet, 38 . Special, Doc Holliday and the list goes on and on....

What were your initial thoughts on Kerrang!'s decision to go weekly?

I initially honestly didn't think it would work. But I guess I was proved wrong!

Many of those writers moved on to Metal Hammer. How much of an impact did that have on Kerrang!?

Kerrang! always had its audience. I must admit I haven't read it in a long time. Metal Hammer was always considered a poor relation to Kerrang!, that of course is not the case today!

Which articles are you most proud of?

I would say my long article for *Extra Kerrang!* on Journey's entire back catalogue, including all the rarities. I remember both Geoff Barton and Derek Oliver were very impressed with the end result. Road stories, I would have to say Molly Hatchet and Metallica. And for sheer off-the-wallness, Celtic Frost when I interviewed them in their legendry 'Dark Room'- just a table with a Skull, holding a Black Candle, surrounded by H.R. Geiger paintings! It was totally weird.

When did you finish writing for Kerrang!?

Mid 1990s. I was getting very busy with my film career and that was my main source of income. Also I think *Kerrang!* was getting stale, the humour that was there for so long had gone!

Did you write for any other metal magazines?

Yes, I have just started doing a few articles and album reviews for *Classic Rock*. I have just got back from Cleveland, Ohio where I saw Metallica being inducted into the Rock And Roll Music Hall Of Fame, it was great to be there!

What do you think of Kerrang! as it stands in 2009?

Can't really say as I have not read an issue for years. I hear the sales figures are down these days.

What do you think of the likes of Classic Rock and Terrorizer?

Terrorizer I read now and again when I need to check up on thrash and *Classic Rock* is great because it covers the music I love!

What were the highlights of writing for Kerrang!?

The Covent Garden days. It was one big party and helping to contribute to 'View From The Bar' was always fun. I'm just glad to have been part of the really magical period of *Kerrang!*.

S

S&M

On April 21 and 22, 1999, Metallica played and recorded both shows with the San Francisco Symphony Orchestra (conducted by the revered Michael Kamen) at the Berkeley Community Theatre. Metallica drew inspiration from the 1969 Deep Purple opus *Concerto For Group And Orchestra* although the original idea for a heavy metal band to play live with an orchestra was perhaps late bassist Cliff Burton who had a deep fondness for classical works. Released in November, 1999, *S&M*, as it was named, reached Number 2 in the United States and Number 1 in Australia. It sold around 300,000 copies in its first week of release. Reviews were mostly positive.

Rolling Stone raved about the album: "... [*S&M*] creates the most crowded, ceiling-rattling basement rec room in rock...[in its] sheer awesomeness...the performance succeeds....the monster numbers benefit from supersizing. The effect is...one of timelessness".

It was the last album to feature bassist James Newsted who left the band on January 17, 2001. He was later replaced by Robert Trujillo, formerly of Suicidal Tendencies and Ozzy Osbourne's band.

SAD BUT TRUE

This was the fifth and final single from *The Black Album* issued in 1993. Metallica released the accompanying music video in October 1992.

SADUS

Founded in Antioch, California in 1984, Sadus were heavily influenced by Slayer and as such there was a lot of heavy riffing and gruff vocals on much of their earlier work before they harnessed their own sound. The band line-up has been fairly consistent with singer/guitarist Darren Travis, singer/bassist Steve DiGiorgio and drummer John Allen with ex guitarist Rob Moore. They released the *D.T.P.* demo in 1986 with their latest album released in 2006, *Out For Blood*.

    Check out the awesome *Illusions* (1988) and *Swallowed In Black* (1990).

SAXON

The Saxon albums *Saxon*, *Wheels Of Steel*, *Strong Arm Of The Leather* and *Denim And Leather* (all released between 1979 and 1981) are benchmarks in British heavy metal and while they struggled to find success in America, serious American metal enthusiasts like Lars Ulrich sought out those early albums via import stores. Saxon were one of the major players in the NWOBHM movement and while they never received the heights of success afforded to Iron Maiden and Def Leppard – whose influences were not metal but glam rock and whose music was not heavy but melodic – Saxon retained a loyal following and their music and legacy endures to this day. Songs like 'Wheels Of Steel', '747 (Strangers In The Night)', 'Motorcycle Man', 'Heavy Metal Thunder' and '20,000 Ft' are classic heavy metal tracks and the fact that Saxon never shied away from being labeled a metal band especially appealed to members of Metallica. Metal fans often talk about the impact Diamond Head and Motörhead had on the early sound of Metallica but the fact is Saxon had just as much of an influence. The relentless riffing, pounding drums, decisive melodies and the gruff but oddly melodic vocals of Biff Byford have become synonymous with British heavy metal. Unknown to many but adored by serious metal enthusiasts, Saxon are one of Britain's greatest metal treasures. Ulrich loved them.

On March 27, 1982, Metallica supported the New Wave Of British Heavy Metal band Saxon fronted by Biff Byford at the Whisky A-Go-Go in LA. It was only Metallica's second live show. McGovney was enquiring about getting Metallica to support Saxon for one of the two shows they were playing there when he bumped into Tommy Lee and

Vince Neil of Mötley Crüe. Glam metal band Crüe were fast becoming a very popular band in the LA area with the likes of fellow hair metal band Ratt, so they didn't want to support Saxon but Ratt did on the first night. McGovney was introduced to the booking lady – who thought Metallica sounded like the Oregon glam metal band Black 'N Blue – by the Crüe guys and got Metallica to support Saxon on the second night. Writing in the *LA Times* on March 29, journalist Terry Atkinson said of Metallica: "Saxon could also use a fast, hot guitar player of the Eddie Van Halen ilk. Opening quartet Metallica had one, but little else. The local group needs considerable development to overcome a pervasive awkwardness".

SEVEN DATES OF HELL TOUR

Metallica supported Venom in front of 7,000 people at the Aardschok Festival in Zwolle, Netherlands as part of Venom's European tour.

SHIT HITS THE SHEDS TOUR

A Metallica tour from May to August 1994 with a performance at Woodstock '94.

SHOW NO MERCY

The debut album by Slayer. It was released in December 1983 through Metal Blade Records after Brian Slagel signed them to his label. He saw them perform Maiden's 'Phantom Of The Opera' and was suitably blown away by the band's performance. The band helped finance the recorded with the combined savings of Tom Araya and Kerry King who borrowed cash from his dad. The album suffers from poor production but was Metal Blade's bestselling album. It remains a pivotal release in the history of metal.

SICK OF THE STUDIO '07

A Metallica tour of European festivals and stadiums.

SIX FEET DOWN UNDER

A Metallica live EP released in 2010 that contains eight songs recorded by fans and live releases from the band's archive.

SIX FEET DOWN UDNER II

A Metallica live EP that was released in 2010 as a follow up to *Six Feet Under*. It features eight songs recorded in Australia and New Zealand.

SLAGEL, BRIAN

Slagel is the founder and CEO of Metal Blade Records. He gave Metallica their first break by giving them coverage on the compilation *The New Heavy Metal Revue Presents Metal Massacre* which thanks to its independent success in 1982 was given distribution by Enigma Records in 1983. Here is an interview the author did with Slagel in 2011.

When did you first come across Metallica?

I was friends with Lars before he started Metallica. We were both into the NWOBHM and used to hang out and listen to music and search for it around LA. He always said he wanted to start a band. I started to put together a compilation album of local LA metal bands and Lars knew this. He mentioned if he had a band could they be on the album. I said yes and he and James recorded 'Hit The Lights' for it.

What were your initial impressions of their music?

I was quite surprised how good it was considering I was not sure how good a drummer Lars could be as I just knew him as a fan.

What were they like live back then?

We were all young so we were all just your typical manic metal heads!

What promoted you to put them on the* Metal Massacre *compilation?

As I said earlier, Lars had mentioned he was starting a band and could they have a slot on the compilation. Being his friend I of course said yes.

What did they think of Metallica's music compared to other American metal bands of the time?

They were certainly different from anything going on in LA at the time or really in the USA as *they* were so influenced by the New Wave Of British Heavy metal and European style metal.

What can you tell me about those first couple of Metallica albums?

I honestly was not a huge fan of *Kill Em All* as I thought James voice was not quite up to par yet. Music was great of course. *Ride The Lightning* was amazing though and that album really I thought launched them big time! It is still my fave Metallica album today.

Did you think at the time Metallica would become such a huge global force?

None of us did, never in a million years. We were all just metal fans trying to do things for the scene. When we get together now, sometimes it is "how did this all happen?" It really is amazing to see how big they have become.

What do you remember about Cliff Burton?

Cliff was a great guy! A bit quiet, but super cool. He knew his metal also and I think he had a huge influence on how Metallica sounded. And an amazing player and stage presence! I saw him first when he was in the band Trauma who were on *Metal Massacre 2*. They played a show in LA and he was incredible. Lars mentioned to me they were looking for a bass player and I told him he should come see Cliff. As soon as he and James saw him, Lars told me that guy would be in Metallica and sure enough he soon was.

Did you think their sound was very similar to the NWOBHM which you covered?

Yes for sure. In their early gigs they mostly played Diamond Head and Blitzkrieg covers. They certainly sounded more European than most bands. They also had a bit of a punk element too that helped set them apart.

Finally, what were your initial impressions of Hetfield and Ulrich and also McGovney and Mustaine?

Well I knew Lars the best since we were friends before Metallica started. Great kid who was super hyper and like me a big time fan. So we got along well and always have. James was pretty shy in the early days, so we did not talk a whole lot in the beginning, but a really good guy always. Ron was a cool guy as well, really kind of a regular guy so to speak. Mustaine I think had rock star in him from the early days. He was great when sober, but he could out drink us all. He was such a great player too, much better than anyone around at that time. I always got along well with Dave as well. All really good guys to this day even!

SLAYER

From Huntington Park in California, Slayer was formed in 1981 by guitarists Kerry King and Jeff Hanneman. Slayer was part of the Big Four of thrash metal with Metallica, Megadeth and Anthrax. Lars Ulrich told *Metal Forces'* Bernard Doe back in 1984: "About a year and a half ago in LA, we were headlining and Slayer were at the bottom of a four band bill. They played all cover versions, like Priest, Purple and Maiden songs and the story is that after seeing us play they decided not to play covers anymore and write their own fast HM [heavy metal] songs".

With singer Tom Araya and drummer Dave Lombardo completing the classic line-up, Slayer released eleven studio albums between their 1983 debut *Show No Mercy* and 2009's *World Painted Blood*. Their latest album, *Repentless*, was unleashed in 2015.

Their most revered work is *Hell Awaits* (1985), *Reign In Blood* (1986), *South Of Heaven* (1988) and *Seasons In Abyss* (1990).

CURRENT MEMBERS:

Tom Araya (Lead vocals, 1982–)

Paul Bostaph (Drums, 1992–1996, 1997–2001, 2013–)

Gary Holt (Guitar, 2011–)

Kerry King (Guitar, 1981–)

FORMER MEMBERS:

Jon Dette (Drums, 1996–1997, 2013)

Jeff Hanneman (Guitar, 1981–2013)

Dave Lombardo (Drums, 1982–1986, 1987–1992, 2001–2013)

TOURING MUSICIANS:

Bob Gourley (Drums, 1983)

Gene Hoglan (Drums, 1983)

Pat O'Brien (Guitar, 2011)

Tony Scaglione (Drums, 1986–1987)

SLIPKNOT

Controversial alternative metal band Slipknot formed in Des Moines, Iowa back in the mid-nineties. Prior to the release of their debut album they went through several line-up amendments but they managed to hit the studio in '98 and their self-titled debut album, released in 1999, was a huge hit. They played on that year's Ozzfest and became a metal phenomenon in what seemed like an instant. Each member of the band wears a unique mask onstage (copied from their idols KISS, GWAR and Mudvayne) and like many nu-metal and alternative metal outfits, they've had their fair share of criticisms and have been constantly mocked by some quarters of the rock music press. Their sophomore album *Iowa* was an even bigger success than its predecessor and won huge acclaim from some major rock publications, including a positive review in *Rolling Stone* by David Fricke. Lead singer Corey Taylor has also enjoyed success as the singer of the metal band Stone Sour whose debut CD was unleashed in 2002. Slipknot worked with producer Rick

Rubin on their third album, *Vol.3: (The Subliminal Verses)*, which hit Number 2 in the *Billboard* 200. From the nu-metal era Slipknot have emerged as by far one of the most successful bands; they constantly sell out some of the world's biggest venues and headline major metal festivals all around the globe. Their fourth album *All Hope Is Gone* was released in 2008 and was followed by *.5: The Gray Chapter* (2014).

S.O.D.

Stormtroopers Of Death was formed in 1985 by Anthrax guitarist Scott Ian after he finished laying down his guitars for the Anthrax opus *Spreading The Disease*. He roped in the talents of fellow Anthrax buddy Charlie Benante on drums, former Anthrax bassist Dan Lilker and singer Billy Milano (Psychos frontman). It's been an on and off project since its inception. They released their debut album *Speak English Or Die* in 1985 and followed it up with the live album *Live At Budokan* three years later. *Bigger Than the Devil* was issued in 1999 and their most recent release was a collection of older, previously unreleased material called *Rise Of The Infidels* (2007).

Their most popular albums are *Speak English Or Die* (1985) and *Bigger Than The Devil* (2007).

SOME KIND OF MONSTER (FILM)

A 2004 documentary showing the making of Metallica's St. Anger.

SOME KIND OF MONSTER (SINGLE)

The fourth single from Metallica's *St. Anger* album. It was released in July 2004.

SOULFLY

This band formed in 1997 by ex-Sepultura frontman Max Cavalera. Although they were often enveloped in the nu-metal genre there is much more to their music; they use all sorts of tribal and South American influences inspired by Cavalera's native Brazil. Their self-titled debut album (1998) was not a huge commercial success but it gave the band some kudos and in the same year they played the mega successful Ozzfest. *Primitive* was a bigger success and their most nu-metal sounding album; it was released in 2000 and features appearances from members of Stone Sour, Slayer, Deftones and Will Haven. Conversely *Prophecy* is a totally different sounding album and features Cavalera with a different line-up of musicians. Cavalera certainly took the album as far away from nu-metal as he could get using more world music influences. More studios albums followed in

2005 (*Dark Ages*) and 2008 (*Conquer*) and Cavalera remains busy with his side-project Cavalera Conspiracy, which was launched in 2007. They released *Omen* (2010), *Enslaved* (2012), *Savages* (2013) and *Archangel* (2015).

SPINESHANK

Nu-metal band Spineshank formed in 1996 and released their debut album *Strictly Diesel* in '98 via Roadrunner Records, however, neither the album or their second release, *The Height Of Callousness*, were immediate commercial hits. The band toured as special guests with some pretty big metal outfits like Coal Chamber, Soufly, Danzig and Sepultura. They played on the 2001 Ozzfest. Their breakthrough album came with 2003's *Self-Destructive Pattern*: the song 'Smothered' was nominated for a prestigious Grammy Award for 'Best Metal Performance'. However, their success seemed short lived because singer Jonny Santos left in 2004 and despite attempts to reignite the band with a new singer the band announced they were to fold and a *Best Of* album was issued. In 2008, Soulfly and Santos reunited and announced plans for a new studio album. *The Height Of Callousness* was released in 2000 and was succeeded by *Self-Destructive Pattern* and *Anger Denial Acceptance* in 2003 and 2012, respectively.

ST. ANGER (ALBUM)

In June, 2003, Metallica released possibly their most reviled album in their career thus far. *St. Anger* was produced by Bob Rock from May, 2002 to April, 2003. In January, 2001, the band had rented an army barracks in the Presidio area of San Francisco and turned it into a makeshift studio. The album was delayed due to the aforementioned departure of Newsted and James Hetfield's stint in rehab for alcoholism. The band were undergoing some massive internal struggles so much so they hired a personal enhancement coach by the name of Phil Towle. The making of the album was caught on film by Joe Berlinger and Bruce Sinofsky and released as the critically acclaimed award-winning rock documentary *Some Kind Of Monster*. It took two years to make and used over one thousand hours of film. During the recording of the album Ulrich turned off the snare sound on his drum snares which created an entirely different sound far removed from his rock and thrash metal roots; this received a massive backlash from fans who did not take to the new drum sound one bit. *St. Anger* sold just over 400,000 copies in its first week of release and hit Number 1 in their native country and Number 3 in the UK. It also hit Number in Australia, Austria, Canada, Finland, Germany, Japan, Norway, Poland and Sweden. Reviews were decidedly mixed.

The *NME* said: "The songs are a stripped back, heroically brutal reflection of this fury. You get the sense that, as with their emotional selves, they've taken metal apart and started again from scratch. There's no space wasted here, no time for petty guitar solos or downtuned bass trickery, just a focused [*sic*,] relentless attack".

"I think with *Load*, *Reload* and *St. Anger* they may have lost their focus too much!" said metal writer Bob Nalbandian to the author back in 2011.

The title-track won the band a Grammy Award for 'Best Metal Performance'. Just four singles were released from the album: 'St. Anger', 'Frantic', 'The Unnamed Feeling' and 'Some Kind Of Monster'.

ST. ANGER (SINGLE)

Metallica released this as the first single from the album of the same name in June 2003. It won the 'Best Metal Performance' at the 46th Grammy Awards.

STAIND

Staind hail from Massachusetts, New England and formed in 1995. They've never been one of the major players but have been consistently hard-working and creative. Their independently released debut album *Tormented* was first issued in 1996 and is famous for its very controversial cover (which even offended Limp Bizkit's Fred Durst). Only a few thousand copies were made available and due to demand it was reissued by the band. Staind have more in common with their post-grunge heroes (Tool, Rage Against The Machine and Korn) than any of the nu-metal lot. Despite Durst's initial response he became friends with the band and he even signed them to his label Flip: Staind's first success came with 1999's *Dysfunction* (Elektra/Flip) which spawned the singles 'Home', 'Just Go' and 'Mudshovel'. The band toured on most of the major metal festivals and released their biggest success (*Break The Cycle*) in 2001; it was a critical and commercial triumph. The album hit Number 1 in the UK and US. Staind toured with Linkin Park on the 2001 Family Values tour in North America. Albums followed in 2003 (*14 Shades Of Grey*), and 2005 (*Chapter V*). Despite the flagging careers of many of the post-grunge and nu-metal band's Staind's 2008 album *The Illusion Of Progress* peaked at Number 3 in the *Billboard* 200 in 2008; it's their sixth album. A self-titled album was released in 2011.

STATIC-X

Formed in 1994 in LA, Static-X signed to the Warner's label in '98 and released their debut album *Wisconsin Death Trip* a year later. The band have more of an industrial metal style than any other influence although there is definitely a nu-metal influence in the melting pot. They have release a total of six studio albums; *Cult Of Static* was released in 2009. They toured with headliners Linkin Park on the 2001 North American Family Values tour. Both bands have remained friends. Guitarist and singer Wayne Static and Linkin Park's Rob Bourdon (on drums) and Dave Farrell (on bass) appear in the music video (Brad Delson, Mike Shinoda and Chester Bennington also make appearances) to The X-Ecutioners 'It's Goin' Down', which features the turntable skills of Joe Hahn (who has also directed videos for the band). The line-up has changed over the years, using session musicians and different musicians on stage. On November 1, 2014, it was announced that Wayne Static died at the age of 48.

STONE COLD CRAZY

Metallica covered this Queen song for *Rubáiyát: Elektra's 40th Anniversary* and subsequently used it as a B-side to 'Enter Sandman'. It features on *Garage Inc*. James Hetfield performed it with Queen and Tony Iommi at the Freddie Mercury Tribute Concert.

STORY OF THE YEAR

Joe Hahn directed the video for 'Anthem Of Our Dying Day', taken from Story Of The Year's 2003 debut album *Page Avenue*. A post-grunge band, Story Of The Year formed in the mid-nineties in St. Louis and were originally called Big Blue Monkey but changed their name to Story Of The Year in 2002, which is the title of their EP. The band scored their first big break when they signed to Madonna's label Maverick Records in 2002. They supported Linkin Park (with P.O.D. and Hoobastank) in 2004 during the band's *Meteora* North American road jaunt. They're not exactly what you'd call prolific having only released three albums: *In The Wake Of Determination* was released in 2005 and *The Black Swan* hit the shelves in 2008. And then came *The Constant* (2010) and *Page Avenue: 10 Years and Counting* (2013).

SUICIDAL TENDENCIES

Formed in 1981 in Venice, LA, Suicidal Tendencies is a thrash-hardcore punk crossover band whose long-lasting founder and only permanent member Mike Muir is one of the genre's leading frontmen. They're hardly prolific with only eight studio albums released between their 1983 self-titled debut and 2000's *Free Your Soul And Save Your Mind* although they have briefly disbanded a couple of times, notably between 1995 and 1997. Despite their hardcore punk inspired beginnings, they have been embraced by thrash metal fans.

Their most important work is *Suicidal Tendencies* (1983), *Join The Army* (1987) and *How Will I Laugh Tomorrow When I Can't Even Smile Today* (1988).

SUMMER SANITARIUM TOUR

From June to August 2000 Metallica were on the road in the USA. Hetfield missed some shows due to back injury and so the vocals were handed to Newsted.

SUMMER SANITARIUM 2003 TOUR

Metallica's tour (June to August) in support of *St. Anger* with Trujillo on bass.

SUMMER TOUR 2013

A Metallica tour from June to September 2013. At the second Orion Music + More festival in Detroit the band performed under the name Dehaan as a reference to the actor Dane DeHaan who starred in *Through The Never*. They played 'Kill 'Em All' in full as a celebration of its 30 years release.

SYSTEM OF A DOWN

Politically inclined, the music of System Of A Down is famous for being very experimental and also for the subject (politics, religion, social issues) matter of the lyrics. The band formed in 1994 in Glendale, California and went on to become one of metal's biggest acts in the new millennium. They're a hard band to pigeon hole; suffice it to say their music is certainly alternative with touches of nu-metal and prog rock. The band decided to lay low from 2006 and have been on a sabbatical ever since. Their self-titled debut opus was released in '98 and a further four studio albums were issued: 2001's *Toxicity*, 2002's *Steal This Album!*, and the two-part album *Mezmerize* and *Hypnotize* were released in 2005. The band reunited in 2010 after a hiatus.

T

TAPROOT

Michigan nu-metal Taproot formed in 1997 and by 2000 they'd signed a record deal with Atlantic Records despite some interest from Limp Bizkit's Fred Durst. After three independently produced and released albums their first major release came in 2000 with *Gift*, but it was *Welcome* which was a breakthrough, making it to Number 17 in the US *Billboard* 100. Always on the lookout for new bands Jack Osbourne, Ozzy's son, became a fan of Taproot and got them a slot on the second stage at the 2000 and 2001 Ozzfests. Singer Stephen Richards made a guest appearance on the track 'P5hng Me A*wy' which features on *Reanimation*. They never became one of the major players in the nu-metal circuit but they're consistent: in 2005 they released *Blue-Sky Research* and followed it with *One Long Road Home* in 2008. The original line-up of the band is singer Stephen Richards, guitarist Mike DeWolf, bassist Phil Lipscomb and drummer Jarrod Montague though Montague has been replaced by Dave Coughlin and DeWolf by Dave Lizzio. *Plead The Fifth* (2010) and *The Episodes* (2012) are their most recent albums.

TATLER, BRIAN

Tatler is the guitarist and co-founder of the NWOBHM band Diamond Head. He is also a good friend of Lars Ulrich and a major influence on Metallica. Here is an interview the author did with Tatler in 2009 and 2011.

When did you first meet Lars?

July 10 1981. Lars had flown over from LA to see Diamond Head at the Woolwich Odeon.

What do you remember about him?

He found his way backstage and introduced himself. We were all very impressed that he had flown all the way from America to see us! No one had ever done that before. His accent was very amusing and unusual, a mix of Danish/American.

Briefly, what do you remember about that period he spent on tour with DH and stayed at your house?

One of my enduring memories of that period is Lars and I staying up late at my parent's house in order to watch a video of Deep Purple at the California Jam 1974. Lars would rave about Ritchie Blackmore and he would mime the guitar solos. He was and still is a huge music fan.

When did you first meet the rest of the band?

At Birmingham Odeon on the September 20 1986.

What did you think of Kill 'Em All when you first heard it?

I did not hear *Kill 'Em All* till about 2005. Lars had sent me several Metallica albums over the years including *Puppets, Justice* and *The Black Album* but I never had the first album. James vocal style owes a debt to Sean Harris on that record and it reminds me of Diamond Head in places but having said that, it is uniquely their own.

When did you first see Metallica live? (What was the line-up?)

On September 20 Lars called me and to say that Metallica (supported by Anthrax) were playing that night at the Birmingham Odeon and would I like to come along. So I caught the No.9 bus to Birmingham, got my backstage pass and a crew guy took me to see Lars. It was the first time we had met up since 1981, and boy, how times had changed! Lars introduced me to James Hetfield, Kirk Hammett and Cliff Burton, we chatted and Lars suggested I play 'Am I Evil?' onstage with them. Well, why not? Lars said they would be playing it in the encore and suggested that I go and watch the show but come back towards the end of the set. They opened with 'Battery' and I could not get over the energy coming from the band and the enthusiasm of the audience, I had played this venue myself but this crowd was definitely crazier than a Diamond Head audience. This was the *Master Of Puppets* tour. I'd thought that Metallica were still quite small, but this night changed all that. I didn't know any of the songs and my first thoughts were that it was terrifically fast and complicated (Lars had sent me a cassette of the new album but I hadn't got into it at that point). They were all so much in synch, I remember thinking that if one of them were to leave, how on earth would the remaining members be able to replace him. After about an hour I went backstage – still wondering how Lars could play that fast – where the guitar tech strapped James's white Flying V onto me and then I was being introduced as "The guy who wrote this next song". The five of us played 'Am I Evil?' up to the fast section, at which point Metallica went into 'Damage Inc' and I scampered offstage.

Did you think they would ever become so big?
No, I am constantly amazed at their incredible success and their longevity. If I had heard *Kill 'Em All* in 1983 I would not have put money on them becoming the biggest metal band of all time, who

would? They have worked extremely hard for it though, this kind of success is not easily achieved.

Metallica have been very helpful to DH by covering your music. That must have pleased you?

Very, very helpful, in fact if Metallica had not covered Diamond Head the band would not have re-formed in 1991 and again in 2000. I reckon Diamond Head would have faded away like so many NWOBHM bands from the '80s. And of course my share of the songwriter's royalties have come in very handy.

Lars Ulrich has written a foreword. Do you think he'll read the book?

I hope so. Lars does love Diamond Head and he is mentioned in the book a lot. I have followed Metallica's ascent to the top for over twenty-five years. The book starts with the story of how I first met him backstage at the Woolwich Odeon in 1981.

Lars has been very supportive of the band over the years. Do you still keep in touch?

Yes, every now and then Lars calls me or I call him. We spoke a few times recently about his foreword and the use of a letter he had written to me in 1982. Every time Metallica have toured the UK since 1986 Lars has been in touch to sort out passes for shows. I have seen them live about twenty times now. They keep improving, I think. It's cool to have played a part in such a phenomenal band's career.

What does it feel like to be included in Guitar Hero: Metallica?
Awesome! The company that make the game (Activision) got in touch and said they wanted to use 'Am I Evil?' in the game but needed the twenty-four track master tapes. I put them in touch with Universal who owns the version on *Borrowed Time* after taking over MCA records. I understand Metallica drew up a list of bands they wanted, but not all the multi-tracks could be traced so some bands missed out. It is a whole new way of reaching a young audience. I have played the game but I didn't get very far, about two minutes into 'Am I Evil?'. I had made too many mistakes and was booed off!

Metallica played some Diamond Head songs on their recent European tour. What does it feel like to know that Metallica played your songs in front of thousands of people on an almost nightly basis?

It means I get performers royalties through PRS so that always nice, but also it helps keep the songs and the name Diamond Head alive. I have been invited on stage three times with Metallica to play various Diamond Head tunes, always a privilege and a lot of fun. God bless 'em!

Do you see them live on their Death Magnetic *tour?*

Yes. I went to the *Death Magnetic* album release party at the O2 Arena in London on 15 September, 2008 and also at the LG Arena in Birmingham on the 25 March, 2009. Both were fantastic shows, the band just get better and better. Tony Iommi was also at the Birmingham show and I got my picture taken backstage with Tony, James and Kirk, The Riffmiesters!

TESTAMENT

A pivotal thrash metal band, Testament formed in Berkeley, California in 1983 and released their debut *The Legacy* in 1987. Testament's profile rose when they supported Anthrax around the United States and Europe in support of Anthrax's *Among The Living* album, which is now a thrash metal classic. The band has gone through a few line-up amendments leaving the only original members, guitarist Alex Skolnick and bassist Greg Christian, to lead the band. They toured

Europe in 2009 with Judas Priest and Megadeth as part of the *Priest Feast* Tour. Between their 1987 debut and 2008s *The Formation Of Damnation* they released nine studio albums in total. They are a revered thrash metal band though outside of the genre they have gained little prominence but continue to have a cult following, globally.

Have a listen to *The New Order* (1988), *Practice What Your Preach* (1989), *Souls Of Black* (1990) and *The Ritual* (1992).

THIN LIZZY

Metallica of course made a metal version of the famed Lizzy song 'Whiskey In The Jar' but Thin Lizzy never cracked America. Some of Lizzy's other known songs are 'Jailbreak' and 'The Boys Are Back In Town'. The band was formed in Dublin in 1969 with founding members drummer Brian Downey and singer/guitarist Phil Lynott who met at school. Lynott died in 1986. There have been various versions of the band since with guitarists Scott Gorham and John Sykes. Gorham and Downey formed Black Star Riders in 2012 which is essentially a version of Thin Lizzy but with new material.

"Those bands, to me, really came out of nowhere", Anthrax's Scott Ian told the author in 2006 when discussing heavy metal originators Black Sabbath and second originators Judas Priest. "Were as with most other bands, you can see the influences more directly. You can see it direct or listen to it direct...I mean I love Iron Maiden but you can hear them in Wishbone Ash and Thin Lizzy. Without Thin Lizzy there's no Iron Maiden".

TOUR 1990

Metallica toured European festivals and played a secret gig under the name The Frayed Ends at the London Marquee. They also played shows in Aerosmith's *Pump* Tour with The Black Crowes and Warrant. They were on the road from May to September.

TRUJILLO, ROBERT

Born Roberto Agustin Trujillo in Santa Monica, 1964. He was a member of Suicidal Tendencies and Infectious Grooves before replacing Newsted in Metallica. He has also worked with Ozzy Osbourne and Jerry Cantrell of Alice In Chains.

TURN THE PAGE

Metallica covered this famed Bob Seger song on their covers album *Garage Inc* released in 1998. It was the first single released from said album.

2 OF ONE

A 1989 video album by Metallica that collected the two versions of the band's first music video 'One'.

U

UFO

Formed in 1969, UFO has existed for over forty years and yet despite the reverence they have earned, the influential albums they have released and the scandalous tales that have followed them around the world for over five decades UFO are sadly not as well-known or even as popular as they should be. Many rock fans would argue that UFO should be a much bigger band especially in the States where they could at one point in the late 1970s fill enormous 15,000 seater venues. In many respects, they are underdogs and they're better off for it. There's no question that UFO are one of the most influential rock bands of all time. Similarly to the likes of Uriah Heep and Nazareth, UFO are iconic rock stalwarts.

Akin to most long-standing rock bands, UFO's career has gone through a number of different eras. Firstly, there is what could be termed the space rock era; the band's first two studio albums and their first live album were essentially space rock, psychedelic albums. Secondly, there is the most important and influential era of the band from when Michael Schenker joined in 1973 to when he left in 1978. It is the era of the band's career which most fans hold in the highest regard. It was an incredibly creative, consistent and thrilling time when the band were at the height of their powers, and when they were seemingly unstoppable both in the studio and onstage. However, it ended rather abruptly, much to the dismay of the band's fans the world over, and it was succeeded by the Paul Chapman era which lasted until 1983 when that particular line-up folded. The band subsequently went on a hiatus. The following period was undoubtedly the least consistent with a number of line-up changes although 1991's *High Stakes & Dangerous Men* incarnation deserved far more time and attention than it was originally given, but it was not meant to be and the band reformed with Michael Schenker in 1993. The second and final Schenker era ended in 2002. After some downtime the band united with new guitarist Vinnie Moore, and a new and highly creative and successful period of the band commenced, which continues to this day, although this particular period did see the departure of original bassist and all-round rock legend, Mr. Pete Way. The band currently consists of Phil Mogg, Andy Parker, Paul Raymond and Vinnie Moore, but with a succession of bassists giving a helping hand in the studio and live onstage. It is without question the strongest, not to say most consistent, line-up the band has had since the late 1970s Schenker era. Vinnie Moore has certainly proven himself to be a vital addition to the band and their recent "resurrection".

James Hetfield named his first band Obsession after this seminal rock album.

UFO's live album *Strangers In The Night* is without question one of the greatest live albums in the annals of rock music. It has a famous fan in former Guns N' Roses guitarist Slash and regularly appears in lists of great live albums such as *Kerrang!*'s '100 Greatest Heavy Metal Albums Of All Time' where it was placed at Number 47. Joe Elliott of Def Leppard, Mike McCready of Pearl Jam and Metallica have also praised the release. Steve Harris – a noted UFO fan – of Iron Maiden even contributed his thoughts on the album to the 2008 CD reissue.

UFO have earned the respect and adulation of some of the world's most popular and best-selling rock bands from Slash of Guns 'N Roses to Metallica and Iron Maiden to Pearl Jam. There are a number of UFO's songs such as 'Lights Out', 'Only You Can Rock Me', 'Doctor Doctor' and 'Love To Love' that are often hailed as some of the most influential rock songs of all time while a fair few of their albums – *Lights Out*, *Obsession* and *Strangers In The Night*, in particular – are often touted as some of the greatest rock albums ever released.

ULRICH, LARS

Lars Ulrich was born on December 26, 1963, in Gentofte, Denmark. He was raised in an upper middle class family. His father Torben was a well-known, respected and successful tennis player but his talents lay not only in the sports field: Torben was also a nifty jazz musician. Lars was surrounded by art, music, film and sport. He came from a cultural, high-brow family that inspired Lars to learn and appreciate new things. Lars Ulrich trained as a tennis player himself in his youth but in February, 1973, Lars was taken to a Deep Purple concert in Copenhagen by his father who had managed to get a handful of free passes although as fate would have it one of his friends dropped out thus giving Lars the chance to attend instead. It's true to say the concert changed his life so much so that one the next day he bought Purple's now legendary *Fireball* album featuring the classic Purple line-up of singer Ian Gillan, guitarist Ritchie Blackmore, bassist Roger Glover, organist Jon Lord and drummer Ian Paice. The album would become Lars' main reason for wanting to become a musician in a band rather than a sportsman. Aged twelve, his grandmother bought him a Ludwig drum kit; his first ever set of drums. Lars quickly became absorbed in hard rock and heavy metal, mostly British. British bands of the 1960s took the sound and feel of black American blues and made it heavier, grittier and ironically, introduced a generation of young Americans to the sound of black American blues which they had not previously appreciated. The British bands were white but they loved black music and the likes of The Who and The Kinks; later Black Sabbath and Deep Purple led to Judas Priest and as such rock music got heavier. Much heavier; louder too. Aged sixteen, Lars and his family moved to Los Angeles to pursue his training as a tennis player. However, he was becoming increasingly obsessed by rock music and it was in America where he finally chose music over sport.

In 1981, the now aspiring drummer discovered a band from Stourbridge in the West Midlands (England) called Diamond Head. Their music owed a lot to Black Sabbath but it was faster and grittier. It was working class metal. It was metal made for factory workers and kids uninterested in a life in academia. Ulrich had bought Diamond Head's debut *Lightning To The Nations* (released in 1980) and was so taken aback by the album that he travelled to London from California to see Diamond Head perform at the Woolwich Odeon on July 10, 1981. Though he loved the gig and was excited to be in London, Ulrich had not planned his visit properly and had nowhere to sleep. He managed to get backstage and Diamond Head's guitarist Brian Tatler and singer Sean Harris were so keen on the young Dane that they offered to let him stay at Tatler's house in the Midlands. Brian Tatler remembered to the author in 2011. "We were all very impressed that he had flown all the way from America to see us! No one had ever done that before. His accent was very amusing and unusual, a mix of Danish/American".

Ulrich toured with the band for a few weeks thereafter. "One of my enduring memories of that period is Lars and I staying up late at my parent's house in order to watch a video of Deep Purple at the California Jam 1974", said Tatler. "Lars would rave about Ritchie Blackmore and he would mime the guitar solos. He was and still is a huge music fan".

What Ulrich liked about Diamond Head's music was the way they used riffs; Diamond Head didn't go for the usual verse/chorus line-up in a song but they used middle breakdowns and developed different parts to songs rather than the standard three part structure. The riffs by Diamond Head were monolithic and gritty; raw and powerful. They caught the attention of critics and metal bands but for various reasons did not make it into the big league of metal players.

Back in the City Of Angels, the young Ulrich put an advertisement – which read "Drummer looking for other metal musicians to jam with Tygers Of Pan Tang, Diamond Head and Iron

Maiden" – in a newspaper called *The Recycler*. The advertisement received an answer from two guitarists from a band called Leather Charm that hailed from the LA area of Southern California. Guitarists James Hetfield and Hugh Tanner were inspired by many of the hard rock and heavy metal bands that influenced Ulrich. Those bands included Deep Purple, Aerosmith, Queen, Ted Nugent and Motörhead. Many of Hetfield's influences leaned towards melody and structure rather than erratic riffs and aggressive melodies.

UNFORGIVEN, THE

'The Unforgiven was the second single from Metallica's *The Black Album*. It is a power ballad and one of the band's slower songs.

UNFORGIVEN II, THE

Metallica's sequel to 'The Unforgiven' which can be found on *The Black Album*.

UNFORGIVEN III, THE

The third song from Metallica in the 'Unforgiven' series. This features on *Death Magnetic*.

UNNAMED FEELNG, THE

This was the third single from the Metallica album *St. Anger*.

UNTIL IT SLEEPS

This was the first song Metallica released as a single from their 1996 album *Load*.

V

2011 VACATION TOUR

Metallica were on the road from April to October and included the first two Big 4 shows.

VENOM

Venom was a massive inspiration to not only Metallica but many of the American and European thrash and death metal bands. Venom formed in Newcastle Upon Tyne in the North East of England in 1979. They were influenced by the likes of Black Sabbath, Judas Priest, Alice Cooper, KISS and Deep Purple. Their first two albums – 1981's *Welcome To Hell* and the following year's *Black Metal* – are landmarks of the metal genre and have been cited as a heavy influence on the thrash metal and extreme metal scene. Of course, the second album led to the extreme metal subgenres death and black metal. Their music and imagery featured many satanic references and the band members each took stage names such as guitarist Jeff Dunn as Mantas, bassist/singer Conrad Lant as Cronos and drummer Tony Bray as Abanddon. KISS may have looked like a demonic band but their music was certainly far from being frightening. Songs like 'Cold Gin' and

'Black Diamond' are fantastic rock songs but Venom wanted to make the kind of metal that fans would associate with such Devilish imagery. They released *At War With Satan* in 1984, which was far more progressive than its predecessors.

The recording of *Ride The Lightning* was squeezed in-between Metallica's support slot on Venom's Seven Dates Of Hell Tour of Europe which had kicked off on February 3 in Switzerland and finished on August 29 in France.

Venom guitarist and co-founder Jeff Dunn gave Metallica author Joel McIver his reminisces of the tour: "It was like *National Lampoon's Vacation*. Metallica went fuckin' nuts on the first night. What had happened was, there were some fans outside, and one of Metallica had broken a window to get to the fans and say hello. By this time the promoters had decided that they were gonna kill them for damaging the venue, so Gem Howard from Music For Nations, who was looking after them on the tour, brought them into our dressing room and said, 'We'll put the guys in here because the security and everybody's looking for them, there's gonna be hell'. And they just sat there in our dressing room like little rabbits caught in the headlights!"

Mike Exley, a writer for the UK magazine *Metal Forces*, said to the author in 2011: "...I think, for Metallica, [Venom] was one of the first things that got the guys into thrash. Ulrich always goes on about the effect of NWOBHM – Diamond Head and their ilk. But, old pictures of the day tended to show Hetfield with hardcore punk T-shirts and those bullet wristbands (which if you ever tried making them, were a complete no-no), around his arms; but I think it was the spirit of Venom that really came through in Metallica. I think they loved the honesty of it, the English punk sound Venom had? What some people forget, is that on that Seven Dates Of Hell Tour, at least in Europe anyway, Metallica were the support band and got a love for crazy European audiences out of it; was just a shame they didn't play at Hammersmith on that night [1984.] The albums that adorned the original tour poster; *Black Metal* for Venom and *Kill 'Em All*, for Metallica, are now seen as the quintessential releases of the period and it was an era of real discovery. One has to feel for Venom sometimes. In 1985 when they did the European (and UK) Tour again, they took out Exodus with them, and when they reformed in Europe and played a big festival in Belgium, Machine Head were on the bill? Look what happened to all of those bands!"

VIEW, THE

A single released from the derided Metallica-Lou Reed album *Lulu*. It was issued in September 2011.

VIO-LENCE

Formed in the Bay Area in 1985, Vio-Lence was initiated by Forbidden guitarist Robb Flynn who later found fame in Machine Head. Perhaps the most known line-up of the band was singer Sean Killian, guitarists Robb Flynn and Phil Demmel, bassist Deen Dell and drummer Perry Strickland. Flynn left in 1992. Their debut album *Eternal Nightmare* was released in 1988 and they followed it up with two more full length studio albums. They reunited briefly in 2002 without Flynn. Also, Demmel joined Machine Head in 2003.

It's certainly worth checking out *Eternal Nightmare* (1988), *Oppressing The Masses* (1990) and *Nothing To Gain* (1993).

W

WE'VE COME FOR YOU ALL

Anthrax's ninth studio album, *We've Come For You All*, was released in 2003. It was the final album to feature singer John Bush and the first to feature guitarist Rob Caggiano. The cover art was designed by famed comic book artist Alex Ross. The album received rave reviews from metal critics.

WHEREVER I MAY ROAM

This was the fourth single released from Metallica's *The Black Album*. It was issued in October 1992.

WHEREVER WE MAY ROAM TOUR

The Metallica tour lasted from October 1991 to December 1992. This was in supported of *The Black Album* and included a performance at the Freddie Mercury Tribute Concert.

WHIPLASH

'Whiplash' was the first single from the Metallica album *Kill 'Em All*. It was first played live on October 23, 1982.

WHISKEY IN THE JAR

Metallica covered this famed Thin Lizzy song on their covers collection *Garage Inc*. The band continue to perform it live.

WORLD MAGNETIC TOUR

A Metallica tour in support of *Death Magnetic*. The band were on the road from September 2008 to November 2010.

WORSHIP MUSIC

Anthrax's tenth studio album was released in 2011 and the first opus to feature singer Joey Belladonna since 1990's *Persistence Of Time*. It was also the second and final album with guitarist Rob Caggiano. The album was delayed as production had started way back in 2008. This was due to the departure of singer Dan Nelson who replace John Bush who actually returned to the band only to drop out again as he could not commit to the album. The album went to Number 12 in the US which was the band's highest charting album since 1993's *Sound Of*

White Noise.

X

XANDADU

Lars Ulrich features on the 2010 Canadian documentary *Rush: Beyond The Lighted Stage*. 'Xanadu' is one of Rush's most famous tracks and features on 1977's *A Farewell To Kings*.

Y

YOUNG, JEFF

Former Megadeth guitarist, Jeff Young played on the band' seminal *So Far, So Good...So What!*. He can be seen in the superlative documentary *The Decline Of Western Civilization Part II: The Metal Years.*

YOUTHANASIA

Megadeth's sixth studio album was released in 1994. The album was widely acclaimed and peaked at Number 4 in the US. It was a progression from 1992's *Countdown To Extinction.*

Z

ZAZULA, JON & MARSHA

The founders of New Jersey's record store Rock 'N Roll Heaven and the record label Megaforce Records. The couple were a prominent part of the US tape-trading scene with such other notable names in metal as Brian Slagel and Rob Quintana. They signed Metallica to Megaforce after hearing the *No Life 'Til Leather* demo. They also released Metallica's debut and signed Anthrax.

ZZ TOP

A Texas based blues rock trio with bearded frontmen Billy Gibbons and Dusty Hill and drummer Frank Beard who is ironically the one without a beard. They were inducted into the Rock and Roll Hall of Fame in 2005. They had a period of commercial success in the eighties with the hit album *Eliminator*, which is notable for its use of synthesizers. They also became really popular on MTV with the videos for 'Gimme All Your Lovin'', 'Sharp Dressed Man' and 'Legs'. Their fourteenth album *Mescalero* was released in 2003 and in 2008 they signed a deal with uber-producer Rick Rubin with plans for their fifteenth opus. Their debut, *ZZ Top's First Album,* was released in 1971.

Metallica and ZZ Top have performed on stage together and shared the bill at the 1985 Monsters Of Rock festival in England. Metallica have also performed loose instrumentals of 'Tush' onstage, a ZZ Top classic which inspired Motörhead's 'No Class'.

Anthrax Pics by Red Shaw

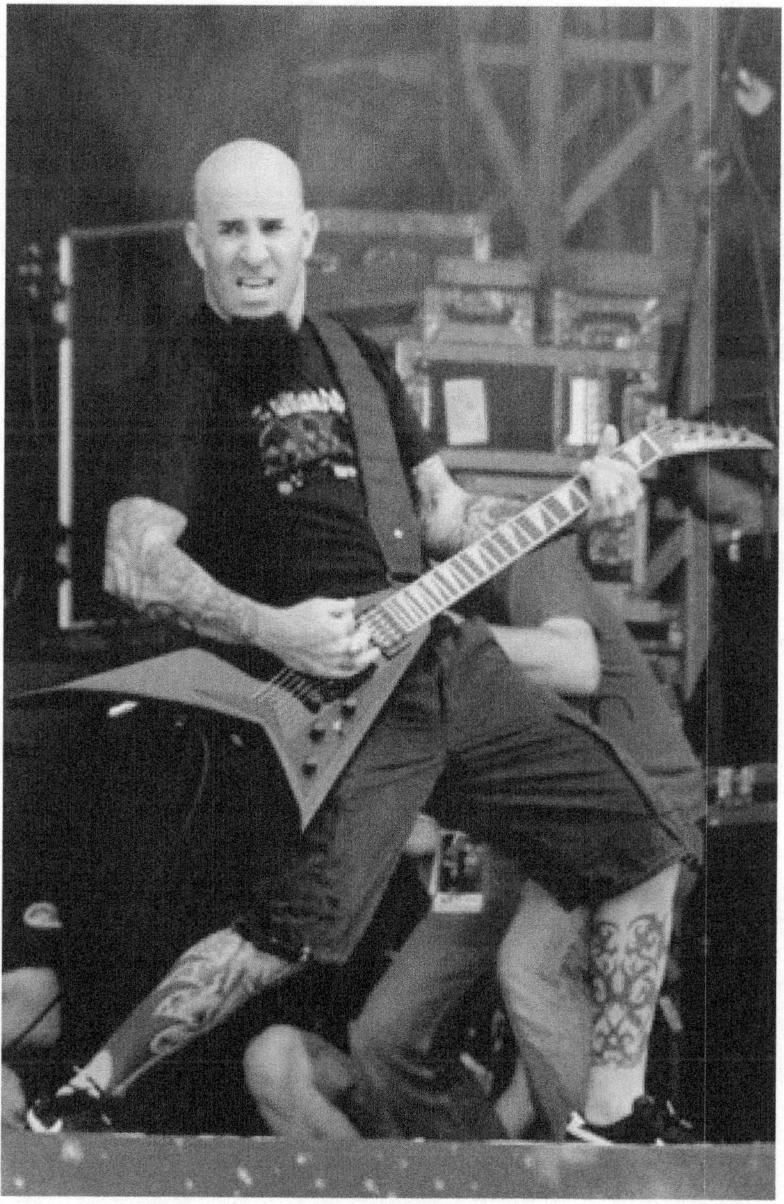

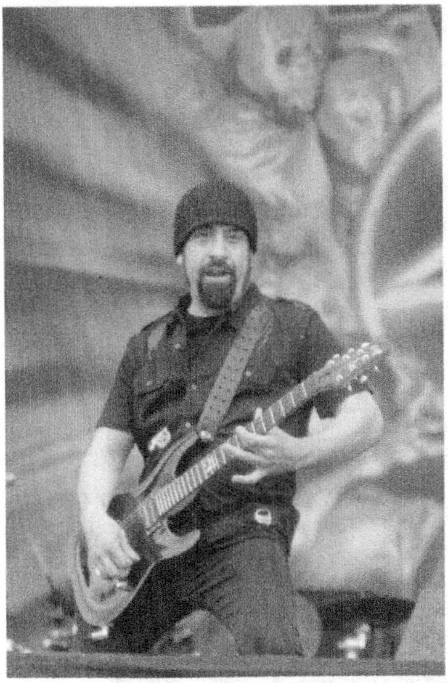

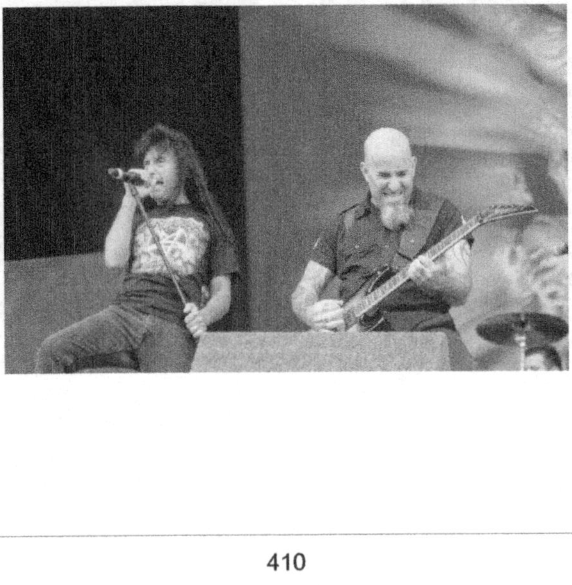

BIG 4 ENCYCLOPEDIA

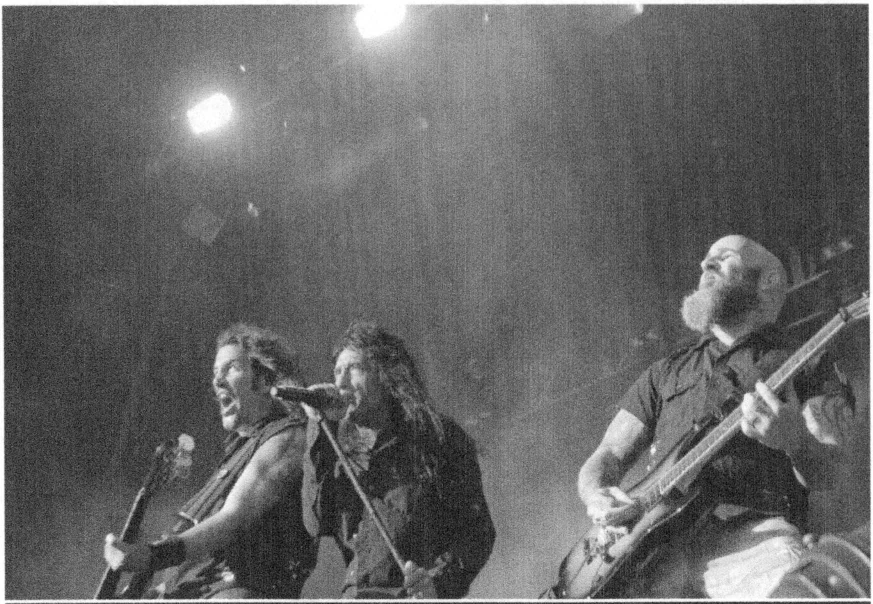

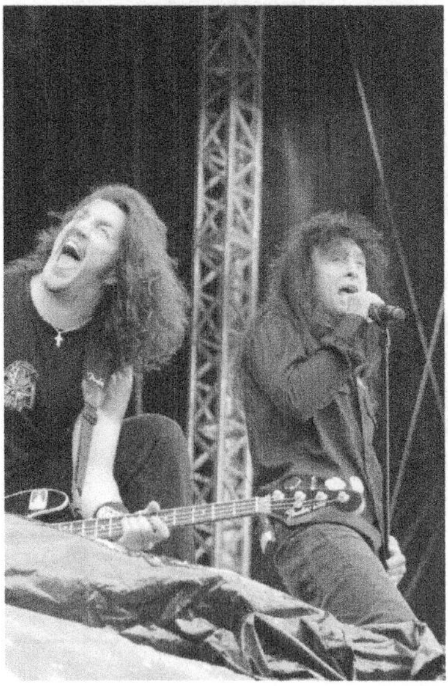

Megadeth Pics by Red Shaw

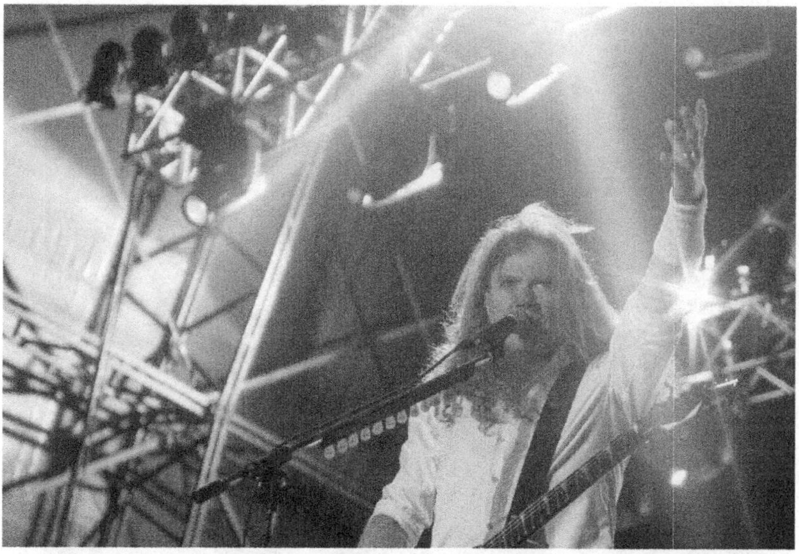

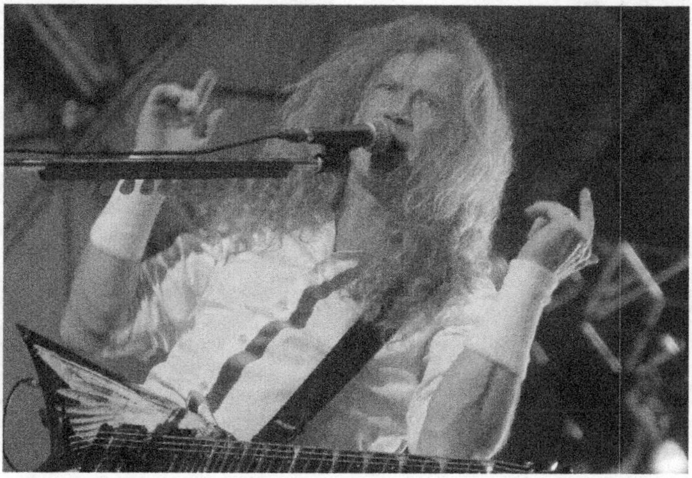

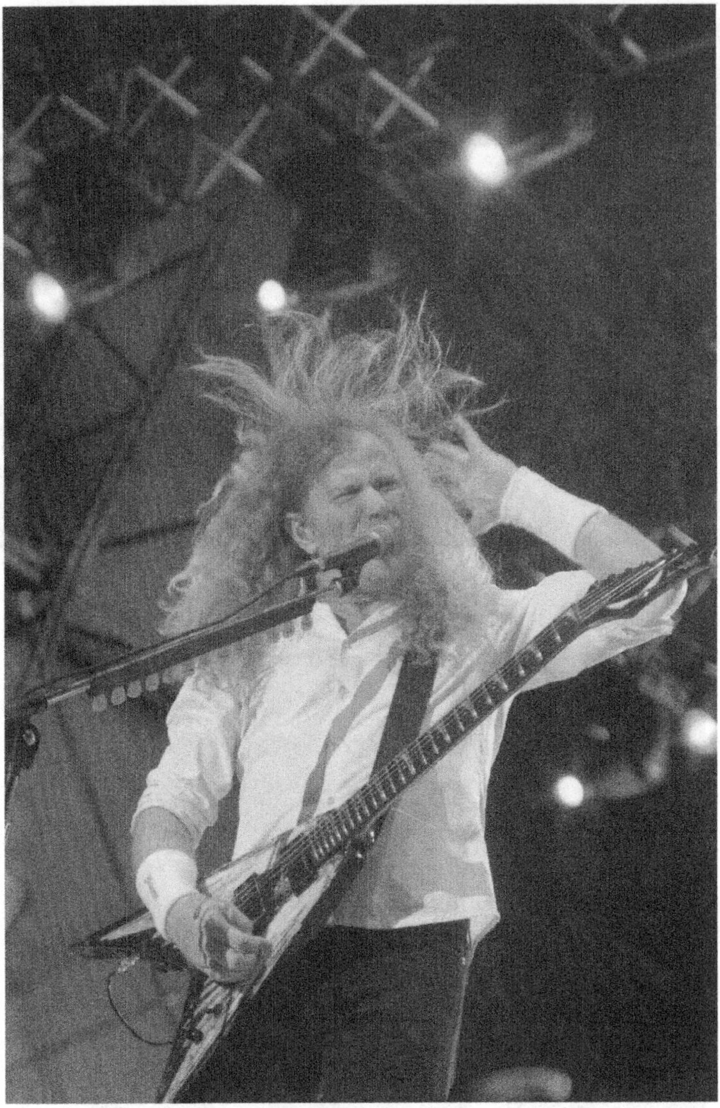

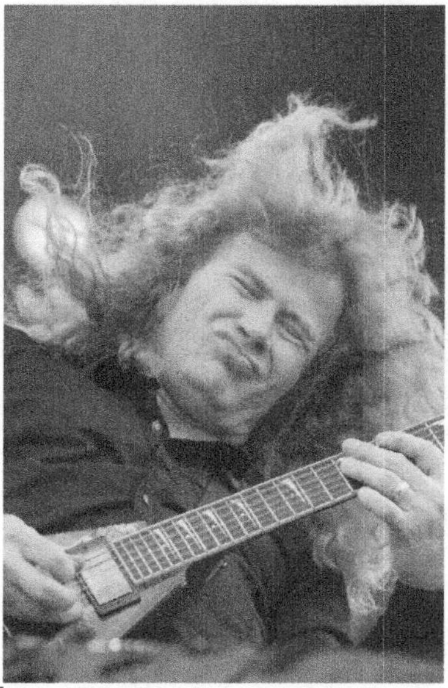

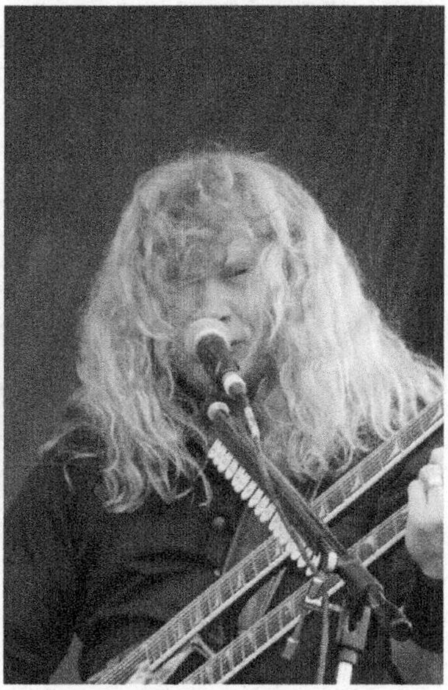

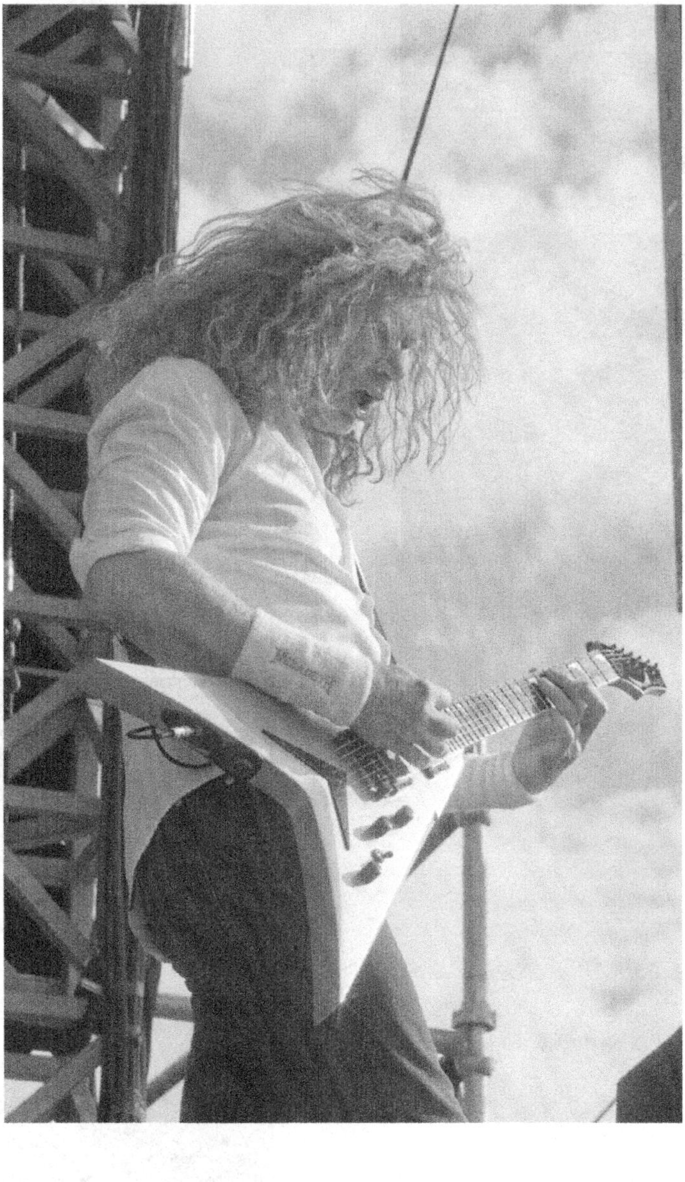

Metallica Pics by Red Shaw

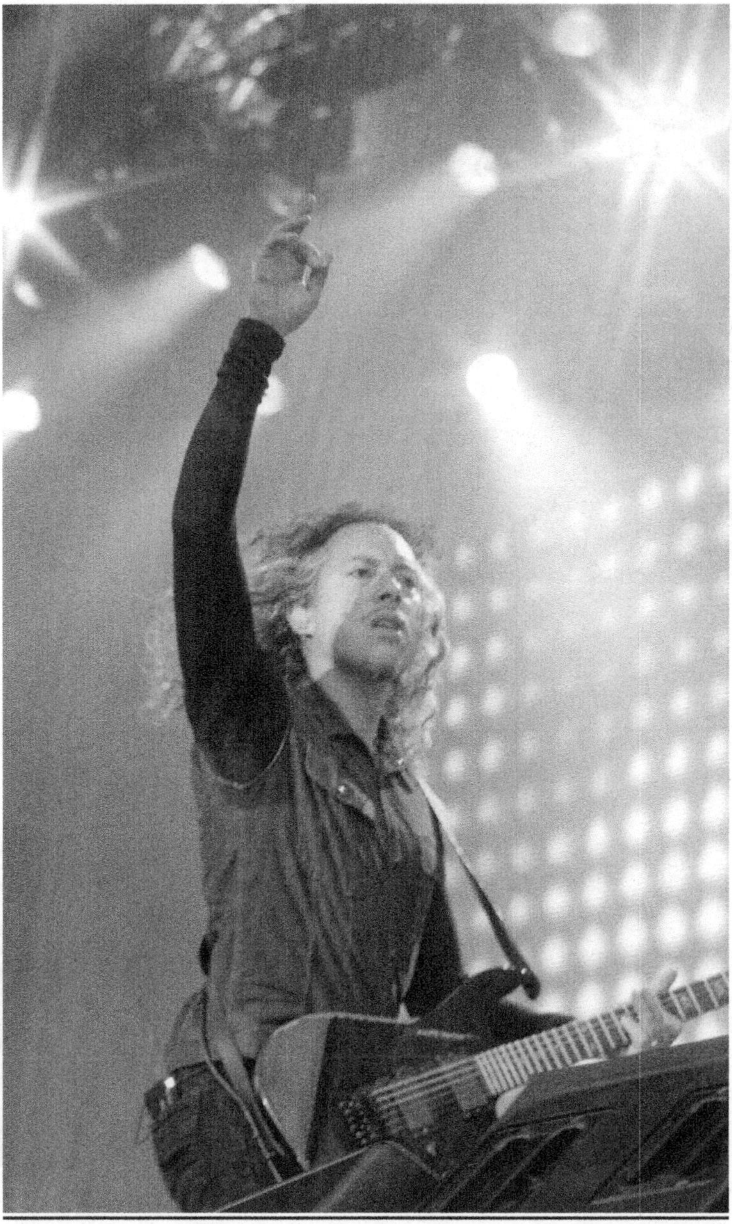

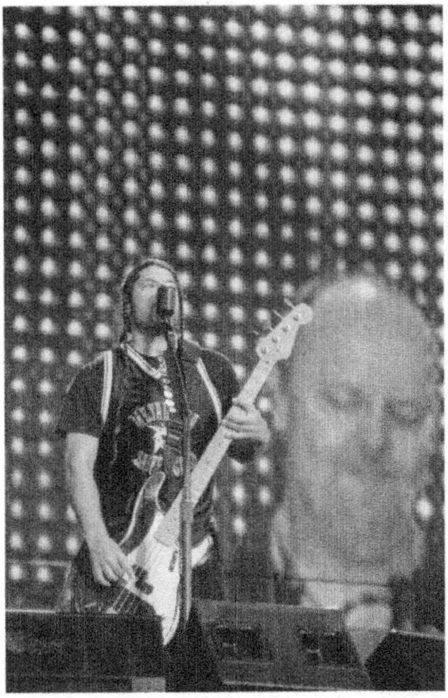

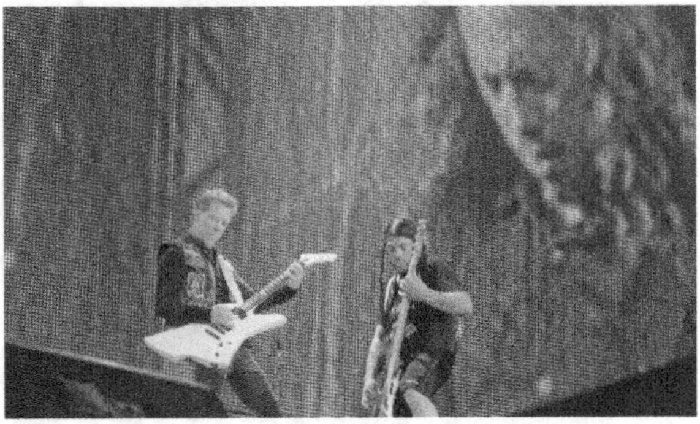

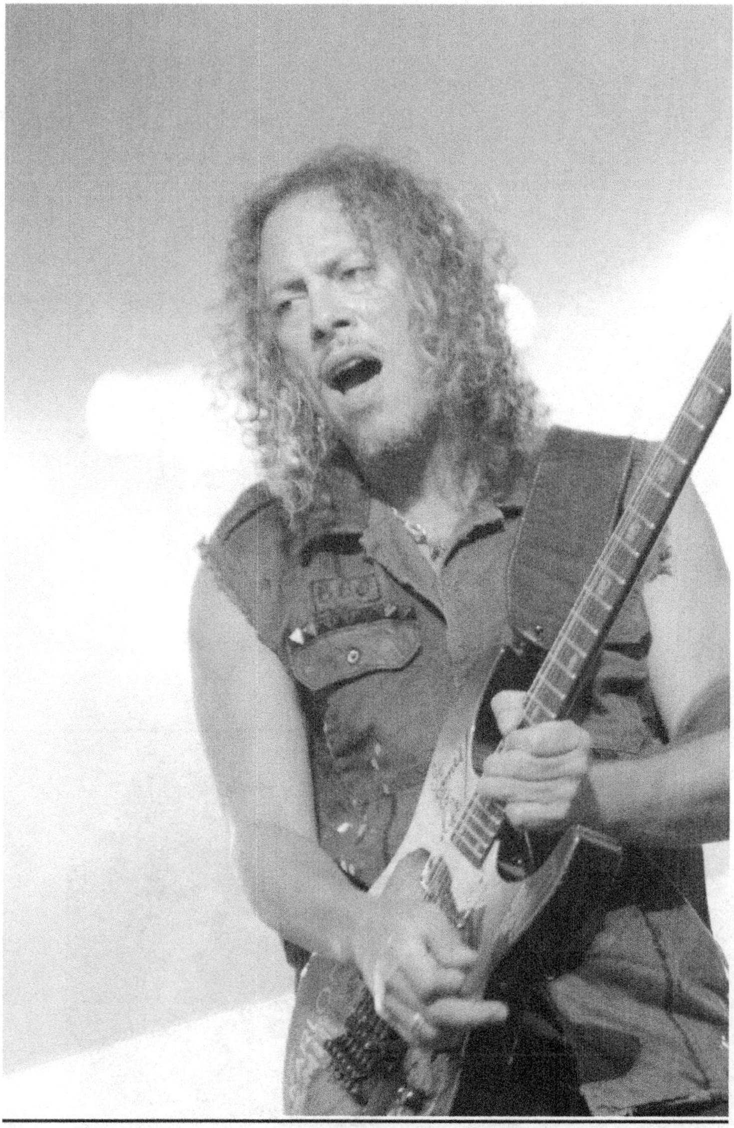

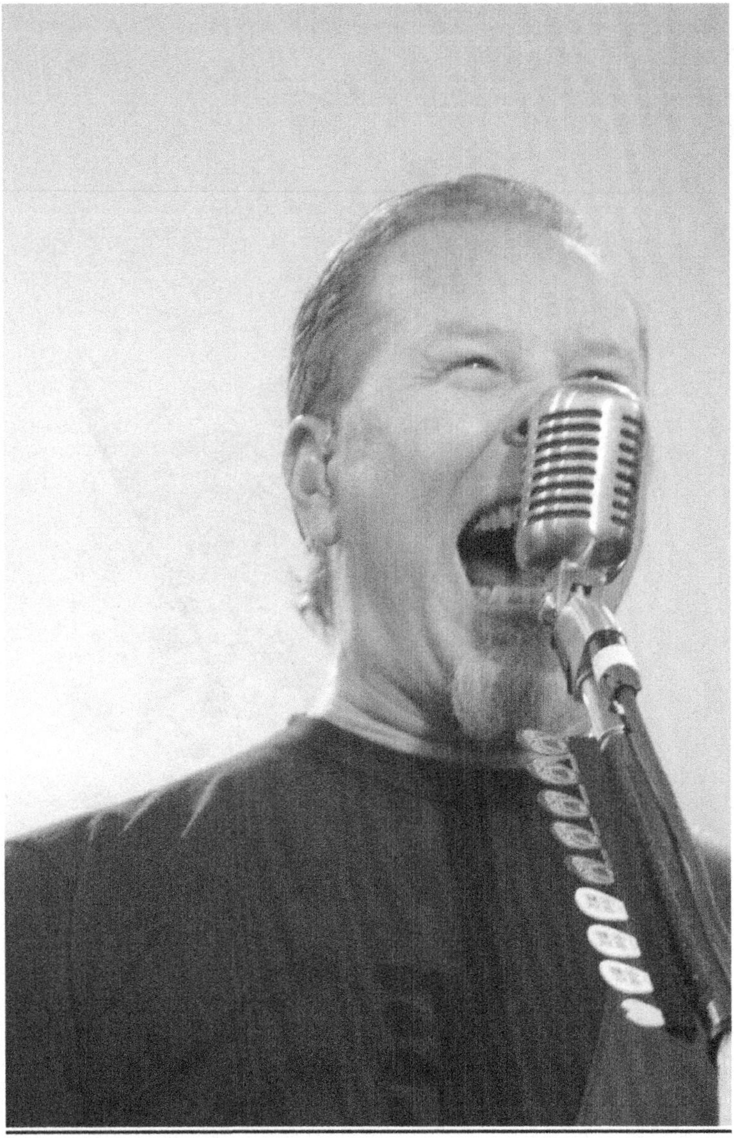

BIG 4 ENCYCLOPEDIA

Slayer Pics by Red Shaw

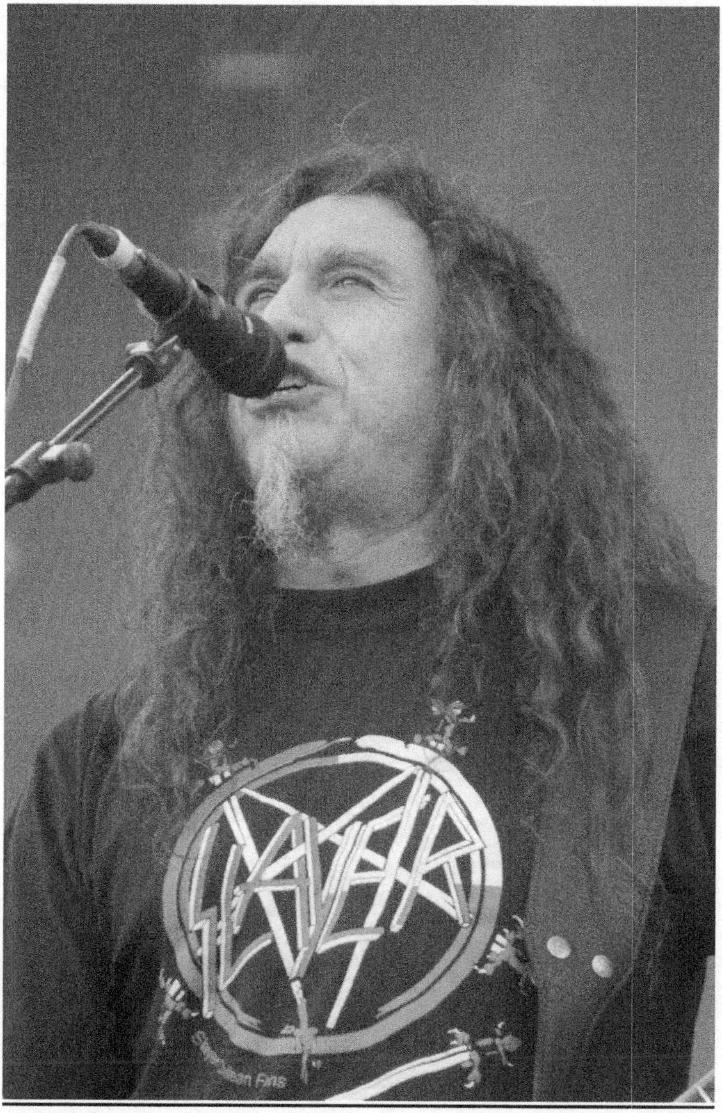
SLAYER

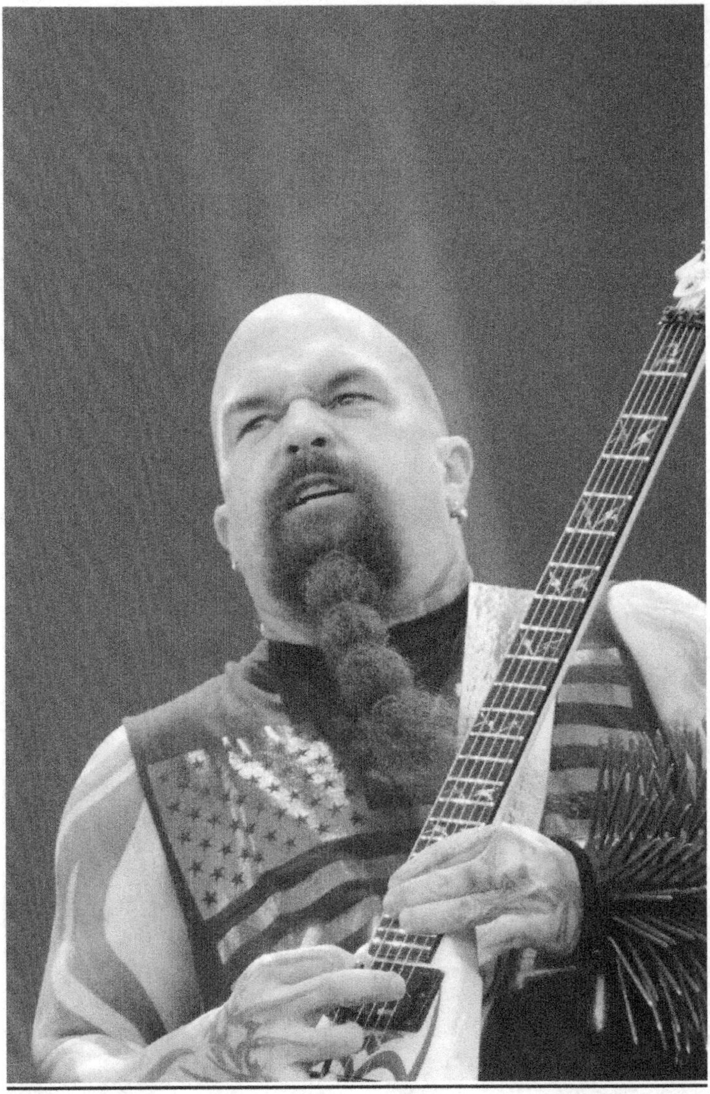

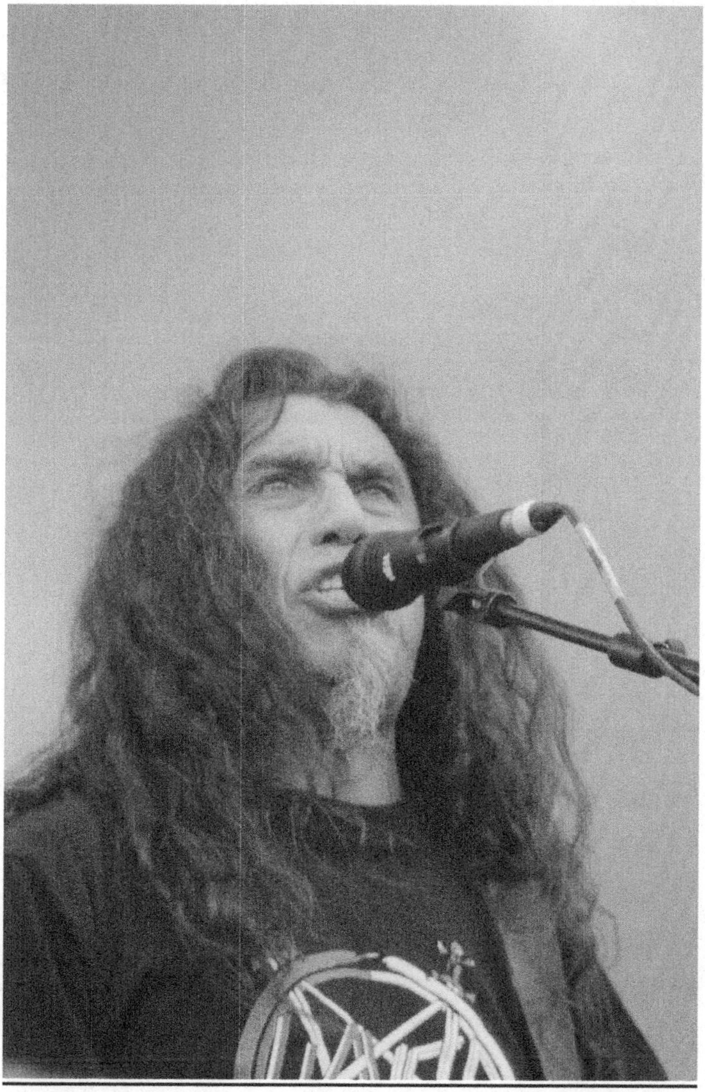

DISCOGRAPHY

Here is a selective (mostly UK) discography of the Big 4's releases...

METALLICA

STUDIO ALBUMS:

KILL 'EM ALL

Megaforce, 1983

RIDE THE LIGHTNING

Megaforce, 1984

MASTER OF PUPPETS

Elektra, 1986

...AND JUSTICE FOR ALL

Elektra, 1988

METALLICA

Elektra, 1991

LOAD

Elektra, 1996

RELOAD

Elektra, 1997

GARAGE INC.

Elektra, 1998

ST. ANGER

Elektra, 2003

DEATH MAGNETIC

Warner Bros. 2008

LULU (w/ Lou Reed)

Warner Bros, 2011

LIVE ALBUMS:

LIFE SHIT: BINGE & PURGE

Elektra, 1993

S&M (w/ San Francisco Symphony Orchestra)

Elektra, 1999

THE BIG FOUR – LIVE IN SOFIA, BULGARIA

Warner Bros., 2010

METALLICA THROUGH THE NEVER

Blackened, 2013

EPS:

THE $5.98 E.P.: GARAGE DAYS REVISITED

Elektra, 1987

SIX FEET DOWN UNDER

Universal, 2010

SIX FEET UNDER PART II

Universal, 2010

LIVE AT GRIMEY'S

Universal, 2010

BEYOND MAGNETIC

Warner Bros., 2011

BOX-SETS:

THE GOOD, THE BAD & THE LIVE

Vertigo, 1990

LIMITED-EDITION VINYL BOX SET

Rhino, 2004

THE METALLICA COLLECTION

Warner Bros., 2009

SINGLES:

WHIPLASH (1983)

JUMP IN THE FIRE (1984)

CREEPING DEATH (1984)

MASTER OF PUPPETS (1986)

HARVESTER OF SORROW (1988)

EYE OF THE BEHOLDER (1988)

ONE (1989)

ENTER SANDMAN (1991)

THE UNFORGIVEN (1991)

NOTHING ELSE MATTERS (1992)

WHEREVER I MAY ROAM (1992)

SAD BUT TRUE (1993)

UNTIL IT SLEEPS (1996)

HERO OF THE DAY (1996)

MAMA SAID (1996)

KING NOTHING (1997)

THE MEMORY REMAINS (1997)

THE UNFORGIVEN II (1998)

FUEL (1998)

TURN THE PAGE (1998)

WHISKEY IN THE JAR (1999)

DIE, DIE MY DARLING (1999)

NOTHING ELSE MATTERS '99 (w/ San Francisco Symphony Orchestra) (1999)

I DISAPPEAR (2000)

ST. ANGER (2003)

FRANTIC (2003)

THE UNNAMED FEELING (2004)

SOME KIND OF MONSTER (2004)

THE DAY THAT NEVER COMES (2008)

MY APOCALYPSE (2008)

CYANIDE (2008)

THE JUDAS KISS (2008)

ALL NIGHTMARE LONG (2008)

BROKEN, BEAT & SCARED (2009)

THE VIEW (w/ Lou Reed) (2011)

PROMOTIONAL SINGLES:

FADE TO BLACK (1984)

FOR WHOM THE BELLS TOLL (1984)

...AND JUSTICE FOR ALL (1989)

STONE COLD CRAZY (1990)

DON'T TREAD ON ME (1991)

BLEEDING ME (1997)

BETTER THAN YOU (1998)

THE ECSTASY OF GOLD (2007)

THE END OF THE LINE (2009)

OTHER SINGLES:

REMEMBER TOMORROW (2008)

THAT WAS JUST YOUR LIFE (2008)

THE UNFORGIVEN III (2008)

HATE TRAIN (2012)

WHEN A BLIND MAN CRIES (2012)

GUEST APPEARENCES:

HIT THE LIGHTS – METAL MASSACRE, VOL. 1 (1982)

STONE COLD CRAZY – RUBAIVAT: ELEKTRA'S 40TH ANNIVERSARY (1990)

I DISAPPEAR – MISSION: IMPOSSIBLE II (2000)

WE DID IT AGAIN (w/ Ja Rule) – *SWIZZ BEATZ PRESENTS G.H.E.T.T.O. STORIES*

53RD & 3RD – *WE'RE A HAPPY FAMILY: A TRIBUTE TO RAMONES*

THE ECSTASY OF GOLD – *WE ALL LOVE ENNIO MORRICONE* (2007)

REMEMBER TOMORROW – *MAIDEN HEAVEN: A TRIBUTE TO IRON MAIDEN* (2008)

YOU REALLY GOT ME (w/Ray Davies) – *SEE MY FRIENDS* (2010)

WHEN A BLIND MAN CRIES – *RE-MACHINED: A TRIBUTE TO DEEP PURPLE'S MACHINE HEAD* (2012)

RONNIE RISING MEDLEY – *RONNIE JAMES DRIO – THIS IS YOUR LIFE* (2014)

MUSIC VIDEOS:

ONE (1989)

ENTER SANDMAN (1991)

THE UNFORGIVEN (1991)

NOTHING ELSE MATTERS (1992)

WHEREVER I MAY ROAM (1992)

SAD BUT TRUE (1992)

UNTIL IT SLEEPS (1996)

HERO OF THE DAY (1996)

MAMA SAID (1996)

KING NOTHING (1997)

THE MEMORY REMAINS (1997)

THE UNFORGIVEN II (1998)

FUEL (1998)

TURN THE PAGE (1998)

WHISKEY IN THE JAR (1999)

DIE, DIE MY DARLING (1999)

NO LEAF CLOVER (1999)

I DISAPPEAR (2000)

ST. ANGER (2003)

FRANTIC (2003)

THE UNNAMED FEELING (2004)

SOME KIND OF MONSTER (2004)

THE DAY THAT NEVER COMES (2008)

ALL NIGHTMARE LONG (2008)

BROKEN, BEAT & SCARED (2009)

THE VIEW (w/ Lou Reed) (2011)

VHS / DVD:

CLIFF 'EM ALL

Elektra, 1997

2 OF ONE

Elektra, 1989

A YEAR AND A HALF IN THE LIFE OF METALLICA

Elektra, 1992

CUNNING STUNTS

Elektra, 1998

S&M (w/ San Francisco Symphony Orchestra)

Elektra, 1999

THE VIDEOS: 1989-2004

Warner Bros., 2006

THE BIG FROM – LIVE FROM SOFIA, BULGARIA

Warner Bros., 2010

QUEBEC MAGNETIC

Warner Bros., 2012

SLAYER

STUDIO ALBUMS:

SHOW NO MERCY

Metal Blade, 1983

HELL AWAITS

Metal Blade, 1985

REIGN IN BLOOD

American, 1986

SOUTH OF HEAVEN

American, 1988

SEASONS IN THE ABYSS

American, 1990

DIVINE INTERVENTION

American, 1994

UNDISPUTED ATTITUDE

American, 1996

DIABOLUS IN MUSICA

American, 1998

GOD HATES US ALL

American, 2001

CHRIST ILLUSION

American, 2006

WORLD PAINTED BLOOD

American, 2009

REPENTLESS

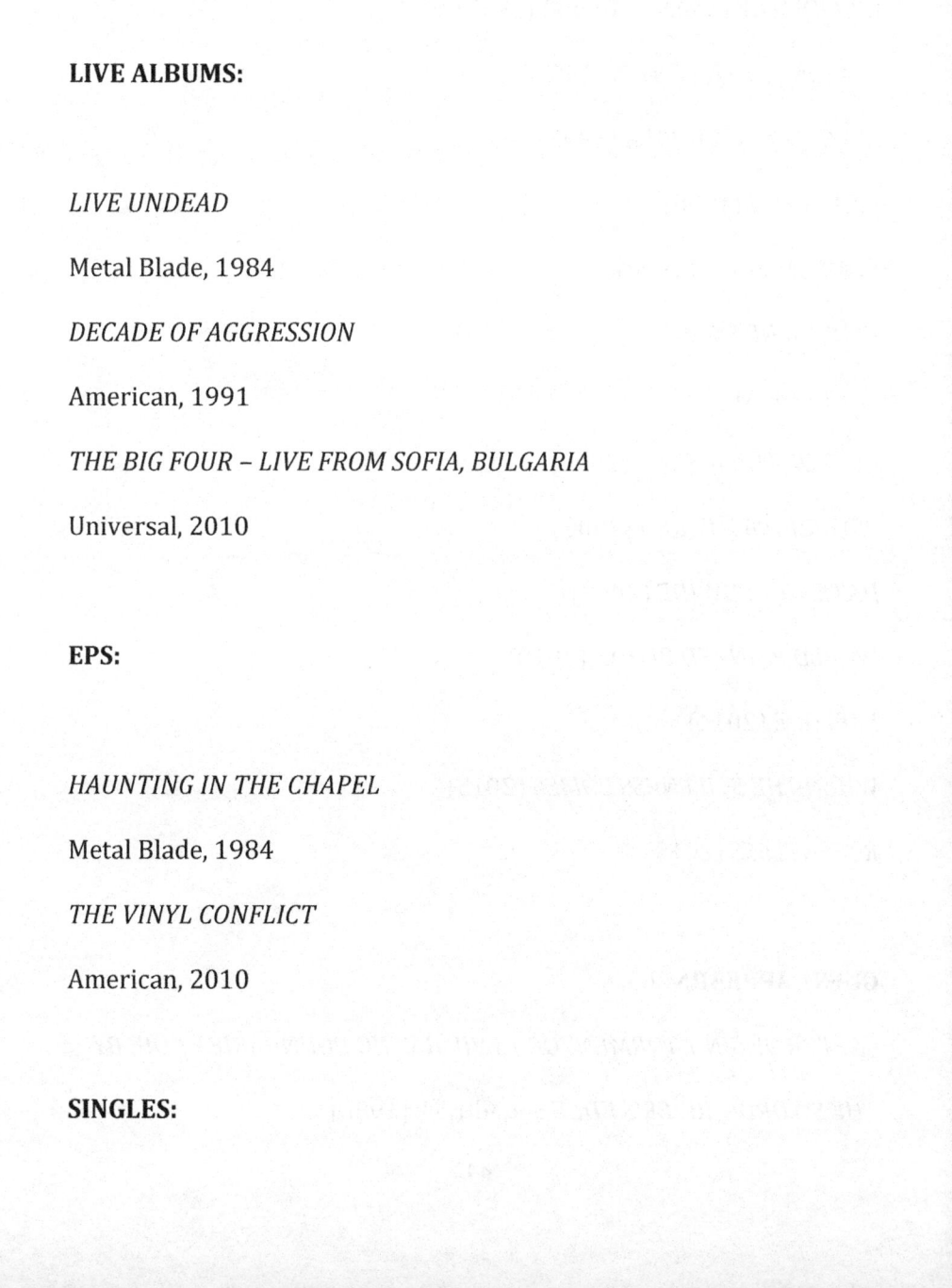

Nuclear Blast, 2015

LIVE ALBUMS:

LIVE UNDEAD

Metal Blade, 1984

DECADE OF AGGRESSION

American, 1991

THE BIG FOUR – LIVE FROM SOFIA, BULGARIA

Universal, 2010

EPS:

HAUNTING IN THE CHAPEL

Metal Blade, 1984

THE VINYL CONFLICT

American, 2010

SINGLES:

RAINING BLOOD (1986)

ANGEL OF DEATH (1986)

POSTMORTEM (1986)

CRIMINALLY INSANE (Remix) (1987)

SEASONS IN THE ABYSS (1990)

SERENITY IN MURDER (1995)

I HATE YOU (1996)

STAIN OF MIND (1998)

BLOODLINE (2001)

CULT (2006)

EYES OF THE INSANE (2006)

PSYOCHOPATHY RED (2009)

HATE WORLDWIDE (2009)

WORLD PAINTED BLOOD (2010)

IMPLODE (2014)

WHEN THE STILLNESS COMES (2015)

REPENTLESS (2015)

GUEST APPEARNCES:

CAPTOR OF SIN / TORMENTOR / EVIL HAS NO BOUNDARIES / DIE BY THE SWORD – RIVER'S EDGE Soundtrack (1986)

IN-A-GADDA-DA-VIDA (Iron Butterfly Cover) – *LESS THAN ZERO* Soundtrack (1987)

ANGEL OF DEATH – *GREMLINS 2: THE NEW BATCH* Soundtrack (1990)

DISORDER (ICE-T Collaboration) – *JUDGEMENT NIGHT* Soundtrack (1993)

NO REMORSE (I WANNA DIE) (Atari Teenage Riot collaboration) – *SPAWN: THE ALBUM* (1997)

HUMAN DISEASE – *BRIDE OF CHUCKY* Soundtrack (1998)

HERE COMES THE PAIN – *WCW MAYHEM: THE MUSIC* (1999)

HAND OF DOOM (Black Sabbath Cover) – *NATIVITY IN BLACK II* (1999)

SPIRIT IN BLACK – *BOOK OF SHADOWS: BLAIR WITCH 2* Soundtrack (1999)

BLOODLINE – *DRACULA 2000* Soundtrack (2000)

ANGEL OF DEATH – *MRS DEATH 2: HELLS FURY* Soundtrack (2000)

BORN TO BE WILD (Steppenwolf cover) – *NASCAR: CRANK IT UP* (2000)

ANGEL OF DEATH – *JACKASS: THE MOVIE* Soundtrack (2002)

DIVINE INTERVENTION – *HAGGARD: THE MOVIE* Soundtrack (2003)

WARZONE – *UFC: ULTIMATE BEAT DOWNS, VOL. 1* (2004)

SPILL THE BLOOD – *JACKASS NUMBER TWO* (2006)

EYES OF THE INSANE – SAW III Soundtrack (2006)

RAINING BLOOD – GUITAR HERO 3: LEGENDS OF ROCK (2007)

RAINING BLOOD – SKATE (2007)

WAR ENSEMBLE – GUITAR HERO: METALLICA (2009)

CHEMICAL WARFARE – GUITAR HERO: WARRIORS OF ROCK (2010)

MUSIC VIDEOS:

WAR ENSEMBLE (1990)

RAINING BLOOD (1990)

SEASONS IN THE ABYSS (1991)

SERENITY IN MURDER (1991)

DITTOHEAD (1994)

I HATE YOU (1996)

STAIN OF MIND (1998)

BLOODLINE (2001)

EYES OF THE INSANE (2006)

BEAUTY THROUGH ORDER (2006)

WORLD PAINTED BLOOD (2010)

REPENTLESS (2015)

VHS/DVD:

LIVE INTRUSION

American, 1995

WAR AT THE WARFIELD

American, 2003

STILL REIGNING

American, 2004

THE BIG FOUR – LIVE FROM SOFIA, BULGARIA

Universal, 2010

MEGADETH

STUDIO ALBUMS:

KILLING IS MY BUSINESS...AND BUSINESS IS GOOD!

Combat, 1985

PEACE SELLS...BUT WHO'S BUYING?

Capitol, 1986

SO FAR, SO GOOD...SO WHAT!

Capitol, 1988

RUST IN PEACE

Capitol, 1990

COUNTDOWN TO EXTINCTION

Capitol, 1992

YOUTHANASIA

Capitol, 1994

CRYPTIC WRITINGS

Capitol, 1997

RISK

Capitol, 1999

THE WORLD NEEDS A HERO

Sanctuary, 2001

THE SYSTEM HAS FAILED

Sanctuary, 2004

UNITED ABOMINATIONS

Roadrunner, 2007

ENDGAME

Roadrunner, 2009

THIRTEEN

Roadrunner, 2007

SUPER COLLIDER

Universal, 2013

DYSTOPIA

Universal, 2016

LIVE ALBUMS:

RUDE AWAKENING

Sanctuary, 2002

THAT ONE NIGHT: LIVE IN BUENOS AIRES

Image, 2007

RUST IN PEACE LIVE

Shout! Factory, 2010

THE BIG FOUR – LIVE FROM SOFIA, BULGARIA

Universal, 2010

COUNTDOWN TO EXINCTION LIVE

Universal, 2013

EPS:

MAXIMUM MEGADETH

Capitol, 1991

HIDDEN TREASURES

Capitol, 1995

COMPILATIONS:

CAPITOL PUNISHMENT: THE CAPITOL YEARS

Capitol, 2000

STILL, ALIVE…AND WELL?

Sanctuary, 2002

GREATEST HITS: BACK TO THE START

Capitol, 2005

WARCHEST

EMI, 2007

ANTHOLOGY: SET THE WORLD AFIRE

Capitol, 2008

ICON

Capitol, 2014

SINGLES:

WAKE UP DEAD (1986)

PEACE SELLS (1986)

MARY JANE (1988)

ANARCHY IN THE U.K. (1988)

IN MY DARKEST HOUR (1988)

HOOK IN MOUTH (1988)

LIAR (1989)

NO MORE MR. NICE GUY (1989)

HOLY WARS...THE PUNISHMENT DUE (1990)

HANGAR 18 (1991)

FORECLOSURE OF A DREAM (1992)

SYMPHONY OF DESTRUCTION (1992)

SKIN 'O TEETH (1993)

SWEATING BULLETS (1993)

CROWN OF WORMS (1994)

TRAIN OF CONSEQUENCES (1994)

A TOUT LE MONDE (SET ME FREE) (1995)

ANGRY AGAIN (1995)

99 WAYS TO DIE (1995)

TRUST (1997)

ALMOST HONEST (1997)

USE THE MAN (1997)

A SECRET PLACE (1998)

CRUSH 'EM (1999)

BREADLINE (2000)

INSOMNIA (2000)

KILL THE KING (2000)

MOTO PSYCHO (1001)

DREAD AND THE FUGITIVE MIND (2001)

DIE DEAD ENOUGH (2004)

OF MICE AND MEN (2005)

THE SCORPION (2005)

GEARS OF WAR (2006)

A TOUT LE MONDE (SET ME FREE) (2007)

SLEEPWALKER (2007)

WASHINGTON IS NEXT! (2007)

NEVER WALK ALONE...A CALL TO ARMS (2007)

HEAD CRUSHER (2009)

THE RIGHT TO GO INSANE (2010)

44 MINUTES (2010)

SUDDEN DEATH (2010)

NEVER DEAD (2011)

PUBLIC ENEMY NO.1 (2011)

WHOSE LIFE (IS IT ANYWAYS?) (2012)

SUPER COLLIDER (2013)

FATAL ILLUSION (2015)

MUSIC VIDEOS:

PEACE SELLS (1986)

WAKE UP DEAD (1987)

IN MY DARKEST HOUR (1988)

ANARCHY IN THE U.K. (1988)

NO MORE MR. NICE GUY (1989)

HOLY WARS...THE PUNISHMENT DUE (1990)

HANGAR 18 (1991)

GO TO HELL (1991)

FORECLOSURE OF A DREAM (1992)

HIGH SPEED DIRT (1992)

SYMPHONY OF DESTRUCTION (1992)

SKIN 'O TEETH (1992)

A TOUT LE MONDE (SET ME FREE) (1994)

RECKONING DAY (1995)

ANGRY AGAIN (1994)

TRAIN OF CONSEQUENCES (1994)

TRUST (1997)

ALMOST HONEST (1997)

A SECRET PLACE (1998)

INSOMNIA (1999)

CRUSH 'EM (1999)

BREADLINE (2000)

MOTO PSYCHO (2001)

DIE DEAD ENOUGH (2004)

OF MICE AND MEN (2005)

A TOUT LE MONDE (SET ME FREE) (2007)

NEVER WALK ALONE...A CALL TO ARMS (2007)

HEAD CRUSHER (2009)

THE RIGHT TO GO INSANE (2010)

PUBLIC ENEMY NO. 1 (2011)

WHOSE LIFE (IS IT ANWAYS?) (2012)

SUPER COLLIDER (2013)

VHS/DVD:

RUSTED PIECES

Capitol, 1991

EXPOSURE OF A DREAM

Capitol, 1992

EVOLVER: THE MAKING OF YOUTHANASIA

Capitol, 1995

BEHIND THE MUSIC

Sanctuary, 2001

RUDE AWAKENING

Sanctuary, 2002

VIDEO HITS

Capitol, 2005

ARSENAL OF MEGADETH

Capitol, 2006

THAT ONE NIGHT: LIVE IN BUENOS AIRES

Image, 2007

RUST IN PEACE LIVE

Universal, 2007

THE BIG FOUR – LIVE IN SOFIA, BULGARIA

Universal, 2010

COUNTDOWN TO EXTINCTION LIVE

Universal, 2013

ANTHRAX

STUDIO ALBUMS:

FISTFUL OF METAL

Megaforce, 1984

SPREADING THE DISEASE

Megaforce/Island, 1985

AMONG THE LIVING

Megaforce/Island, 1987

STATE OF EUPHORIA

Megaforce/Island, 1988

PERSISTENCE OF TIME

Megaforce/Island, 1990

SOUND OF WHITE NOISE

Elektra, 1993

STOMP 442

Elektra, 1995

VOLUME 8: THE THREAT IS REAL

Ignition, 1998

WE'VE COME FOR YOU ALL

Sanctuary, 2003

WORSHIP MUSIC

Megaforce, 2011

LIVE ALBUMS:

THE ISLAND YEARS

Island, 1994

MASS OF MUSIC DESTRUCTION

Sanctuary, 2004

ALIVE 2: THE MUSIC

Sanctuary, 2005

CAUGHT IN A MOSH: BBC LIVE IN CONCERT

Universal, 2007

THE BIG FOUR – LIVE FROM SOFIA, BULGARIA

Warner Bros., 2010

EPS:

ARMED AND DANGEROUS

Megaforce, 1985

I'M THE MAN

Island, 1987

PENIKUFESIN

Island, 1989

INSIDE OUT

Ignition, 1999

SUMMER 2003

Nuclear Blast, 2003

ANTHEMS

Megaforce, 2013

COMPILATIONS:

ATTACK OF THE KILLER B'S

Island, 1991

RETURN OF THE KILLER A'S

Beyond, 1999

THE GREAT OF TWO EVILS

Sanctuary, 2004

ANTHROLOGY: NO HIT WONDERS

Island Def Jam, 2005

SINGLES:

SOLDIERS OF METAL (1983)

MADHOUSE (1985)

I AM THE LAW (1987)

INDIANS (1987)

MAKE ME LAUGH (2988)

ANTISOCIAL (1988)

GOT THE TIME (1990)

IN MY WORLD (1990)

BRING THE NOISE (w/Public Enemy) (1991)

ONLY (1993)

BLACK LODGE (1993)

HY PRO GLO (1993)

ROOM FOR ON MORE (1993)

FUELED (1995)

NOTHING (1996)

BORDELLO OF BLOOD (1996)

INSIDE OUT (1998)

BORN AGAIN IDIOT (1998)

BALL OF CONFUSION (1999)

CRUSH (2000)

SAFE HOME (2003)

TAKING THE MUSIC BACK (2003)

FIGHT 'EM TILL YOU CAN'T (2011)

THE DEVIL YOU KNOW (2011)

I'M ALIVE (2012)

NEON KNIGHTS (2014)

MUSIC VIDEOS:

METAL THRASHING MAD (1984)

MADHOUSE (1985)

INDIANS (1987)

I'M THE MAN (1987)

CAUGHT IN A MOSH (1987)

I AM THE LAW (1987)

AMONG THE LIVING (1987)

GUNG-HO (1988)

ANTISOCIAL (1988)

WHO CARES WINS (1988)

IN MY WORLD (1990)

GOT THE TIME (1990)

BELLY OF THE BEAST (1991)

BRING THE NOISE (w/ Public Enemy) (1991)

ONLY (1993)

BLACK LODGE (1993)

ROOM FOR ONE MORE (1994)

HY PRO GLO (1995)

FUELED (1995)

NOTHING (1996)

INSIDE OUT (1998)

SAFE HOME (2003)

WHAT DOESN'T DIE (2004)

DEATHRIDER (2004)

CAUGHT IN A MOSH (Version 2) (2005)

THE DEVIL YOU KNOW (2012)

A SKELETON IN THE CLOSET (2014)

VHS / DVD:

N.F.V.: OIDIVNIKUFESIN

PolyGram, 1987

THROUGH TIME P.O.V.

PolyGram, 1991

ATTACK OF THE KILLER B'S VIDEOS

PolyGram, 1991

LIVE NOIZE

PolyGram, 1992

WHITE NOISE: THE VIDEOS

Elektra, 1994

RETURN OF THE KILLER A'S: VIDEO COLLECTION

Beyond, 1999

ROCK LEGENDS

Wienerworld, 2004

ALIVE 2: THE DVD

Sanctuary 2005

ANTHROLOGY: NO HIT WONDERS – THE VIDEOS

Island Def Jam, 2005

THE BIG FOUR – LIVE FROM SOFIA, BULGARIA

Warner Bros., 2010

CHILE ON HELL

Nuclear Blast, 2014

METALLICA
SLAYER
MEGADETH
ANTHRAX
THE BIG 4
LIVE
FROM SOFIA, BULGARIA

ASSORTED REVIEWS

Here are some reviews the author has written for various publications about the Big 4 bands and their music ...

ANTHRAX

AMONG THE LIVING

CD/ ALBUM

Among The Living is often hailed as Anthrax's best album and an all-time classic thrash metal opus. With songs like 'Indians', 'I Am The Law' and 'Caught In A Mosh' you can't really argue with such bold statements. It is a magnificent album of its kind and still sounds fresh, exciting and vibrant some 23 years after its initial release. The band had already made a worthy claim for inclusion in the highest ranks of American thrash metal bands with their 1984 debut *A Fistful Of Metal* and 1985's *Spreading The Disease* but with this beauty they took it one giant step further. They may have looked more juvenile than the likes of Metallica and were not seen as an enigma like Dave Mustaine, and though there has been some controversy over the years they certainly haven't caused outrage with the American far right the way Slayer have, yet when it comes to duel guitars, pounding bass lines, powerful vocals and catchy choruses, Anthrax were/are a hard band to beat.

It is inevitable that with all the fuss surrounding the band and vocalists Dan Nelson and John Bush over the past few years that some of their older material would be reissued. Dedicated to the deceased Metallica bassist Cliff Burton, *Among The Living* was produced by Eddie Kramer and the album's title was inspired by Stephen King's immense novel *The Stand*. Anthrax have created a reputation over the years for an abundance of pop culture references in their lyrics and artwork; and Scott Ian and Charlie Benante will be the first ones to admit they are geeks. The classic 'I Am The Law' was based on the 2000AD comic strip *Judge Dredd*. If these album was to be scored out of five it would get full marks.

This deluxe edition is great value for money. The original album comes with a few bonus tracks, including different versions of some songs, the B-side 'Bud E Luv Bomb And Satan's Lounge Band', a live version of 'I Am The Law' and the instrumental 'I Am The Man'. The sleeve notes by the American actor/comedian and friend of the band Brian Posehn don't really do the album reissue justice. The DVD, which is the section disc of this two disc edition, is a blast and shows just how amazing the band were live. Recorded at London's Hammersmith Odeon (now the Apollo) in 1987, the set-list features 'Madhouse', 'Metal Thrashing Mad' and songs from *Among The Living*, including 'Caught In A Mosh' and 'I Am The Law'. Metal fans will not be disappointed with this set.

ANTHRAX
CAUGHT IN A MOSH: BBC LIVE IN CONCERT
CD / ALBUM

The past few years have been a bit of a shambles in the Anthrax camp concerning three singers: Joey Belladonna, Dan Nelson and who I think is their best ever singer (and they've had a few!), Mr. John Bush. Most fans are asking: What the hell is going on? While we're waiting for the new album, this archive collection will fill the time in nicely. It's a fantastic release and well your time and money.

Caught In A Mosh is two concerts on two discs. Both shows were recorded during a crucial time in the band's career when they went from being a something of cult thrash band to being a major force to be reckoned with. Anthrax was/is a member of the holy quartet of thrash: "The Big Four". The others are obviously Metallica, Slayer and Megadeth. There has always been a comedic side to Anthrax derived from their love of pop culture, in particular comic books. 1987 saw the release of their legendary studio opus *Among The Living* which is still a damn good album. It followed the kiss-arse *Fistful Of Metal* and *Spreading The Disease*. They had a lot of great material of their own to play with and it shows in the setlists to both shows though they are fairly similar.

OK, the first disc was recorded at the band's sold out show at the Hammersmith Odeon in London on 15th February, 1987. Needless to say the band are on fire as they fly through 12 songs like Concord. Like I said, though I prefer John Bush, Belladonna was a fantastic frontman and singer for Anthrax. He hits some really high Halford style notes and really knew how to fire up a crowd. Included in the setlist are chest beating anthems like 'I Am The Law', 'Madhouse' and a strong cover of the Sabbath's classic 'Sabbath Bloody Sabbath'. The sound quality is excellent and just listening to the audience alone makes me wish I was there. The second disc was the band's stunning performance at Monsters Of Rock at Donington Park on 22nd August, 1987. The band blitz through nine songs, including 'Caught In A Mosh' and 'A.I.R'.. As with the first disc, the sound is spot on and the band were in fine form on the day. The sleeve notes by James McNair tell a potted history of the band up to 1987. They're one of those bands that are better onstage than in the studio. *Caught In A Mosh* is a reminder of how great Anthrax can be when they get their act together.

ANTHRAX

MANCHESTER ACADEMY 2, JUNE 15, 2004

LIVE

Despite Hatebreed's lame excuse of not filling the support slot because their bus broke down, Anthrax induced enough headaches and muscle pains to clear the local supermarket of aspirin. It was a highly-charged night were the perspiration could have filled a swimming pool, the walls literally vibrated and the floor almost cracked open.

Moving around the diminutive stage with facial expressions and chest beating movements resembling Hulk Hogan, lead vocalist John Bush worked the excitable audience like a U.S General gearing his troops up for war; which seems an apt description while they are promoting their new live album and DVD, *Music Of Mass Destruction*. It was almost freighting watching the speed at which guitarist and founding member Scott Ian banged his head in unison with the hungry crowd, it's surprising that they did not simultaneously combust.

The setlist was as tight as a ballerina's costume and as raw as an uncooked steak. Anthrax were excruciatingly loud and unbelievably fast, yet they still retained those catchy melodious choruses. Classic thrash metal creations like 'Anti-social', 'Got The Time' and 'Bring The Noise' were gloriously played with aplomb and they even bothered to resurrect 'Death Rider' – the first song from their debut album, *Fistful Of Metal*.

One thing is for sure, Anthrax deserve far more reverence. They are working the small circuit trying to regain popularity after years of record company conflicts. Not content with playing one round, the '80s thrash metal titans have toured the UK four times in the last eighteen months, including a tour with the mighty Motörhead.

Tonight's stunning gig was a throbbing attack on the fragile mind that left the majority weeping for more and rejoicing in the new faith of this bands amazing comeback. This ladies and gentlemen is the cream of metal holiness.

MEGADETH

TH1RT3EN

CD/ ALBUM

Megadeth are back with – you guessed it! – their thirteenth studio album and for a band with such a tumultuous history as Megadeth's the fact that they've lasted this long may come as quite a shock to some rock and metal fans. The curiously misspelled title, which for reviewers is irritating to type, is a way of celebrating the band's latest release which is something of a minor gem. This particular writer was a big fan of the band's last release but this time around bassist Dave Ellefson is back playing on his first Megadeth album since 2002's not-quite-so-good *Rude Awakening*.

This album contains some of Megadeth's finest work in years, including the bone-crunching 'Never Dead' and the mental 'Public Enemy No. 1'. Other excellent tracks include the powerful 'Sudden Death' and the catchy 'Guns, Drugs & Money' which are surely some of the most famous commodities in rock! Whereas Metallica know how to alienate their fanbase – who let's face it don't like change – Megadeth stick to what they know best: thrash metal! The only obvious flaw with this album is that Dave Mustaine's voice grates more than usual, which leaves this particular reviewer feeling cold. As a musician, his guitar work is exemplary but as a singer, well, Lemmy can do better and that says something. (I'm a Motörhead fan, by the way).

Lyrically, Mustaine explores his demons and makes references to his past mistakes and his volatile personality. Those who have read his excellent memoir *A Life In Metal* will know that Mustaine has certainly lived a colourful life. The production of the album is top-notch but like Metallica, Megadeth will probably never make anything as powerful as their first few releases. Having said that, *Th1rt3en* is a fine effort and proof that this band is far from over. They have a lot more to say and what they do say is worth listening to for sure.

MEGADETH

MANCHESTER ACADEMY, FEBRUARY 7, 2005

LIVE

Being a support group to a band with a hefty and controversial reputation isn't the easiest job in the world but Diamond Head pull it off with sweaty confidence. The audience loved practically every minute of it as the queue outside the venue grew shorter and the crowd watching Diamond Head grew larger.

Megadeth are emphatically an acquired taste. It is certainly the case that they are not every body's cup of tea but one thing is for sure; they have a decidedly enthusiastic fanbase. Even though tonight's show at one Manchester's Universities larger venues was purported to be a sell-out there was plenty of room to move around. The whole place literally vibrated as if sticks of TNT had been activated outside and that was only during the sound check! The actual gig sounded like a demented frenzy of electric chords and heavy drumbeats.

The problem with the set, especially for newcomers to Dave Mustaine's furious brew of thrash metal, is that it was difficult to tell when one song ended and the next one started. The biggest cheers inevitable came from their older material while fans still managed to enjoy stuff from their recent creation *The System Has Failed*.

About half-an-hour into Megadeth's gig, Mustaine stopped for a breather to tell the audience that about three years ago he was told by his doctor that he would never play the guitar again because of tendon damage in one of his hands. Here, Mustaine is to prove him and everybody wrong, while his guitar playing was evidently frantic his voice was bordering on humiliation.

There were some minor sound problems with Mustaine's microphone at the beginning of show, but even so, Mustaine has certainly never been the best of metal singers and this evening his voice proved almost nauseating as he spluttered streams of incomprehensible lyrics despite some awesome guitar playing. The band sounded much better when he kept quiet and just played. With Glen Drover on guitar, bassist James MacDonough and Shawn Drover on drums, Megadeth certainly proved a tight force to be reckoned with when it came to creating some serious sonic bursts that were frighteningly loud.

Looking at how many people were head banging, playing air guitar – rather aggressively I might add – and singing along, the system had definitely not failed them. Regardless of my lack of fondness for

Mustaine's vocal capability, being at the Manchester Academy this evening was like being on an express train driven by a bunch of drug-induced maniacs. It was a loud, fast and tiresome journey – certainly an experience that is not for the whole family.

MEGADETH
PRIEST FEAST: TESTAMENT/MEGADETH/JUDAS PRIEST
MANCHESTER APOLLO, FEBRUARY 17, 2009
LIVE

Testament singer Chuck Billy looked like he was having an absolute blast through their 40 minute set. Maybe it's because (and Billy acknowledged this) Testament made their first trip to the UK in '87 supporting Anthrax and the band played this very venue. They were super-tight and really enthusiastic. Alex Scholnik is a terrific metal guitarist and their latest album – the acclaimed *The Formation Of Damnation* – got a good airing.

Megadeth kicked off their hour set with 'Sleepwalker' the opening song to their last album the excellent *United Abomination*. And for once the sound was pretty good at a Megadeth show. As usual Mustaine did not interact with the audience as much as he could have done but it was obvious there were just about as many fans to see him as there was to see the mighty Priest. He was technically brilliant throughout and his voice sounded much better than usual but somehow their set lacked passion. It's the classics that went down well especially *'Peace Sells'*.

The first half of Priest's world tour was last year and it was mostly a festival run. Sadly Priest got some of the worst live reviews of their career: messy setlist and poor vocals were mostly to blame. Fortunately for British fans they've ironed out their problems and Halford is sounding surprisingly strong (albeit it at times). The tour was blighted by poor ticket sales (Nottingham was cancelled; Birmingham was half empty and this Manchester shows a downgraded from the MEN Arena) but that did not dented their confidence. Halford really did try hard and surprised me with some high notes, most notably 'Between The Hammer And The Anvil' and 'Eat Me Alive'; although about two thirds though the set 'Dissident Aggressor' (which is a hard song anyway) and 'Rock Hard Ride Free' gave him a tough time. 'Sinner' was brilliantly played but a little too long (it gave Halford the stage too nip backstage and cool down). If truth be told,

Halford did go off stage a bit too much in between songs which ruined the flow of the evening. And it has to be said the cod theatrics were embarrassing. At one point during the new song 'Messenger Of

Death' Halford was pushed onstage in a chair by a roadie who was dressed in a gown from head to toe and what Halford was dressed in when they opened with 'Prophecy' has to be seen to be believed. Not a great Priest show but a good one by their current standards. They are still capable of being a truly great live band; they just need to concentrate on the music rather than the spectacle and one idea is to focus on albums between *Sad Wings Of Destiny* and *Screaming For Vengeance,* now that would be killer setlist!

All in all it was an entertaining night but some could justifiably claim that for three major metal bands on the one bill it was a little underwhelming.

METALLICA
...AND JUSTICE FOR ALL
CD / ALBUM
(NOTE: Originally written for Martin Popoff's illustrated book on Metallica).
...And Justice for All, the band's fourth album, is certainly less melodic than its predecessors; but more direct and forceful yet intricate. After the death of bassist Cliff Burton, who was probably the most musical member of the band, Metallica had to deliver the goods. Does *...And*

Justice for All sound so different from its three predecessors because Burton was not involved? Most definitely.

The band came out of the studio on May 1, 1988 armed with an album that would split the fanbase. In the 1980s it was felt that the synthesizer was going to replace the guitar with bands such as ZZ Top and even Judas Priest experimenting with new sounds and studio effects, including the dreaded synthesizer. At that point Metallica set about making an album that was different from the first three albums.

Although *...And Justice for All* is not a concept album per se there are consistent themes running rippling throughout the nine lengthy tracks. Perhaps inspired by futuristic novels like George Orwell's *1984*, the themes present in the album include political, legal and social injustice in a world of censorship, war and nuclear weapons. Metallica had become so popular with a generation of kids that they could write and say what they wanted to and kids would probably take it literally. Lyrically, the one thing Metallica did stay away from was the occult, which had been tried and tested by bands since the early beginnings of metal from Black Sabbath to the blood thirsty NWOBHM band Venom to the tongue-in-cheek lyrics and imagery of Iron Maiden *et al*. Heavy metal had been perceived as a sexist genre due in the main to bands such as Mötley Crüe but Metallica had distance themselves from such subjects.

In terms of the musicianship, many fans had noticed the double-bass drum sound on the song 'One', for example. Ulrich was certainly one of the leading pioneers of the thrash metal drum beats and just as he'd proven with 'Metal Militia' (*Kill 'em All*), 'Fight Fire With Fire' (*Ride The Lightning*), 'Battery' (*Master of Puppets*), and with the *...And Justice for All* track 'Dyers Eve' Ulrich became one of metal's most distinctive drummers. His style of drumming is fast, fierce and aggressive often with simplified drum beats and a double bass technique which many metal drummers adopted in the 1980s and subsequent decades.

After recording the band hit the road for some shows, which included the Monsters Of Rock Tour with Van Halen headlining and other bands such as the Scorpions, Dokken and Kingdom Come, Ulrich and Hetfield had to fly back and forth to Bearsville in New York where they were mixing *...And Justice for All* with Steve Thompson and Michael Barbiero. It proved very tiring for the Metallica duo.

The production is clinical and cold and though it remains Metallica's most progressive album, there are obvious flaws present. *...And Justice for All* doesn't quite have the same power; the same guttural kick as its three predecessors but it does have some profound moments, some moments of absolute metal genius. The songs are not quite as engaging as those on *Master Of Puppets* but having said that much of the guitar work is exemplary.

Fans had waited two and a half years since *Master Of Puppets* and some felt it was too long but the band had a lot to deal with because of Burton's tragic death and Hetfield's highly-publicized skateboarding accident. *...And Justice for All* was released in August 1988 and was the band's first Top 10 hit in the USA, reaching Number 6. Whatever criticisms that were aimed at the album clearly had no effect on its sales. It did great for the band in the UK peaking at Number 4. 'Harvester Of Sorrow' was a hit single in the UK reaching Number 20 and 'Eye Of The Beholder' reached Number 27. The band also released the title-track as a single. With a hit album had Metallica now become a mainstream band?

METALLICA

AURAL AMPHETAMINE

DVD / DOCUMENTARY

This documentary is not specifically about Metallica but as the sub-heading says "...The Dawn Of Thrash". There's a surprising amount of depth, discussing what lead up to the dawn of thrash (punk and the

NWOBHM in particular) and the impact thrash had on the metal world. There are many references to bands like Motörhead, Judas Priest, Iron Maiden and Saxon discussing how much of a role they played in developing a fast style of metal that led up to the Bay Area thrash scene.

About half of the running time is dedicated to the NWOBHM with interviews from Brian Tatler of Diamond Head and Exlir. Perhaps the film-makers overstate their case a little but they do make some very good points and we all know how much of a NWOBHM nut Lars Ulrich is. As it's an unofficial DVD there are no original interviews with big players like Metallica, just archive footage and old interviews. There are appearances from obscure players like Sacrilege BC, Laaz Rockit and Neurosis as well as interviews with journalists/author's like Joel McIver and Malcolm Dome. This is a good documentary, insightful and entertaining with a surprising amount of detailed discussion.

METALLICA
MANCHESTER EVENING NEWS ARENA, FEBRUARY 26, 2009
LIVE
As soon as tickets were announced for Metallica's UK they were

snapped up like freshly baked hot cakes from a bakery. Even though there are many Metallica fans out there who don't really dig the band's music post *Metallica* (or even post *Master Of Puppets*) they continue to watch the band live simply because Metallica know how to put on a great show. Being (still) relatively young and given the fact that Metallica don't really visit the North West this was my – ahem – first Metallica live experience. All I can say is it damn well won't be my last. They were stunning.

I'd heard from the previous show, which was the band's first night on their European tour, that they leaned heavily on new material from *Death Magnetic* (which I like) but I didn't expect them to open the show with the album's first two songs: 'That Was Just Your Life' and 'The End Of The Line'. The lasers were stunning to watch but it was when the stage finally lit up and when they burst into 'For Whom The Bells Toll' when the show really got moving. The audience were whipped into a state of frenzy when the classic stuff was played ('One', 'Wherever I May Roam' and 'Master Of Puppets'). They were tight, well-rehearsed and full of energy; the fact that they played until around 11:15 and Hetfield was often shouting "Manchester" goes to show that the success of *Death Magnetic* has given them a new lease of life and reinvigorated them.

The setlist was actually quite different from the previous show in Nottingham but by all accounts the new material held up well with the old stuff: 'The Judas Kiss', 'Cyanide' and 'Broken, Beat And Scared' were all finely played. Surprisingly they played a cover of Bob Seger's 'Turn The Page' from 'Garage Inc'. midway through the set; and the second (covers) encore consisted of 'Blitzkrieg', 'The Prince' and Diamond Head's 'Helpless'. When it past eleven o'clock it seemed as though they weren't going to leave the stage but they finally finished with a brilliant version of 'Seek And Destroy' (but no 'Whiplash' unfortunately).

The stage lights and flames were excellent but my only criticism (and it's a minor one) is that when Hetfield had his back to my side of the venue the microphone clarity was not that great. Kirk Hammett is a great metal guitarist and he was consistently excellent throughout the night and Ulrich was also on form as was bassist Robert Trujillo. It was a great show but let's just hope their next road trek includes a date in the North West.

METALLICA

***THE MUSIC AND THE MAYHEM* BY MICK WALL & MALCOLM DOME**

BOOK

The Metallica library continues to grow with this latest addition; there must be almost as many books published on the San Francisco thrash metal band as there are about Led Zeppelin. Acclaimed rock journo Mick Wall has just released a major biography of Metallica called *Enter Night* and Malcolm Dome has published his own books on the band too. This neatly packaged book is an update of *The Complete Guide To The Music Of....* of which there are many other titles in the series. Essentially, this 144 page book is an illustrated discography beginning with their 1983 debut *Kill 'Em All* and ending with the massively successful *Guitar Hero: Metallica*. In that sense it gives a potted history of their career through their music; the albums and the songs. Perhaps it is not detailed or "meaty" enough for real Metallica aficionados but for casual fans and those with a general fondness for Metallica it makes for good toilet reading.

METALLICA

JAMES HETFIELD: THE WOLF AT METALLICA'S DOOR BY MARK EGLINTON

BOOK

The Metallica book shelf is getting almost as heavy as the Led Zeppelin one with so many books published over the past few years on San

Francisco's most famous metal band. What makes this particular biography stand out amongst the crowd (like most major rock artists there have been some excellent tomes on Metallica and some not so excellent ones) is the obvious fact that it is not a bio of Metallica per se but rather a bio of the band's great frontman, Mr. James Hetfield. The Story is told from his point of view and on that score, the familiar stories of Metallica's rise to fame and the success of certain albums, etc., becomes much more interesting. This is Mark Eglinton's first book and it is well-written, researched and informative. It's not an authorised book but that doesn't mean a damn thing; in fact, unauthorised works tend to be far more in depth and never fail to gloss over the controversial periods thus giving the full picture without prejudice. Cheesy title aside, Eglinton is good on Hetfield's youth and battling his personal demons. As this is the first (and so far only book) on Hetfield, *"The Wolf At Metallica's Door"* gives an illuminating story of his turbulent yet exciting life.

METALLICA

***THE ENCYCLOPAEDIA METALLICA* BY MALCOLM DOME & JERRY EWING**

BOOK

Joel McIver's huge biography of Metallica *Justice For All: The Truth About Metallica* cannot be bettered so self-confessed metal-head's and revered journalist's Malcolm Dome and Jerry Ewing have devised an alternative take on the band's fascinating history by authoring a 288 page encyclopedia. The book chronicles the history of the band in an A-Z format detailing what seems like everything that has ever been involved in the crazy world of thrash metal's most respected and entertaining band. As you can tell by the title (or any book with the word "encyclopaedia") *Encyclopaedia Metallica* is not meant to be read from start to finish; instead the reader will prefer to dip in and out of it.

The problem is you only learn about the band through mini-biographies and snippets of information about other artists such as Venom, W.A.S.P and their heroes Motörhead. But there's some really random stuff here that still relates to Metallica's past such as the animated US TV series *South Park* so clearly Dome and Ewing know their stuff. Indeed the book does go into a lot of detail – sometimes scarily – which will please the hardcore fan while still being interesting to the newcomer. Some of the pictures (black-and-white) are good to look at, especially the shots from earlier in their career. *Encyclopaedia Metallica* is an interesting idea and a refreshing way of examining the history of a legendary and tumultuous band.

NEWSTED

HEAVY METAL MUSIC

CD/ ALBUM

Former Metallica bassist Jason Newsted returns to the metal limelight with this excellent album of hard-hitting, heavy tunes. This is the kind of stuff Metallica should be making, and the quality of the tracks is enough to make Newsted's former band green with envy but of course the only green they seemingly care about these days is money. So let's get down to the nitty gritty of it. *Heavy Metal Music* has a lot to offer the metal fan from double kick drums, distorted bass and beefy guitars to catchy solos and above average melodies. Newsted's voice is surprisingly powerful and what he and his band offered on their *Metal* EP debut has been stepped up several notches with this album. It's a refreshing album even though it's totally immersed in an old school metal sound and the mixing is crystal clear.

It's great to see Newsted taking centre stage after seemingly disappearing from view since his post Metallica stints with Ozzy and Voivod. The album is free from pretensions – he doesn't mean to reinvent metal or amaze everyone with a new sound. Instead, he's happy to play the music of his youth. Newsted produced the album himself and gathered together a band consisting of Jesus Mendez Jr. on drums, Jessie Farnsworth on guitar and vocals and Mike Mushok on guitar. Some of the standout tracks include the terrific 'Soliderhead', the trail-blazing 'Love Time Dead' and the ass-kicking 'King Of The Underdogs'.

Heavy Metal Music isn't like a Metallica album though it is better and more effective than any Metallica album since *The Black Album*, released over twenty years ago. Newsted has done himself and his fans proud with this little gem. There's no question that *Heavy Metal Music* is one of the top metal releases of 2013.

SLAYER

UNHOLY ALLIANCE TOUR CHAPTER 3: AMON AMARTH [7] MASTADON [6] TRIVIUM [7] SLAYER [8]

MANCHESTER APOLLO, OCTOBER 27, 2008

LIVE

Feeling the weight of the credit crunch, the Unholy Alliance Chapter 3 was downsized from the massive MEN Arena to the more intimate Apollo theatre.

Amon Amarth are not quite as seasoned as Slayer but they've

been a dominant force in the scene for over a decade. Their brand of Viking themed metal is not to everyone's tastes but tonight they do their best to win over some new fans. Songs from their latest album *Twilight Of The Thunder God* get an airing; it's a shame many spent their time at the merchandise stand or the bar.

Mastadon are sadly underwhelming. Still promoting *Blood Mountain* they sound great on CD but tonight their set sounds like one massive opus rather than a selection of songs. Sure, it isn't entirely their fault: the mucky sound gives off lots of distortion and the Trivium fans are, well, waiting impatiently for Trivium to hit the stage. There's some boos and hisses. Nevertheless they show loads of energy; guitarist Brent Hinds and bassist Troy Sanders blitz through the likes of 'The Wolf Is Loose' with gusto.

Trivium seems to be the band the younger members of the crowd are waiting for. Credit goes to the band for injecting so much enthusiasm into the venue and for involving the crowd as much as possible. Matt Heafy has the makings of a great front man and the trio of Heafy/ Corey Beaulieu/Paolo Gregoletto have some choreographed moves that would make K.K. Downing and Glenn Tipton envious. A powerful version of 'Down From The Sky' from their latest album *Shogun* is a hit. And they try to win over the reluctant Slayer fans with

'Becoming The Dragon' and 'Down from The Sky'.

Slayer stands tall as they arrive in stage at 9:50pm, later than scheduled. Speaking to the crowd for the first time, Tom Araya says playing in an intimate venue is good because "you can hear the f**k ups". They fly into a powerful version of 'Chemical Warfare'; a screen, which is the stage's centrepiece, displays all sorts of visual images, including their name just in case we forget. During 'Ghosts Of War' the screen shows images of the US flag and Osama Bin Laden. A screaming version of 'Cult' shakes the earth. Their latest album, the acclaimed *Christ Illusion*, has rejuvenated the band but tonight Araya looks a little fatigued and again the sound is not great. Other songs played include 'Jihad', 'South Of Heaven' and 'Live Undead' before they finish with 'Angel Of Death'. Tonight Slayer prove they're still one of the best metal band's out there.

AFTERWORD BY

BOB NALBANDIAN

I was truly honoured when Neil offered me to write the afterword for his forthcoming book on the Big 4. I pondered on the approach and angle I should take and seeing that I've not only been a huge fan of these four bands since their inception, but I've also live in Southern California my whole life and I knew three of the Big 4 bands intimately. And I also played a major role in introducing these bands to a worldwide metal audience via my fanzine *The Headbanger* and other fanzine publishers I traded cassette demos with in the early '80s. So I thought for this Afterword I would share with you all my experience and involvement in the humble beginnings of the Big 4.

  First time I saw Metallica perform was on March 14, 1982 at a small venue in Orange County, CA called Radio City. This was Metallica's first-ever performance and it was unlike any local OC or LA show that I've witnessed. Instead of parroting the usual VH meets Mötley style of the LA club bands in the early '80s, this band, which featured James Hetfield on vocals, Dave Mustaine on guitar, Lars Ulrich on drums and Ron McGovney on bass, did an entire set of NWOBHM covers from Diamond Head, Blitzkrieg, Sweet Savage and Savage, as well as one brand new original song titled 'Hit The Lights'. The crowd had no idea if these were covers or original songs as practically nobody in LA had ever heard of these bands, and the crowd also couldn't figure out if they were witnessing a heavy metal band or a punk band as no hard rock or metal band in California at the time was playing music that fast and aggressive. While most local LA and OC honed their craft playing backyard parties or VFW halls before playing the club circuit, Metallica valiantly decided to debut at a well-established nightclub. And it honestly showed in their set, although they performed great renditions of those classic songs, their overall performance was quite lacklustre. If anyone was to tell me or anyone else in the club that night, including the members of Metallica, that in ten years from now this group of four amateur musicians will be the biggest heavy metal band in the world, we likely would have likely laughed that fucker straight out of the club. A couple weeks later I would witness Metallica open up NWOBHM legends Saxon for two sold-out shows at the Whisky-A-Go-Go in Hollywood. And that my friends was the spark that set the band underway to world domination.

The Woodstock was my favourite nightclub in the early '80s, located next door to Radio City in Anaheim, I would frequent that club on a semi-weekly basis. I recall seeing a damn good cover band in late '82/early '83 that did very impressive renditions of Judas Priest, Iron Maiden and Deep Purple songs. I couldn't recall the name of that band until I came across a flyer a week later and recognized their photo below a stick-like logo spelling out SLAYER. My immediate thought was, really good cover band with a killer drummer, but what a stupid logo. After a few weeks, a good friend of mine… a burly 14 year-old kid named Gene Hoglan (mind you, I was 17 at the time) called me up and said: "I just saw GOD!" I responded: "Gene, don't tell me you've became a born again Christian too?" He replied: "No, I just witnessed SLAYER!" I said: "Yeah, they're a cool cover band, I recently saw them at the Woodstock". And Gene passionately responded: "They're not a cover band anymore. Slayer has become America's answer to Venom!" Even though Gene was a few years younger than I, he had an older sister Lisa who would often take him along to clubs like the Troubadour in Hollywood, and apparently the previous night they went to the Troubadour to watch the headlining band and Slayer either opened or closed that show. Gene convinced me to check out Slayer the following week at the Woodstock and he was absolutely right, the band had totally transformed into a first-rate speed metal band with masterful originals combining the speed and satanic imagery of Venom and Mercyful Fate with the traditional British metal barrage of Priest and Maiden. In the weeks that followed, I became close with the band and they would buy centre spread ads in my fanzine (for a whopping $25.00). Gene and I also did the very first (advance) album and live reviews of the band in *The Headbanger*. The members of Slayer and then manager Steven Craig would often come over to my house and we would dub videos of their early Woodstock shows and advance cassettes of their forthcoming debut album *Show Now Mercy* and mail them out to fanzine and magazine publishers worldwide along with a copy of *The Headbanger*. Within the next few years Slayer would become arguably the greatest thrash metal band in the world.

Soon after the news broke about Metallica parting ways with their then illustrious guitarist and sending him on a cross country bus journey back to Los Angeles, my phone rings. "Hey Bob, it's Dave Mustaine, I just put a new band together with some killer players", and with that now infamous snarl, Mustaine boasts "This new band is gonna fuckin' blow away Metallica... we're faster, heavier and way more sophisticated than anything Metallica has ever done! Bob, would you be willing to interview me for *The Headbanger* as I want you to be the first to expose my new band...MEGADETH!" My response of course was "Fuck yeah!"

A couple weeks later I met up with Dave Mustaine and his new bassist David Ellefson at my buddy Patrick Scott's house in Huntington Beach to do the first ever interview with Megadeth. I have since remained close friends with both Dave and David still till this day. Megadeth's debut album *Killing Is My Business...And Business If Good*, despite its poor production, I consider to be the most groundbreaking thrash metal album of all-time. Megadeth brought forth a totally original sound and style combining ultra-fast speed-metal riffs with unique and very sophisticated fusion-based tempo changes.

Being an avid tape-trader in southern California since 1981, I was already familiar with the East Coast underground metal scene courtesy of penpals, tape traders and fanzines. All us underground metal collectors were well familiar with NY powerhouse metal bands Riot, Manowar, Twisted Sister, and The Rods, but we were also collecting demos from embryonic bands like Virgin Steele, Cities, Americade, and a band recently signed to Megaforce Records called Anthrax. Not long after the band's debut release, *Fistful Of Metal*, they supported NWOBHM greats Raven on a nationwide club tour. I caught Raven the year before with Metallica as support on their *Kill 'Em All For One* tour which was absolutely stellar, but this time it was Anthrax that had something to prove and they proved themselves well at this sold out show at the Country Club in Reseda. Anthrax were powerful, tight and very heavy but it seemed fairly evident to me that they were riding the coattails of Metallica. But by the band's third full-length record, *Among The Living*, it was evident that Anthrax had evolved into something very special and totally original. Incorporating ultra-fast double-bass "blast beats" with bone-crushing rhythms, Anthrax offered something completely unique to thrash metal...A sense of humour. While most thrash bands wrote about death, destruction and Satan, Anthrax brought forth a comedic and somewhat satiric edge to thrash metal music which would set them apart from their west coast contemporaries.

So, you may ponder, why a Big Four as opposed to a Big Five, Six or Seven? Many argue that other US bands such as Exodus, Overkill and even Testament (then Legacy) should fall under that banner of thrash metal. Not that I disagree, as those aforementioned bands also played a crucial role in the evolvement of thrash metal. But I look at the Big 4 as the primary colours...Red, Blue and Yellow. From those three colours you can create every other colour imaginable. That's how I see Metallica, Slayer, Megadeth and Anthrax when it comes to thrash. All four bands introduced something absolutely unique to speed/power-metal music and I believe it was the accumulation of these four bands that lead to the coining of the term "Thrash". And while other thrash bands have established a distinctive identity, many would rather consider them as the branches of the thrash metal tree rather than the roots. And not to discredit the stalwarts rooted in Europe that were also forerunners to thrash/death/black metal such as Destruction, Sodom, Kreator, Hellhammer, Bathory and of course Britain's overlords Venom and Motörhead (although arguably not a true thrash band but highly influential in inspiring the genre). But it was the Big 4 bands that set the standard for thrash on a worldwide level, and interestingly enough, after over 30 years, these four bands continue to dominate the thrash and heavy metal scene today.

No. 17
£1.00
METAL
KING DIAMOND
MÖTLEY CRÜE
DOKKEN
METALLICA
MASTERS OF METAL

80 PAGES
MR. BIG
TRIXTER
MINISTRY
DAVE LOMBARDO SPEAKS OUT
JUDAS PRIEST · BANG GANG
HEATHEN · ENUFF Z'NUFF · HEARTLAND
MORGOTH · DAVID LEE ROTH · SEPULTURA
TYKETTO · THE LAW · TANGIER · R.D.P

FORCES
D.R.I.
RAGE
MORE BEER!
PLUS: TOKEN ENTRY · SLAVE RAIDER · ADVERSITY · ANGEL DUST · YOUTH OF TODAY

FORCES
U.K. £1.50
FREE ARTCH FLEXI-DISC!
SCORPIONS
TESTAMENT
VOIVOD
DOKKEN
FREHLEY'S COMET
FLOTSAM AND JETSAM
WARFARE
PIRANHA
ATOMKRAFT
PANTERA
VIRUS
CRUMBSUCKERS
EXODUS POSTER
ANTHRAX
· ANGEL OF DEATH · NASTY SAVAGE · LAAZ ROCKIT ·

FREE
POSTER
TROUBLE
SAVATAGE
SALTY DOG
LOUDNESS
MEGADETH
KAI HANSEN

METAL FORCES
PEARL JAM
LITA FORD
MSG
YNGWIE
METALLICA
THE READERS' CHOICE
GUNS N' ROSES • SOUNDGARDEN
MORBID ANGEL • BABY ANIMALS
AGNOSTIC FRONT • PINK CREAM 69
LAW AND ORDER • ZODIAC MINDWARP

APPENDECIES

BIBLIOGRAPHY & SOURCES

The following publications and websites were integral in the making of this book. I am deeply indebted to them all...

BOOKS

Berlinger, Joe. Milner, Greg. *Metallica: This Monster Lives.* (USA: Griffin Trade Paperbacks, 2005).

Byford, Biff. Tucker, John. *Never Surrender (Or Nearly Good Looking).* (Germany: Iron Pages, 2002).

Chirazi, Steffan. *So What!: The Good, The Mad And The Ugly.* (USA: Broadway Books, 2004).

Christe, Ian. *Sound Of The Beast: The Complete Headbanging History Of Heavy Metal.* (London: Allison & Busby Limited, 2004).

Crocker, Chris. *Metallica: The Frayed Ends Of Metal.* (London: Boxtree, 1995).

Daniels, Neil. *Metallica: The Early Years & The Rise Of Metal.* (UK: IMP Books, 2012).

Dome, Malcolm & Ewing, Jerry. *The Encyclopaedia Metallica.* (Surrey: Chrome Dreams, 2007).

Ellefson, David. McIver, Joel. *My Life With Deth: Discovering Meaning In A Life Of Rock & Roll.* (London: Simon & Schuster, 2013).

Eglinton, Mark. *James Hetfield: The Wolf At Metallica's Door.* (Shropshire: IMP Books, 2010).

Hadland, Sam. *Metallica: Fuel & Fire – The Illustrated Collector's Guide.* (Canada, Collector's Guide Publishing, 2004).

Hale, Bill. *Metallica: The Club Daze.* (Canada, ECW Press, 2009).

Hale, Bill. Megadeth: *Another Time, A Different Place.* (US: Powerhouse Books, 2012).

Halfin, Ross. *Ultimate Metallica.* (USA: Chronicle, 2010).

Hotten, Jon. *Metallica.* (London: Music Book Services, 1994).

Ian, Scott. Wiederhorn, Jon. *I'm The Man.* (New York: De Capo Press, 2014).

Ingham, Cliff. *Metallica: The Stories Behind The Biggest Songs.* (London: Carlton, 2009).

Irwin, William. *Metallica And Philosophy.* (USA: Wiley-Blackwell, 2007).

Konow, David. *Bang Your Head: The Rise And Fall Of Heavy Metal.* (London: Plexus, 2004).

MacMillan, Malc. *The New Wave Of British Heavy Metal Encyclopaedia.* (Germany: Iron Pages, 2001).

McIver, Joel. *Metallica: And Justice For All.* (London, Omnibus Press, 2009) (3rd Ed)

McIver, Joel. *To Live Is To Die: The Life And Death Of Metallica's Cliff Burton.* (London: Jawbone, 2009).

McIver, Joel. *The Bloody Reign Of Slayer.* (London: Omnibus Press, 2008).

Mustaine, Dave. *A Life In Metal.* (USA: HarperCollins, 2010).

Popoff, Martin. *The Collector's Guide To Heavy Metal – Volume 2: The Eighties.* (Canada: Collector's Guide Publishing, 2005).

Popoff, Martin. *Metallica: The Complete Illustrated History.* (US: Voyageur Press, 2013).

Putterford, Mark. Heatley, Michael. *Metallica: In Their Own Words.* (London: Omnibus Press, 1994).

Sharpe-Young, Gary. *Thrash Metal.* (London: Zonda Books, 2007).

Stenning, Paul. *Metallica: All That Matters.* (London: Plexus, 2010).

Tatler, Brian. Tucker, John. *Am I Evil? The Music, The Myths And Metallica.* (Self-Published: http://www.diamond-head.net, 2010).

Tucker, John. *Suzie Smiled…The New Wave Of British Heavy Metal.* (Shropshire: IMP Books, 2006).

Wall, Mick. Dome, Malcolm. *Metallica: The Complete Guide To Their Music.* (London: Omnibus Press, 2005). (2nd Ed)

Wall, Mick. *Enter Night.* (London: Orion, 2010)

MAGAZINES

Classic Rock / Fireworks / Kerrang! / Metal Hammer / Powerplay / Record Collector / Rock Sound

WEBSITES

www.musicomh.com

BAND WEBSITES

Metallica:

www.metallica.com

www.loureedmetallica.com

www.myspace.com/metallica

www.facebook.com/Metallica

www.encycmet.com

www.metallicaworld.co.uk

www.allmetallica.com

www.metallicabb.com

www.1metallica.s5.com

www.metallifukinca.com

https://metallicablogmagnetic.com

Slayer:

www.slayer.net

www.slayer.net/uk/home

www.facebook.com/slayer

https://slayer.backstreetmerch.com

https://twitter.com/slayer

Megadeth:

www.megadeth.com

www.facebook.com/Megadeth

https://twitter.com/megadeth

https://www.youtube.com/user/MegadethTV

Anthrax:

https://anthrax.com

https://www.facebook.com/anthrax

https://twitter.com/anthrax

www.anthraxukoffical.com

ACKNOWLEDGEMENTS

Thank you to the following writers whose work I have quoted in this book. I am deeply indebted to them all. Their articles, reviews and interviews have provided invaluable insight into the music of Metallica, Slayer, Megadeth and Anthrax...

Thanks to the following folks for their input: *Biff Byford, Michael Christopher, Dave Ferris, Bill Hale, Joel McIver, Mike McPadden, Bob Nalbandian, Tim "Ripper" Owens, Harry Paterson, Rob Quintana, Brian Slagel, Brian Tatler* and *John Tucker.*

The following printed music magazines proved invaluable: *Classic Rock, Fireworks, Kerrang!, Metal Hammer, Powerplay, Record Collector* and *Rock Sound.*

Thank you too all the publications and websites in the acknowledgments as well as the writers quoted in the main text.

Special thanks to Red Shaw for her photos.

Apologies if I have missed out any names. It was not intentional!

DISCLAIMER

The author gratefully acknowledges permission to quote and use references from the sources as referenced in the main text and repeated in the *Bibliography*. Every quote and reference taken from selected sources is fully acknowledged in the main text and in the *Bibliography & Sources* and/or *Acknowledgements*.

However, it has not been entirely possible to contact every copyright holder, but every effort has been made to contact all copyright holders and to clear reprint permissions from the list of sources. If notified, the publishers/author will be pleased to rectify any omission in future editions. The opinions of the contributing writers/journalists do not reflect those of the author.

ABOUT THE AUTHOR

NEIL DANIELS has written about rock and metal for a wide range of magazines, fanzines and websites. He has written over a dozen books on such artists as Judas Priest, Paul Stanley, Joe Perry, Rob Halford, Bon Jovi, Linkin Park, Journey, Bryan Adams, Neal Schon, Richie Sambora, Brian May, Iron Maiden, You Me At Six, 5 Seconds Of Summer, Metallica, AC/DC, Pantera, UFO, ZZ Top and Robert Plant. He also co-authored *Dawn Of The Metal Gods: My Life In Judas Priest And Heavy Metal* with original Judas Priest singer/co-founder Al Atkins. His third book on Judas Priest is the CD sized *Rock Landmarks – Judas Priest's British Steel*, published by Wymer.

His acclaimed series, *All Pens Blazing – A Rock And Heavy Metal Writer's Handbook Volumes I & II*, collects over a hundred original and exclusive interviews with some of the world's most famous rock and metal scribes.

His second duel collection of rock writings, *Rock 'N' Roll Mercenaries – Interviews With Rock Stars Volumes I & II*, compiles sixty interviews with many well-known rock stars and scribes. The former collections were republished via Createspace as *Rock 'N' Roll Sinners* while the latter books were republished in an omnibus edition titled, *Hard Rock Rebels – Talking With Rock Stars*.

His Createspace books are *AOR Chronicles, Rock & Metal Chronicles, Hard Rock Rebels – Talking With Rock Stars, Rock 'N' Roll Sinners – Volumes I, II & III, Rock Bites, Love It Loud, Get Your Rock On – Melodic Rock Shots, Bang Your Head – Heavy Metal Shots, In A Dark Room – Exploits Of A Genre Fan* and the fictional rock 'n' roll novel, *It's My Life*.

His books have so far been translated into Brazilian, Bulgarian, Czech, Finnish, French, German, Italian, Japanese, Polish and Swedish with more foreign titles in the works.

His reviews, articles and interviews on rock music and pop culture have been published in *The Guardian, Classic Rock Presents AOR, Classic Rock Presents Let It Rock, Rock Sound, Record Collector, Big Cheese, Powerplay, Fireworks, MediaMagazine, Rocktopia.co.uk, Get Ready To Rock.com, Lucemfero.com, musicOMH.com, Ghostcultmag.com, Drowned In Sound.com, BBCNewsOnline.co.uk, Carling.com, Unbarred.co.uk* and *Planet Sound* on Channel 4's Teletext service.

He has also written several sets of sleeve notes for Angel Air and BGO Records.

His website is *www.neildanielsbooks.com*

PUBLISHED BOOKS BY NEIL DANIELS

MUSIC BIOGRAPHIES

The Story Of Judas Priest: Defenders Of The Faith

(Omnibus Press, 2007).

Robert Plant: Led Zeppelin, Jimmy Page And The Solo Years

(Independent Music Press, 2008).

Bon Jovi Encyclopaedia

(Chrome Dreams, 2009).

Dawn Of The Metal Gods: My Life In Judas Priest And Heavy Metal

(with Al Atkins)

(Iron Pages, 2009).

Linkin Park – An Operator's Manual

(Chrome Dreams, 2009).

Don't Stop Believin' – The Untold Story Of Journey

(Omnibus Press, 2011).

Rock Landmarks: Judas Priest's British Steel

(Wymer Publishing, 2011).

Metallica – The Early Years And The Rise Of Metal

(Independent Music Press, 2012).

Iron Maiden – The Ultimate Unauthorised History Of The Beast

(Voyageur Press, 2012).

You Me At Six – Never Hold An Underdog Down

(Independent Music Press, 2012).

AC/DC – The Early Years With Bon Scott

(Independent Music Press, 2013).

Reinventing Metal – The True Story Of Pantera And The Tragically Short Life Of Dimebag Darrell

(Backbeat Books, 2013).

High Stakes & Dangerous Men – The UFO Story

(Soundcheck Books, 2013).

Beer Drinkers & Hell Raisers – A ZZ Top Guide

(Soundcheck Books, 2014).

Killers – The Origins Of Iron Maiden: 1975-1983

(Soundcheck Books, 2014).

Let It Rock – The Making Of Bon Jovi's Slippery When Wet

(Soundcheck Books, 2014).

From American Idol To British Rock Royalty – The Amazing Story Of Adam Lambert

(Createspace, 2015).

Pop Punk From Down Under – The Story Of 5 Seconds Of Summer

(Createspace, 2015).

FILM BIOGRAPHIES

Matthew McConaughey – The Biography

(John Blake, 2014).

The Unexpected Adventures Of Martin Freeman

(John Blake, 2015).

J.J. Abrams – A Study In Genius: The Unofficial Biography

(John Blake, 2015).

CASUAL GUIDES

Electric World – A Casual Guide To The Music Of Journey's Neal Schon

(Createspace, 2014).

Reckless – A Casual Guide To The Music Of Bryan Adams

(Createspace, 2014).

Stranger In This Town – A Casual Guide To The Music Of Bon Jovi's Richie Sambora

(Createspace, 2014).

Made Of Metal – A Casual Guide To The Solo Music Of Judas Priest's Rob Halford

(Createspace, 2014).

Back To The Light – A Casual Guide To The Music Of Queen's Brian May

(Createspace, 2015).

Once A Rocker, Always A Rock – A Casual Guide To The Music Of Aerosmith's Joe Perry

(Createspace, 2015).

Live To Win – A Casual Guide To The Music Of KISS Frontman Paul Stanley

(Createspace, 2015).

COLLECTED WORKS

All Pens Blazing: A Rock And Heavy Metal Writer's Handbook Volume I

(AuthorsOnline, 2009).

All Pens Blazing: A Rock And Heavy Metal Writer's Handbook Volume II

(AuthorsOnline, 2010).

Rock 'N' Roll Mercenaries – Interviews With Rock Stars Volume I

(AuthorsOnline, 2010).

Rock 'N' Roll Mercenaries – Interviews With Rock Stars Volume II

(AuthorsOnline, 2011).

CREATESPACE

AOR Chronicles – Volume 1

(Createspace, 2013).

Rock & Metal Chronicles – Volume 1

(Createspace, 2013).

Hard Rock Rebels – Talking With Rock Stars

(Createspace, 2013).

Rock 'N' Roll Sinners – Volume I

(Createspace, 2013).

Rock 'N' Roll Sinners – Volume II

(Createspace, 2013).

Rock 'N' Roll Sinners – Volume III

(Createspace, 2013).

Rock Bites

(Createspace, 2013).

Love It Loud

(Createspace, 2013).

Get Your Rock On – Melodic Rock Shots

(Createspace, 2013).

Bang Your Head – Heavy Metal Shots

(Createspace, 2013).

In A Dark Room – Exploits Of A Genre Fan

(Createspace, 2013).

FICTION

It's My Life – A (Fictional) Rock 'N' Roll Memoir

(Createspace, 2013).

PRAISE FOR THE AUTHOR'S PREVIOUS WORKS

"Neil Daniels is great on the early years of Brummie metal legends Judas Priest..."

- *Classic Rock* on **The Story Of Judas Priest: Defenders Of The Faith**

"'I've never reached the top...but I gave it a bloody good go!' says original Judas Priest singer Al Atkins in the introduction to his autobiography. With a foreword by Judas Priest bassist Ian Hill ... Metal Gods covers the pre-fame years of the second-ever metal band in entertaining detail".

- *Metal Hammer* on **Dawn Of The Metal Gods: My Life In Judas Priest And Heavy Metal**

"The book also has a curious appendices exploring – among other things – Percy's interest in folklore and mythology".

- *Mojo* on **Robert Plant: Led Zeppelin, Jimmy Page And The Solo Years**

"Prolific rock and metal author Neil Daniels does a very good job in detailing a veritable smorgasbord of the events, places, people, releases

and merchandises of the band, the writer displaying his customary attention to detail and enthusiasm for accuracy".

- *Record Collector* on **Bon Jovi Encyclopaedia**

"...in terms of writing, content and presentation I think it's probably his best... Linkin Park - An Operator's Manual *is an attractive book with black and white photos on every page*".

- *Fireworks* on **Linkin Park – An Operator's Manual**

"... the aggregate of this book is an at minimum interesting and at max fascinating read for any rock fan, 'cos you get the whole deal, the history of Sounds, Kerrang!, Metal Hammer, BW&BK, all the mags, plus the mechanics of book writing, and more mainstream, who's a good interview and bad plus proof, crazy road stories...friggin' well all of this would be interesting to any rocker. Period".

- *Bravewords.com* on **All Pens Blazing: A Rock And Heavy Metal Writer's Handbook Volume I**

"But once again, this rollercoaster ride through some of rock's back pages will bring a glow to the cheek, and perhaps even moistness to the mouth, of any self-respecting rock fan who has ever bought a music paper or mag since the 1970s".

- Get Ready To Rock.com on **All Pens Blazing: A Rock And Heavy Metal Writer's Handbook Volume II**

"These two volumes of interviews celebrate the art of rock journalism".

- Classic Rock on **All Pens Blazing: A Rock And Heavy Metal Writer's Handbook Volumes 1 & 11**

"As a lone-time yet casual fan of the band, I found the band's story very interesting and quite surprising... I received the book on Thursday, used every possible opportunity to read it and finished it on Sunday. That's a recommendation if any".

- Rock United.com on **Don't Stop Believin' – The Untold Story Of Journey**

"With a track by track analysis, tour dates and photos from the period this is everything you needed to know about what is arguably Priest's finest thirty-odd minutes wrapped up into in one handy bite sized paperback at a budget price".

- Sea Of Tranquility.org on **Rock Landmarks – Judas Priest's British Steel**

"It's an insightful look at one of metal's most important bands, and though there have been many books written about them, Metallica have never seemed as easy to understand as after reading this".

- Curled Up.com on **Metallica – The Early Years And The Rise Of Metal**

"In all, Daniels has crafted a very high-level and easy read with Iron Maiden – The Ultimate Unauthorized History Of The Beast, *and top it all off, it's packaged expertly, prime for your coffee table, where Eddie's piercing eyes await".*

- Blistering.com on **Iron Maiden – The Ultimate Unauthorised History Of The Beast**

"This book was a great read. 154 pages crammed with the wonderfully written story of You Me At Six... With some lovely photos and a very handy discography at the back, You Me At Six – Never Hold An Underdog Down *is a must have for any YMAS fan".*

- Get Ready To Rock.com on **You Me At Six – Never Hold An Underdog Down**

"Daniels style is engaging and covers in excellent detail the first six years of the band...Each chapter covers a year and Daniels provides great detail on the various Australian vs. International pressings of the first few albums. It's very detailed and well researched".

- *Metal-Rules.com* on **AC/DC – The Early Years With Bon Scott**

"The tours, the music, the fun, the life, and the death, of one of the best metal acts of the '90s...it's all here. Nice job once again by Mr. Daniels".

- *Sea Of Tranquility.org* on **Reinventing Metal – The True Story Of Pantera And The Tragically Short Life Of Dimebag Darrell**

"Overall, I wouldn't hesitate to recommend this book to not only the diehards (who will snap it up anyway), but also those who want to delve just a little further than Michael Schenker, Phil Mogg (who emerges as quite the dictatorial figure in places), and the band's often horrendous choice of stage outfits!"

- *Classic Rock Society* on **High Stakes & Dangerous Men – The UFO Story**

"The book is an insight into the group's rise to fame, the funny times and their rise to become iconic bearded rocking heroes. I really enjoyed the section on ZZ Top trivia, there's funny and intriguing examples to make *you smile and laugh out loud".*

- *The Mayfair Mall Zine.com* on **Beer Drinkers & Hell Raisers – A ZZ Top Guide**

"This is a book for the superfan, to be honest. But for the superfan, it is a fantastic volume collecting a ton of information on a great player that you wouldn't be able to find in one place otherwise".

- *Music Tomes.com* on **Electric World – A Casual Guide To The Music Of Journey's Neal Schon**

"...if you thought you knew everything there was to know about Iron Maiden, then think again, as Daniels manages to turn up nugget after nugget of trivia and fact. This is a very rewarding read and I would wholeheartedly recommend this to any rock music fan, in fact buy it now and pack it away in your suitcase for your summer holiday read".

- *Planet Mosh.com* on **Killers – The Origins Of Iron Maiden: 1975-1983**

"Told in straightforward language and amazingly concise as for the time span it covers, Let It Rock: The Making Of Bon Jovi's Slippery When Wet *is a fine, solid work".*

- *Hardrock Heaven* on **Let It Rock – The Making Of Bon Jovi's Slippery When Wet**

"…Mr Daniels has applied his knack of bringing you right into the subject here and Bryan Adams fans will love Reckless - A Casual Guide To The Music Of Bryan Adams".

- *Get Ready To Rock* on **Reckless – A Casual Guide To The Music Of Bryan Adams**

"Made Of Metal *is a excellent guide to the long, sometimes magnificent, sometimes frustrating, sometimes downright horrible solo career of the Metal God*".

- *Metal-Rules* on **Made Of Metal – A Casual Guide To The Solo Music Of Judas Priest's Rob Halford**

VISIT **WWW.NEILDANIELSBOOKS.COM** FOR MORE INFORMATION

ALSO BY NEIL DANIELS

METALLICA: THE EARLY YEARS AND THE RISE OF METAL

NEIL DANIELS

WHAT THE PRESS SAID

ONLINE REVIEWS

"Fans of Metallica will find plenty to sink their teeth into with Metallica: The Early Years And Rise Of Metal. *Their journey from an obscure bar band to the biggest metal group in world has been an interesting one, and the time frame covered in this book is what started it all. There's also an appendix that covers Metallica's later years, and also an interesting section on other thrash bands of the era*".

- **Chad Bower –** *About.com: Heavy Metal* **(*http://heavymetal.about.com*)**

"*We do get some good stories though about how Lars Ulrich introduced pretty much everyone in L.A. to the British and European metal of the time. There's no denying that this is interesting stuff*".

- **Ken McGrath –** *Blistering.com* **(*www.blistering.com*)**

"*This book focuses on the band's first four discs (I love the track-by-track rundown of each), the impact that the NWOBHM had on the band, and the influence the band in turn gave to other metal bands. An easy, breezy read whose worth lies in the atmosphere the stories give more than any newfound knowledge to be plucked off the pages".

- **Greg Pratt –** *BW&BK (*[*www.bravewords.com*](www.bravewords.com)*)*

"UK superscribe Neil Daniels writes about as many metal books as me an' Joel McIver these days, and his latest captures the cozy feel of his innovative All Pens Blazing duo, what with all the writers (disclosure, me included) getting to drop their two cents in on all things metal".

- **Martin Popoff –** *Freelance Metal Author (*[*www.bravewords.com*](www.bravewords.com)*)*

"Daniels is a music bio vet who has a unique way making any story interesting...Daniels does a fine job of telling the tale of four of the most groundbreaking albums in the Thrash genre. This is a fine read from beginning to end".

- **Jeb Wright –** *Classic Rock Revisited (*[*www.classicrockrevisited.com*](www.classicrockrevisited.com)*)*

"It's an insightful look at one of metal's most important bands, and though there have been many books written about them, Metallica have never seemed as easy to understand as after reading this".

- **Steven Rosen –** *Curled Up With A Good Book*

    (*www.curledup.com*)

"*The book has some interesting photos of memorabilia dotted throughout it and a selected timeline/discography...A good read recommended for fans of the band, new and old (although maybe not so many new fans after the abomination that was the* Lulu *album!)*".

- **Jason Ritchie –** *Get Ready To Rock*

    (*http://getreadytorock.me.uk*)

"*Daniels has done just this through* Metallica – The Early Years And The Rise Of Metal, *focusing on an era where Metallica weren't just another money making machine intent on hammering out tunes we've all heard before, instead focusing on a period where everything was new and exciting, and Metallica could really make their mark. Whether you're a fan or not – this is a read which will inform, captivate and intrigue you – well worth looking into*".

- **Dave Nicholls –** *Loud-Stuff* (*www.loud-stuff.com*)

"*This is a book that can easily be dipped into from time to time on a casual basis or read in one or two sessions. For a biography of the early years of Metallica, you'll be hard pushed to find a better book than this. Highly recommended".*

- **Mick Burgess –** *Metal Express Radio* **(www.metalexpressradio.com)**

"There are many good bonus features, a Foreword by Brian Tatler of Diamond Head, an introduction by Daniels, quite a few black and white photos of cool memorabilia, timelines, a discography, lots of references and additional materials and an Afterword by author and NWOBHM expert, John Tucker. The most interesting bonus feature (above and beyond the biographical account of the 1980-1989) is an appendix with a collection of succinct and well-written mini-biographies about various American bands that (for the most part) were part of the rise of Thrash Metal".

- **Joshua Wood -** *Metal-Rules* **– (www.metal-rules.com)**

"Each album is covered in detail, including not just a look at the music but also how the cover art was conceived. One interesting element is the rare memorabilia pictured throughout the book. There are flyers of early shows, ticket stubs, t-shirts, and, amusingly, a letter to the fan club

apologizing for being slow to answer correspondence... 3/5"

- **Gillian G. Gaar – *Powerline Mag* (*www.powerlinemag.com*)**

"This is a well researched and executed insight into what it takes to be Metallica; a band who wouldn't compromise their beliefs, played it harder and faster and in time evolved into a formidable monster that is Metallica... It's a good read; it's unauthorised and unofficial but informative and entertaining".

- **Bailey Brothers – *Rock United* (*http://rockunitedreviews.blogspot.co.uk*)**

"The voices of the band are heard via the wealth of existing interview material and the author does a good job of keeping the narrative moving along at an even pace. An entertaining read and a book that can easily be digested in a couple of sessions this is another very well researched effort from Daniels".

- **Dean Pedley – *Sea Of Tranquility* (*www.seaoftranquility.org*)**

"The Early Years And The Rise Of Metal *is definitely worth checking out whether you're a fountain of knowledge when it comes to the Bay Area's finest or you want to learn more about some of the greatest music ever* recorded. Buy it, read it, then force you friends/mum/little brother to read it while you blast out the first four albums whilst flashing the devil horns and head banging like it's 1986".

- **Stuart Patterson –** *Subba Cultcha* **(www.subba-cultcha.com)**

"*Metallica: The Early Years And The Rise Of Metal* offers a fantastic overview of the period before the Black Album, it clearly defines Metallica's importance in the scene they helped create and pay homage to those that made it possible. Some interesting contributions from a range of their peers adds some colour and the archive quotes from the band are insightful and show the progression the band made from wannabes to world beaters".

- **Julian Alpin –** *Tape To Tape* **(http://tapetotape.co.uk)**

MAGAZINE REVIEWS

"...*the real strength of* The Early Years *is the passion and strength with which it tackles Metallica's initial development. So much so that I listened to the first three albums as I read the opening chapters, although an even bigger compliment coming from the fact that I was inspired to purchase* ...And Justice, *so I could revisit it for the first time in* sixteen years. No many books have the power to make me go shopping!"

- **Steven Reid –** *Fireworks*

"...for anyone needing an entry level introduction to the origins of Metallica and their place in the bigger metal picture, this is not a bad place to start".

Marcus Jervis – *Powerplay*

OTHER REVIEWS

"...It's like all of us just having beers around the kitchen table with the band. Man, like a gathering of friends, band and other rock stars included. Highly readable, totally useful, and a real addition to the Metallica books out there... nice job. Classy design too".

- **Martin Popoff – Author (*www.martinpopoff.com*)**

ALSO AVAILABLE FROM

NEIL DANIELS BOOKS

PUBLISHED BY

CREATESPACE

BIG 4 ENCYCLOPEDIA

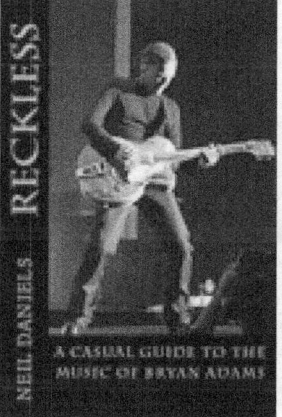

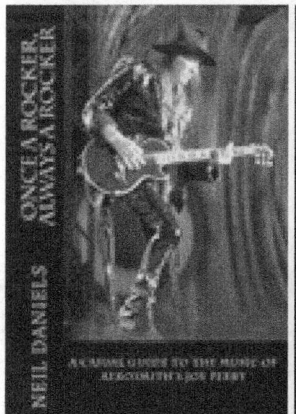

Neil Daniels – From American Idol To British Rock Royalty: The Amazing Story Of Adam Lambert

Neil Daniels – Pop Tunes From Down Under: The Story Of 5 Seconds Of Summer

BIG 4 ENCYCLOPEDIA

AOR CHRONICLES - VOLUME 1
Neil Daniels

Rock & Metal Chronicles - Volume 1
Neil Daniels

HARD ROCK REBELS - TALKING WITH ROCK STARS
Neil Daniels

LOVE IT LOUD
Neil Daniels

Bang Your Head - Heavy Metal Shots
Neil Daniels

Get Your Rock On - Melodic Rock Shots
Neil Daniels

ROCK 'N' ROLL SINNERS VOLUME I
Neil Daniels

ROCK 'N' ROLL SINNERS VOLUME II
Neil Daniels

ROCK 'N' ROLL SINNERS - VOLUME III
Neil Daniels

Rock Bites
Neil Daniels

IN A DARK ROOM
NEIL DANIELS

IT'S MY LIFE
*A (Fictional) Rock
'N' Roll Memoir*
Neil Daniels

NEIL DANIELS BOOKS

AUTHOR / CRITIC / MUSIC JOURNALIST / WRITER

QUALITY BOOKS ON ROCK & METAL MUSIC AND POP CULTURE

For details on Neil Daniels Books visit:

www.neildanielsbooks.com

THE BIG 4

BANG YOUR HEAD!

Photos by Red Shaw

BIG 4 ENCYCLOPEDIA

Made in the USA
Monee, IL
11 September 2025